Germanic Phylogeny

OXFORD STUDIES IN DIACHRONIC
AND HISTORICAL LINGUISTICS

General editors
Adam Ledgeway and Ian Roberts, University of Cambridge

Advisory editors

Cynthia L. Allen, *Australian National University*; Ricardo Bermúdez-Otero,
University of Manchester; Theresa Biberauer, *University of Cambridge*;
Charlotte Galves, *University of Campinas*; Geoff Horrocks, *University of Cambridge*;
Paul Kiparsky, *Stanford University*; David Lightfoot, *Georgetown University*;
Giuseppe Longobardi, *University of York*; George Walkden, *University of Konstanz*;
David Willis, *University of Oxford*

RECENTLY PUBLISHED IN THE SERIES

For a complete list of titles published and in preparation for the series, see pp. 276–80

Germanic Phylogeny

FREDERIK HARTMANN

OXFORD
UNIVERSITY PRESS

OXFORD
UNIVERSITY PRESS

Great Clarendon Street, Oxford, OX2 6DP,
United Kingdom

Oxford University Press is a department of the University of Oxford.
It furthers the University's objective of excellence in research, scholarship,
and education by publishing worldwide. Oxford is a registered trade mark of
Oxford University Press in the UK and in certain other countries

Published in the United States of America by Oxford University Press
198 Madison Avenue, New York, NY 10016, United States of America

British Library Cataloguing in Publication Data
Data available

Library of Congress Control Number: 2023930750

ISBN 978-0-19-887273-3

DOI: 10.1093/oso/9780198872733.001.0001

Printed and bound by
CPI Group (UK) Ltd, Croydon, CR0 4YY

Contents

Series preface

Modern diachronic linguistics has important contacts with other subdisciplines, notably first-language acquisition, learnability theory, computational linguistics, sociolinguistics, and the traditional philological study of texts. It is now recognized in the wider field that diachronic linguistics can make a novel contribution to linguistic theory, to historical linguistics, and arguably to cognitive science more widely.

This series provides a forum for work in both diachronic and historical linguistics, including work on change in grammar, sound, and meaning within and across languages; synchronic studies of languages in the past; and descriptive histories of one or more languages. It is intended to reflect and encourage the links between these subjects and fields such as those mentioned above.

The goal of the series is to publish high-quality monographs and collections of papers in diachronic linguistics generally, i.e. studies focussing on change in linguistic structure, and/or change in grammars, which are also intended to make a contribution to linguistic theory, by developing and adopting a current theoretical model, by raising wider questions concerning the nature of language change or by developing theoretical connections with other areas of linguistics and cognitive science as listed above. There is no bias towards a particular language or language family, or towards a particular theoretical framework; work in all theoretical frameworks, and work based on the descriptive tradition of language typology, as well as quantitatively based work using theoretical ideas, also feature in the series.

Adam Ledgeway and Ian Roberts
University of Cambridge

Acknowledgements

A myriad of people have contributed in one way or another to this book through advice and support such that I cannot possibly acknowledge every single contribution in the way it deserves. I thus want to, at least in a few sentences, mention all of you, who helped in making this book happen. To those who I may have inadvertently forgotten in this list, I sincerely apologize.

As this book grew out of my PhD work, it was supported financially by the Studienstiftung des Deutschen Volkes and Deutsche Forschungsgemeinschaft (grant no. 429663384, 'Germanic dispersion beyond trees and waves') who funded me during this period.

I am greatly indebted to my supervisor George Walkden whose support throughout and beyond my PhD cannot be overstated. This book has benefited greatly from his advice and his input, but he has been even more influential on my work in general by fostering my academic personality and by helping me pursue my linguistic enthusiasm in productive ways. I am so grateful that he has been my mentor ever since the first time I walked into his office in June 2018.

Likewise, I want to thank my second PhD supervisor Gerhard Jäger who encouraged and supported my academic endeavours since I was a master's student in Tübingen at the Department of Linguistics. In matters of computational linguistics, it was often ultimately him who pointed me in the right direction whether or not he realized it at the time. He incited me to pursue Bayesian modelling and agent-based models which today make up a large proportion of my methodological toolbox.

Many thanks are due to Karsten Donnay who helped me grasp the topic of simulation models during multiple long discussions early on. He was a strong influence on my views on agent-based models and my first approaches to implement these models in a linguistic setting.

I would like to thank all of those whose expertise helped me with this project. Specifically, I want to thank Patrick Stiles and Johanna Nichols for giving me feedback on individual aspects of Germanic phylogeny. Further, Andy Wedel,

Henri Kauhanen, and Katerina Kalouli have given me helpful advice especially at the early stages of the project which has enabled me to navigate the difficulties of starting a big computational project.

In particular I want to thank Hans-Jörg Karlsen who helped me put my findings in the archaeological context. Without him, the sections on historical influences on the linguistic diversifications in Germanic would not be in this book.

The project benefited from many discussions with colleagues about the ins-and-outs of Germanic cladistics and modelling complex systems, most notably Richard Blythe, Jiaming Luo, Rolf Bremmer, and Nelson Goering. In particular, I want to thank Anne Popkema and Johanneke Sytsema who were mainly responsible for organizing the Old Frisian Summer School in Oxford and Groningen which I had the great fortune of attending in 2019 and to be invited to as a speaker in 2021. In both years, we had great discussions about earlier Germanic languages in general and the role of Old Frisian in the diversification of West Germanic. In this vein, I want to thank the other speakers and also the attendees who truly made the summer school a hotspot for lively debate and a place-to-be for early Germanic linguistics during those weeks.

I am grateful to Miriam Butt and her group at the University of Konstanz who took me in as a fellow computational linguist, enabled me to go to conferences with them, and gave me access to computing power of which I was in dire need.

Special thanks are due to my student assistant Chiara Riegger for her help with checking, organizing, and formatting the data and bibliography. Moreover, this book greatly benefited from our joint work on Burgundian which helped in fleshing out the Burgundian data.

I want to thank my father Jörg Hartmann whose graphic design skills helped me with the implementation of the wave model graphs.

Lastly, I want to thank all the unsung heroes who have supported (and continue to support) me on my academic way, namely my family and my friends who, in more ways than they might realize, made it possible for me to write this book. Most of all, I am incredibly grateful to my lovely wife Sigrid for always believing in me and for giving me strength, support, and distraction when I most needed it.

Preface

The general field of Indo-European cladistics is one of the most well researched fields in the study of genealogical relationships between languages. We have relatively precise information on how individual Indo-European subclades split up from their most recent common ancestor. However, for some Indo-European subfamilies, such as Germanic, we still have open questions as to the nature and the detailed structure of the diversification of this family.

The aim of this book is twofold: firstly, it aims to examine the Germanic language family with computational methods while building on the rich pool of previous research. The goal is, ideally, to be able to tell the most accurate story of the linguistic diversification of Germanic from the break-up of Proto-Germanic to the individual daughter languages. Secondly, this book introduces a novel method for a computational implementation of the wave model that can be used to investigate similar problems concerning wave-like diversification processes in language families.

The reader might find that this book involves a high level of intricate cladistical aspects of Germanic. I attempt to convey the computational aspects in a way that is accessible to all readers, computational and non-computational alike. Although parts of this book can be used as an introduction to phylogenetic algorithms and simulation-based models of language, it is, at its core, a study on Germanic, phylogenetics, and computational wave-model implementations. The structure of this book is such that the first chapters focus on introducing, justifying, and applying the models whereas the chapter on Germanic phylogeny then pools the insights gained from the computational analyses together with previous research to describe the process of Germanic diversification. That is, this chapter seeks to unify all computational and non-computational studies on Germanic phylogeny to paint the most complete picture of this genealogy to date.

This book is the outcome of my PhD work at the University of Konstanz, the topic of which came to me during my work on Vandalic during my graduate studies in Tübingen. Thus, my 2020 book on the Vandalic language is in some ways the spiritual prequel to this book at hand. After I had worked on the Vandalic relationships with other Germanic languages, I felt the need to re-examine the Germanic family more in detail and with methods that have not yet been applied to Germanic.

List of figures

List of tables

1

Introduction

The linguistic history of the Germanic languages is among the best understood areas in the field of historical linguistics. Since the early days of linguistic investigations, generations of researchers have provided the foundation of what we know today. We have reconstructed the Germanic protolanguage *Proto-Germanic* (PGmc) to a degree where gaps in our knowledge are only found on minor or peripheral issues, at least as regards the phonology, morphology, and lexicon of the language.

But despite this detailed coverage, Germanic phylogeny (i.e. the linguistic relatedness within the family) is comparably unclear. The reasons for this is that early Germanic linguistics faces what can be described as a black-box problem. We can reconstruct Proto-Germanic in detail but the earliest extensive textual evidence, except minor text fragments in runic inscriptions, is not attested for at least 800 years (even more than 1,000 for some languages) after the demise of Germanic linguistic unity. This leaves a gap of many hundred years in the records which can only be filled by investigating the later attested languages and reconstructing their possible diversification from a somewhat coherent unity into the individual daughters.

Germanic linguistic research has also yielded insights into the further subgrouping of the family. We have a fairly good understanding that there are North and West Germanic subgroups that are themselves descended from a Northwest Germanic clade (cf. Grønvik 1998: 134–135; Seebold 2013). Unfortunately, this grouping is rather coarse given that the language family comprises at least six well-attested and diverse daughters from which the modern Germanic languages descend. Not only is this subgrouping in itself coarse, but solely assigning languages to these subfamilies does not yield insights into how these subfamilies evolved out of the common ancestor of Proto-Germanic. Those endeavours that aim at shedding light on the questions in detail are often very much debated. Some of the current issues can be listed in the following comprehensive overview.

The earliest definable—now commonly accepted—subgroup is that of Northwest Germanic, yet the language that is excluded from Northwest Germanic, Gothic, is often assigned to a coarsely defined 'East Germanic'.

Germanic Phylogeny. Frederik Hartmann, Oxford University Press. © Frederik Hartmann (2023).
DOI: 10.1093/oso/9780198872733.003.0001

However, the notion of East Germanic as a Germanic subgroup next to North-west Germanic has been called into question (e.g. Hartmann 2020; Hartmann and Riegger 2022). Moreover, what was the situation that yielded the split between these groups? Some have argued that the split was brought forth by Northwest Germanic undergoing certain subgroup-defining changes that left behind a conservative East Germanic (e.g. Grønvik 1998: 148). Yet it is still unclear whether the data warrant such conclusions as such a notion requires finding clear innovations indicative of a common development among the East Germanic languages which is not the case (see e.g. Hartmann 2020: 115–124). Furthermore, various smaller Germanic languages such as Burgundian and Vandalic have rarely been scrutinized regarding their position in the family and are often assumed to be 'East Germanic' without a clear definition of what this subgroup constitutes.

Having established that Northwest Germanic is its own subgroup, the question arises of why we find so few Northwest Germanic innovations and what this implies about the earliest diversification of Germanic.

Even within Northwest Germanic, especially as pertaining to West Germanic, we find a long-standing debate about whether or not West Germanic constitutes a protolanguage which would in turn suggest the West Germanic languages to either descend from a fairly homogeneous subgroup or from a loosely connected dialect continuum. This issue is connected to two somewhat linked debates about the validity of further subgroups such as Anglo-Frisian or Ingvaeonic (for a comprehensive overview see Stiles 1995). It becomes increasingly clear that we have to see Germanic, and especially West Germanic, as a highly connected area where contact and horizontal transmission of changes frequently occurs and for which it is difficult, if not impossible, to draw clear family trees.

Given these problems, I consider research into the Germanic languages to be in need of a thorough investigation using methods that go beyond, but complement, the traditional methods. Computational research has received much attention in historical linguistics in recent decades as the field of linguistics in its entirety moves towards increased use of quantitative and computational models. The advancement of widely available computational resources and methods calls for a detailed examination of early Germanic linguistics.

The study at hand attempts to be such an investigation. The goal, as will be more precisely defined in later sections, is to apply both computational tree-based phylogenetic and wave-model oriented approaches to the Germanic family to gain novel insights in long-standing debates. In this, I will apply both previously used Bayesian phylogenetic models to the problem and create a novel algorithm which represents a computational implementation of the wave model by means of agent-based simulations modelling linguistic spread, geographical factors, and diachrony. In some sense, the study itself therefore pursues two aims: modelling Germanic linguistic diversification up to the earliest attested languages *and* presenting and evaluating a novel approach that can be used as a method to model linguistic diversification based on wave-like transmission.

The investigation is therefore chiefly computational, drawing heavily on previous research in historical Germanic linguistics. Without the thorough work of generations of researchers, it would not be possible for the models to build on this knowledge. This, however, entails that the study predominantly discusses linguistic issues and issues pertaining to Germanic phylogeny on a meta-level. In other words, examining the intricate details of certain linguistic changes as arguments for a specific subgrouping is beyond the scope of this endeavour. This is not to say that detailed analysis is irrelevant, but rather that the methods and the viewpoint of the present investigation build on these previous studies rather than re-examining the evidence in detail. The conclusions about Germanic phylogeny therefore stem from a confluence of previous research and novel methods building on this research to obtain a clearer picture of certain issues.

It needs to be stressed that this work seeks not to replace previous research by computational models but attempts to thoroughly investigate the problem at hand using quantitative and computational methods based on traditional research to enrich the picture with powerful tools in order to improve our understanding of these processes.

1.1 A note on the definition of the term *cladistics*

The term 'cladistics' does not, as of yet, have a fixed definition in diachronic linguistics and is sometimes used interchangeably with 'phylogenetics'. For this reason, I henceforth adopt the following definitions: 'Linguistic cladistics' as used in this book describes the linguistic inquiry into language relationships based on the (commonly accepted) assumption that languages descend from one another and linguistic families diversify from a common ancestor.[1] 'Linguistic phylogenetics' is a way of studying cladistical relationships

---

[1] Note that in this definition, the process of the descent is unspecified, meaning that not just tree-like diversification models can be used in cladistical investigations. Hence, cladistics contains investigations of genetic relationships between languages without assumptions about the shape of the descent process.

by employing methods that model linguistic traits across time to analyse phylogenies, chiefly in the form of evolutionary tree models.

1.2 Summary of cladistical theories concerning Germanic subgroupings

Over the decades, there have been a number of theories regarding potential subgroupings of the Germanic languages. The most prominent of the discussed theories are summarized here to outline the basic proposals and their research history. Note that these proposals are reviewed in detail in sections 5.1 to 5.6.

1.2.1 North Germanic, West Germanic, East Germanic

The first and earliest grouping of the Germanic languages was a tripartite split of the Germanic languages in North, West, and East Germanic languages. This notion can be found in the earliest linguistic research, for example in Krahe (1948); Prokosch (1939); Schleicher (1860); Wrede (1886). This idea was based both on linguistic considerations but also on Roman and Greek historiographic work where, for example, we find the proposal of a common origin of the 'Gothic peoples', among which the East Germanic languages were counted (cf. Braune and Heidermanns 2004: 4). Very early, the tripartite division of Germanic was challenged from multiple angles with researchers proposing two potential further subgroupings of the three languages: Gotho-Nordic and Northwest Germanic.[2] To this day, the tripartite division is still found as the basic assumption of Germanic subgrouping in many books and studies, including introductory works.

1.2.2 Gotho-Nordic

A close relationship between Gothic (or East Germanic in general) and North Germanic first was appealing to many early researchers who based their investigations partly on historiographic work (cf. Grønvik 1998: 70). In his *Getica*, Jordanes uses the foundational myth of Gothic origins in Scandinavia (cf. Miller 2019: 1–2) which, were this to be believed, would warrant closer

---

[2] There is also the notion that East and West Germanic were more closely related (see e.g. Kortlandt 2001), yet since this theory has never in the past had a strong following, I omitted the proposal at this point. I do not consider it further here.

inspection of Northeast Germanic relations. Further, some supposed linguistic changes common to Gothic and Old Norse brought the Gotho-Nordic hypothesis some adherents (e.g. Schwarz 1951; Krahe and Meid 1969: 37–38), yet it was ultimately abandoned in the common consensus in favour of Northwest Germanic.

1.2.3 Northwest Germanic

Northwest Germanic is the commonly accepted second-order subgrouping of Germanic at least starting with Kuhn (1955), which proposes a closer relationship of the North and West Germanic languages to the exclusion of Gothic. Examples for such changes are, for instance, lowering of earlier *ē to *ā or the loss of several inflectional categories (see Ringe and Taylor 2014: 10–24). Although this theory is accepted in most contemporary research, criticisms of the concept are found in earlier research (chiefly pre-1980) suggesting alternative groupings such as Gotho-Nordic.

1.2.4 Ingvaeonic and Anglo-Frisian

Further subgroupings have been proposed predominantly in the context of West Germanic with *Ingvaeonic* being a subgroup consisting of Old Saxon, Old English, and Old Frisian (e.g. Schwarz 1951), and *Anglo-Frisian* which is proposed by some as a linguistic ancestor to Old English and Old Frisian (for an extensive survey see Nielsen 1981). However, the research history into these subgroupings is intricate as Old Saxon is suggested to be a hybrid language which does not fit perfectly into an Ingvaeonic subgroup (e.g. Nielsen 1989: 79). Moreover, some have cast doubt on whether or not the languages can in fact be regarded as related via their own linguistic ancestors or whether their similarities are due to geographical proximity and membership of a larger dialect continuum (e.g. Stiles 1995, 2013).

1.3 Computational modelling of the Germanic languages

There have been computational studies in the past investigating Germanic phylogeny at least as a by-product of their analyses.

Among the first quantitative attempts to model early Indo-European language relatedness was Ringe, Warnow, and Taylor (2002) who base their investigation on a lexical dataset. The results of their findings do not contain Germanic interrelationships but cast light on some of the difficulties of placing Germanic in a larger Indo-European family tree.

In the early 2000s, Gray and Atkinson (2003) published a Bayesian phylogenetic study that received much attention in the following years with many researchers heavily criticizing the approach for a variety of reasons (e.g. Chang et al. 2015; Pereltsvaig and Lewis 2015). In this study, they attempt to date the break-up of the Indo-European languages in order to investigate the question of the most likely Indo-European homeland. They eventually estimate an early date for the Indo-European disintegration, 8,700 years before present (Gray and Atkinson 2003: 437), thus concluding the Anatolian homeland theory to be correct. Their analysis also includes the Germanic languages, albeit only in the form of modern variants, inferring a split between North and West Germanic languages 1,750 years before present.

As a Bayesian phylogenetic reevaluation of the Gray–Atkinson model, Chang et al. (2015) presented a study which provided evidence against their claim using a model incorporating fixed ancestral states. In particular, the authors constrained certain extinct languages in their dataset to be treated as ancestor nodes of extant languages (e.g. Latin as an ancestor node of the Romance languages). In the Germanic branch of their model results, they arrive at the traditionally assumed Gothic–Northwest Germanic split with a further division of Northwest Germanic into a branch containing English, Dutch, and German and a lineage comprised of, among others, Norwegian and Swedish.

More recent studies, such as Verkerk (2019), aim at a compromise between strictly tree-like structures common in Bayesian phylogenetics and notions of other forms of diversification, namely horizontal contact and linguistic spread. The ideas to display a language family—in this case Germanic—as a horizontal diversification process ('wave-like') is not unique to computational modelling. Traditional linguistics has debated the *wave theory* since it was proposed by scholars such as Schmidt (1872) and applied to Germanic language relatedness (e.g. Kufner 1972). Today, the notion is that Germanic can be understood as a chain of dialects occupying a defined geographical area (Roberge 2020). This assumption of Germanic as a dialect continuum raises the question whether or not it would be beneficial to further the understanding of this language family by computationally modelling the development of the Germanic languages as a gradual diversification process, starting from a geographically influenced dialect continuum.

1.4 Wave model, tree model, and Germanic phylogeny

The process of linguistic development from a common ancestor language has often been framed as running along two different models of linguistic descent: the tree and wave models.

The origins of the viewpoints of tree and wave models can be traced back to research into Indo-European linguistic relationships in the mid-nineteenth century. One of the researchers, to whom an early version of the tree model idea is attributed, is August Schleicher who was among the first to describe Indo-European cladistics using a family tree (Schleicher 1860). A short time later, Schmidt (1872) put forth the theory of a wave-like diversification of the Indo-European languages, suggesting that languages emerge through over-laying isoglosses rather than through splitting from an earlier ancestor. The diagram below shows the most widely accepted family tree of Germanic with the second-order grouping Northwest Germanic.

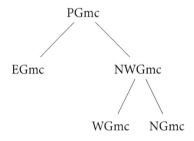

Traditional family tree

The wave model itself has never received a commonly accepted definition as the tree model had but most current research encompassing aspects of wave-like relationships define the wave model as a model which uses inter-secting isoglosses to define linguistic subgroups. These concepts are closely related to the notions behind *dialect geography* which investigates the geo-graphical distribution of languages, variants, and linguistic features in a given area or for a given linguistic family. For Germanic, Nielsen (1989: 116–133) summarizes the earlier research into dialect-geographical aspects of early Germanic.

The wave theory describes a diversification process in which innovations occur in a linguistic community and spread through the area either encom-passing all members (or sub-units) of the speech community or stopping earlier, thus only affecting a subset of members. When repeated multiple times

with multiple innovations, this process yields a linguistic area that is char-
acterized by overlaying innovations. As a result, areas will arise that tend to
share more innovations with their nearest neighbours than with communities
farther away by virtue of more intensive contact and exchange.

While in earlier research, both models were seen as mutually exclusive, more
recent overviews point out that both capture different aspects of linguistic
diversification (e.g. Hock 1991: 454).

The emergence of linguistic subgroups through innovation spreading has
strong ties to the geographical space they occur in, as shown in recent Labo-
vian sociolinguistic studies (summarized in Labov 2001: 35–73). Although linguistic spread is not (always) congruent with geographical distance, the spread
of an innovation permeating through a speech community which eventually
dies out is less likely to affect communities at the other end of the dialectal
region. Knowledge of the geographical position therefore complements and
aids the modelling of the diversification process in question.

Some approaches forego the geographical component and rely solely on linguistic data, such as historical glottometry (as presented in François 2015) (see
section 6.2).

While the wave models come closer to how certain languages diversify
into subgroups, especially in high-contact and close proximity situations, they
are considered to be less easily visualized and harder to summarize with a
small number of parameters. Tree models, on the other hand, can be regarded
as easier to interpret. This is especially true for the dimensionality of the
display. Whereas trees are by definition two dimensional, exhibiting unidirec-
tional branches which can have a certain length and a determinable split time
and ordering. Wave-like diversification processes, at least in the most simple
definition, operate in three dimensions: two dimensions for the geographical
spread of the waves with one temporal dimension for the development of the
spread of innovations over time, whereas by definition, wave model diagrams
are necessarily two-dimensional (see for discussion Anttila 1989: 300–310).
This makes them inherently more complex and less well interpretable. Moreover, from a modelling perspective, a linguistic stemma is more clear and
less complicated to devise for a given family, as they mostly only require
approximate estimates of similarity and linguistic history of each branch to
be collected. Wave-model displays rely on either certain distance measures or
measures of group coherence, or they require the researcher to plot a large
number of isoglosses on a geographical map. A study that previously used geographical information incorporated in a phylogenetic model is Bouckaert et al.
(2012).

With the advent of computational methods in linguistics and large computational resources being readily available, more complex problems that could not be analysed with earlier methods are now in reach.

Germanic is, in some ways, a model case for this issue as the diversification of certain Germanic subgroups is increasingly seen as a diversification of dialect continua in more recent literature (e.g. Seebold 2013; Stiles 2013). Moreover, the family is reasonably well-understood and recent such that we have large datasets and a rich research history which makes it ideally suited to being analysed quantitatively. The present study therefore aims to present a computational wave-model approach that has previously not been applied in cladistics. It is a computational agent-based implementation of the wave theory taking into account temporal and diachronic aspects. In this, it is distinct from previous implementations such as historical glottometry insofar as it operates on computational simulations, statistical principles, and specifically aims at modelling the diversification process rather than displaying single numerical relationships between languages in the form of subgroups.

In short, the approach rests on multiple individual simulations of the Germanic diversification process under the assumption of wave-like innovation spreading. Those simulations that show an isogloss pattern that comes close to the observed linguistic data can then be further analysed to see if there are common patterns of diversification under these best-fit simulations. These simulations take in the factors of time, geography, and linguistic features to approximate the spreading process in order to reconstruct the possible pathways of how the disintegration unfolded.

2

Data

The data for this study were drawn from previous work by Agee (2018) to a great extent. In this study, Agee applies the glottometric framework developed in François (2015) to Germanic. The basis of this glottometric approach is to use a binary innovation dataset to estimate association strength between members of subgroups of a given language family. For his investigation, Agee devised a large database for the Germanic languages containing a large set of innovations from Proto-Germanic to the earliest attested daughter languages. Included in this database are phonological, morphological, syntactic, and lexical innovations. Here, the definition of *innovation* is a change pattern in the structure of a language. According to this definition, a phonological innovation is an identifiable sound change, whereas a syntactic innovation is a change to the syntactic structure of the language. Not that this type of data, with regard to syntactic innovations, is different from the parametric approach taken in some other phylogenetic analyses using syntactic data (such as Longobardi, Guardiano, et al. 2013). Parametric data involve a binary specification of particular structural properties, whereas innovation data involve a binary specification of whether a particular change has occurred or not.

The survey strategy in that study was to extract information of post-PGmc innovations from secondary literature (Agee 2018: 19–20). Although other sources were used, especially for non-NWGmc languages, Agee reports that he relied mostly on the outlines and analyses by Ringe (2017) and Ringe and Taylor (2014). The decision of which innovations were included was based on whether they occur in the 'core vocabulary', a notion the study draws from François (2015) and defined as the top 200 words (Agee 2018: 23). This means that, 'a lexically specific sound change, lexical replacement, lexically specific levelling, etc. is only considered if it affects a word within the core vocabulary' (Agee 2018: 23). This limits the number of innovations to be considered to a certain occurrence frequency. In other words, as the database aims at reflecting the major decisive innovations, Agee decided to omit smaller changes that are mainly word-specific.

For the languages Old Frisian and Old Saxon, the database does not include innovations that are regarded by Agee as exclusively belonging to these

Germanic Phylogeny. Frederik Hartmann, Oxford University Press. © Frederik Hartmann (2023).
DOI: 10.1093/oso/9780198872733.003.0002

languages as the author regards them as too under-researched (Agee 2018: 21–22). Therefore, these innovations were added to the database for the study at hand (see Appendix) by drawing on Bremmer (2009) and Rauch (1992). Moreover, the languages Burgundian and Vandalic are not included in the database and were therefore added to the final dataset. Wherever it is unknown whether a specific innovation is found in Vandalic or Burgundian due to the scarce availability of data, the innovation was given a '?' in the respective field to indicate uncertainty. It is important to stress that this part (Old Frisian and Old Saxon individual innovations and Vandalic and Burgundian in general) is based on original research as these innovations were added to extend the database for the purposes of the study at hand.[1]

To illustrate how the innovations were coded and fed into the database, I extracted four innovations from the dataset to be discussed here (see Table 2.1). The first two entries are present in the original database in Agee (2018) whereas the latter two were added to the database as part of the present investigation.

The first innovation represents the Northwest Germanic lowering of earlier $*\bar{e}$ to Proto-Northwest Germanic $*\bar{a}$ which can be found in Old Norse, Old English, Old Frisian, Old Saxon, and Old High German (see Ringe and Taylor 2014: 10–13). This is clearly preserved in ON *ráð* and OHG *rāt* < PGmc *rēdaz* ('advice'). Fulk (2018: 60–61) notes that this change started in the south of the Germanic-speaking area spreading northward whereas at the same time in the northern parts of the later West Germanic area, onomastic material suggests an un-lowered state. This innovation excludes Gothic and both Vandalic (see Hartmann 2020: 99–107) and Burgundian (see Hartmann and Riegger 2022).

Table 2.1 Sample innovations from the dataset

Innovation	GO	ON	OE	OF	OS	OHG	VAND	BURG
$*\bar{e} > *\bar{a}/$ [+stress]	0	1	1	1	1	1	0	0
dual > emptyset	0	1	1	1	1	1	?	?
$*\bar{o} > *\bar{u}/$ [+stress]	0	0	0	0	0	0	1	0
$*e, *i > i$	1	0	0	0	0	0	0	1

---

[1] After further inspection, it was found that most innovations of Old Saxon that are considered uncontroversial are already in the original database as they are either parallel or common innovations with other languages. However, it was confirmed in preliminary model runs that adding dummy innovations does not change the model estimates in meaningful ways. This means that should independent innovations need to be added to Old Saxon due to different coding decisions or future research, they would not significantly change the model results presented here.

Gothic, for example, shows a continuation of this phoneme in the words Goth. *slepan* < PGmc *slēpaną ('to sleep') and Goth. *ufblesan* < PGmc *blēsaną ('to blow') (Ringe and Taylor 2014: 11). In Vandalic, we find that PGmc *ē is preserved in its quality as observed in words such as Vand. *rēþ *rēða- < PGmc *rēdaz ('advice') (cf. Goth *garēdaba*, OHG *rāt*) or Vand. *mērV- < PGmc *mērijaz ('famous') (cf. OHG *māri*) (see Hartmann 2020: 132–133). It has to be noted that although it is difficult to ascertain vowel quantity in Vandalic due to the attestation situation, the continuation of the vowel quality is apparent. In Burgundian, the preservation of earlier *ē is likewise present: thus we find Burg. *rēða- < PGmc *rēdaz ('advice') attested in, for example, *Leubaredus* and Burg. *mērja- < PGmc *mērijaz ('famous') attested in, for example, *Sigismerem*. For this reason, the innovations for all three languages need to be coded as **0**, i.e. the innovation *ē > *ā is not present in these languages.

The Proto-Germanic dual in verbs was inherited from Proto-Indo-European (see Ringe 2017: 260) and subsequently lost in the daughters Old English, Old High German, Old Norse, Old Frisian, and Old Saxon (Ringe and Taylor 2014: 20–21). In these languages, the number category was replaced by the plural. Thus we find that in Gothic, the Proto-Germanic dual forms are retained while Old High German lost them in favour of the plural. Table 2.2 shows the contrast between Gothic and Old High German in the paradigm of the verb 'to take' (see also Fulk 2018: 273).

Both in Burgundian and in Vandalic, the scarcity of the data does not permit determining whether the dual was present or absent in both languages (Hartmann 2020; Hartmann and Riegger 2022). Thus, Gothic is coded as **0** in this dataset, since it retains the dual forms; both Vandalic and Burgundian receive **?**, since presence or absence of dual cannot be determined and all other languages that exhibit no dual forms are coded as **1**.

The Vandalic raising of stressed *ō > *ū can be determined to be a Late Vandalic change (see Hartmann 2020: 105–106). It can be observed in the forms Vand. *blūma < PGmc *blōmô 'flower' (cf. Goth *blōma*, OE *blōma*) and Vand. *mūþ *mūða- < PGmc *mōdaz 'anger, mind' (cf. Goth *mōþs*, OE

Table 2.2 Sample innovations from the dataset

	PGmc	Gothic	Old High German	
Singular	*nemō	*nima*	*nimu*	'I take'
Dual	*nemōz	*nimōs*	–	'We (both) take'
Plural	*nemamaz	*nimam*	*nemamēs*	'We take'

mōd). In Vandalic, this change yielded a merger between *ō and *ū in stressed syllables, so, for example, PGmc *rūnō 'rune' (cf. Goth *rūna*) > Vand. *rūna, PGmc *blōmô > Vand. *blūma. In Burgundian, this change cannot be found; we instead see retention of earlier *ō. Examples of this are Burg. *mōða- (e.g. attested in *Baltamodum*) < PGmc *mōdaz 'anger, mind' and Burg. *hrōþa- (e.g. attested in *Hrodehildis*) < PGmc *hrōþiz 'fame' (cf. OE *hrēþ*) (see Hartmann and Riegger 2022). For this reason, the coding is **1** for Vandalic and **0** for all other languages.

The final innovation is the raising of Proto-Germanic *e to *i in Gothic and Burgundian. In both languages, we find attestations of this raising in words such as Goth *giba*, Burg. *morginegiba* < PGmc *gebō 'gift' (Hartmann and Riegger 2022). In other early Germanic languages, original *e is retained or subsequently changed due to other changes operating on that phoneme. Examples include OE *ġiefu*, OHG *geba*, ON *gjǫf*, Vand. *geba as attested in, for example, <geba-> (Hartmann 2020: 129). As a result, Burgundian and Gothic are coded with **1** (showing this innovation) whereas all other languages receive **0**.

The final dataset includes 479 possible innovations which were used for all computational methods in this study. Of these, 426 were drawn from the original study by Agee (2018) and fifty-three were added for this study. It needs to be noted that the dataset is by no means exhaustive, nor can it be regarded as representing a larger consensus. The innovations that are included are those that were identified as such in previous research. This means that what constitutes an innovation is always dependent on the scope of view (e.g. whether or not allophonic changes are considered to be equally important as phonemic ones) or the general take on unresolved issues in research. For example, some researchers may group two or more changes together as one phenomenon (breaking and labial mutation are results of the same underlying phenomenon; Hartmann, 2021) or have different views on whether an innovation has taken place.[2] As a result, a dataset including innovations from Proto-Germanic to the individual daughter languages cannot fully meet the assumptions of every viewpoint down to the individual innovation. Rather, they present a middle ground devised from some of the more well-known textbooks and reference works (e.g. Braune and Reiffenstein 2004; Noreen 1923; Ringe and Taylor 2014). Moreover, the methods that are used in this study are devised to account for uncertainty in the individual innovations. This means

---

[2] See, for example, the debate surrounding the phonetic realization of */h/ in West Germanic. Consult e.g. Ringe and Taylor (2014: 106); Barrack (1987); and Iverson, Davis, and J. C. Salmons (1994) for different viewpoints on this matter.

that the interpretation of individual innovations does not have a strong impact on the outcome—only more frequent, systematic errors or biases would have the power to influence the model results notably.

For the same reason, data uncertainty for the Burgundian and Vandalic data has a minor impact on the outcome. Both Bayesian phylogenetic models and the agent-based model have mechanisms to address the issue of missing data and mitigate the effect of fewer datapoints for these languages.

It was detected that in the list by Agee (2018), there is one innovation (the occurrence of OE *heardra*) which is marked as not present/insecure in Old English. This results in an all-zero vector for this innovation. Rather than removing this innovation from the dataset, I decided to leave it in to check the innovation occurrence time dating of the agent-based model which should clearly identify this as a dummy innovation (see section 4.11).

A potential caveat of using an innovation-based dataset is that it relies heavily on previous research into the state of the protolanguage. While it is not an issue to assume a certain reconstructed origin in a computational analysis, the decision whether or not a linguistic feature constitutes an innovation might, in some cases, be influenced by a preconceived idea of a family tree. This might make some innovations biased towards a certain diversification path over another path. Although the researcher can scrutinize the dataset used to ensure no bias in the reconstruction, one cannot exclude that some innovations might be biased towards a certain tree topology. Fortunately, the computational models used in linguistics (and in the study at hand) do not rely on individual innovations too heavily as they have means to compensate for fluctuations in the data. One caveat here is that this only holds true if there are no large-scale systematic errors or biases in the data of which we cannot be entirely sure. As far as the basis for the dataset is concerned, the dataset was checked for major distortions and none were found. This, however, does not rule out systematic errors or biases in the sources regarding reconstructions of Proto-Germanic and post-Proto-Germanic innovations by previous research. As a result, this dataset aims to be an accurate representation of previous research into the topic, which necessarily assumes no major flaws in said research. This underscores the importance of rigorous, detailed philological work as a basis for the datasets included in large-scale comparative studies such as this one.

3

Tree-based phylogenetics

3.1 Phylogenetic algorithms

A large part of computational methods for cladistical analysis are centred around inferring family relationships from data with a family tree structure as the aim. Such methods opt for finding the best tree representation of language relatedness from patterns given in the data. The various computational methods differ not only in the methods with which trees are built but also in how the trees are created from the input data.

Computational phylogenetic tree models ask the questions of how languages are related with regard to their subgrouping, their time of origin, the splitting times of these subgroups, and their coherence as subgroups (Bowern 2018). Further, some methods, chief among those Bayesian inference, aim to estimate the reliability of certain family trees and subgroupings within these trees. In general, the idea of computational phylogenetics is to derive quantitative solutions to these questions from linguistic data.

Two types of data are prevalent in phylogenetic linguistic analyses: state and numeric data. State data are data that encode different states of a feature or pattern in the languages in question. This can be cognate data where different types of cognates are encoded in the data as different states. For example, in a lexical approach akin to the dataset used in Ringe, Warnow, and Taylor (2002), one would assemble words for a specific concept in different languages. This dataset would contain information of, for instance, the concept of 'sea' in English (*sea* < PGmc *saiwiz), Dutch (*zee* < PGmc *saiwiz), German (*Meer* < PGmc *mari), and Swedish (*hav* < PGmc *habą). The English and Dutch words descend from a common PGmc form whereas the German and Swedish correspondences have no common origins with any of the other three languages. In a lexical dataset, we could assume three possible cognates of which English and Dutch share type A (i.e. the *saiwiz-type), German shows type B (i.e. the *mari-type), and Swedish type C (i.e. the *habą-type). This is of course a simplification to outline the properties of a lexical dataset (for a more in-depth discussion, see Heggarty (2021)). The challenges of this are not trivial as the notion of *concepts* must be reasonably defined, especially since what

Germanic Phylogeny. Frederik Hartmann, Oxford University Press. © Frederik Hartmann (2023).
DOI: 10.1093/oso/9780198872733.003.0003

counts as lexical correspondences is not always clear. In the above example, both Swedish and German have reflexes of the *saiwiz-type which assumes the meaning of 'lake' or 'small body of water' which, if included, would also be cognate to the English and Dutch forms. It may therefore not be uncontroversial to assume a specific scope for including or excluding wider meanings into the dataset as semantic change may interfere with cognacy judgements.

Other than lexical or cognate data, there can be innovation-based data that encodes the presence or absence of a linguistic pattern or feature in different languages. The other datatype that is used chiefly in distance-based analyses is numeric data which usually are counts of certain sounds or other linguistic measures with numeric outcomes. From these data, *alignments* are created which means that across different features, the states or counts are collected and aligned for all languages in the analysis in such a way that, for every feature, is recorded how it behaves in different languages (i.e. which states it has; if it is present or absent).

Intuitively, one would assume that the goal of phylogenetic algorithms should be to detect these patterns and to find similarities between patterns from which a family relationship can be derived. Further, it seems intuitive to assign a closer family relationship to languages which share the most similarities.

This is the idea behind distance-based algorithms and, although not without merit, it exhibits significant shortcomings:[1]

In distance measures, differences between two languages regarding their features in the data are collapsed into one single number which oversimplifies the relationship between two languages to a degree that might be inadequate for certain linguistic problems.

Moreover, grouping languages by similarity disregards the strength of the connection and excludes significant patterns in the process. If, for example, language A shares eleven features with language B and another set of ten features with language C, the algorithm decides the grouping of A and B based on the majority of shared features and rejects subgrouping with language C. This can yield groupings where two languages that are estimated to be distantly related share strong similarities which were then overridden by stronger patterns in other subgroups.

Further, we want to ensure that the similarities we see are compatible with certain tree structures while keeping in mind that there is uncertainty regarding which specific structure has led to the data. Only going by the

---

[1] For an extensive review of both Bayesian inference and distance-based methods see Nichols and Warnow (2008).

majority of shared patterns introduces false attributions into the analysis. That is, there are several processes which can obscure the true relationship by introducing parallel innovations due to homoplastic events, convergent developments of either larger linguistic patterns such as morphological restructuring of case systems which has an effect on several different individual linguistic features or changes of a smaller scale such as parallel monophthongization of certain diphthongs. Moreover, problems arise with shared retentions in methods relying on distance measures since, if not weighted, shared innovations and retentions are treated as equal in those models.

Lastly, datasets can only capture a limited sample of linguistic feature space, meaning that all datasets are solely an approximation of the developments that take place over the course of linguistic change. Although this statement is a trivial fact common to all qualitative and quantitative analyses in linguistics, in this situation it is an important reminder to take this issue into account when applying phylogenetic algorithms. Uncertainty that arises due to data being less than perfectly representative of linguistic systems needs to influence the interpretation and results of the models.

3.1.1 Distance-based methods

Before we examine the Bayesian phylogenetic inference models in more detail, we first need to start with inspecting the distance-based methods that can be seen as the structural predecessor of phylogenetic models. This is not to say, however, that distance-based models are not still used in linguistics and other fields such as biology. Due to the limitations of their scientific value for cladistical analysis, distance-based methods have become less frequent specifically for family tree building and analysis. Nevertheless these methods have merit for approaches and problems outside investigations into linguistic relatedness. Therefore the discussion below needs to be seen purely as a review of these methods in the domain of cladistical analysis.

The figures and calculations in this section, with the exception of Figure 3.4, were created with the phylogenetic software *SplitsTree* (Huson and Bryant 2006). The UPGMA algorithm in Figure 3.4 was run in the R package *phangorn* (Schliep 2011) before being visualized in *SplitsTree*.

The neighbour joining algorithm

The *neighbour joining* algorithm, introduced by Saitou and Nei (1987), is a method of clustering languages by means of their respective distances in the form of a network. The process operates iteratively on a transformed version

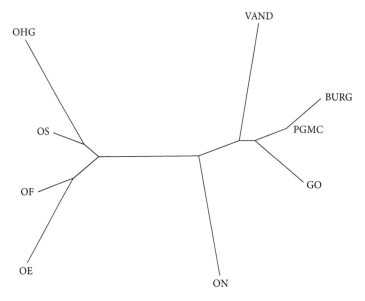

Figure 3.1 Neighbour joining network

of the distance matrix (called Q-matrix) by joining together the pair of closest languages (i.e. the two languages for where the paired distance is lowest in the Q-matrix). After updating the initial distance matrix by the new node created by the earlier joining of two languages, this process is repeated for all remaining languages and nodes. This results in a network of languages in which the edge lengths between nodes correspond to the amount of estimated change between them.

When applied to the Germanic dataset, we are able to display the neighbour joining network for these data as can be seen in Figure 3.1.

What we can observe here is that PGmc is clustered in the close vicinity of Burgundian, Gothic, and Vandalic whereas the West Germanic languages are clustered on the far left end of the graph. Old Norse is relatively closer to PGmc than to West Germanic.

In a second step, this originally unrooted graph can be rooted and transformed into a phylogram. Since the taxon **PGMC** represents the actual root of the family, we can root the phylogram on PGmc. The result of this is the phylogram shown in Figure 3.2.

The most salient feature of this phylogram is that the now rooted tree shows very short branch lengths between the early splits between the ancestral nodes

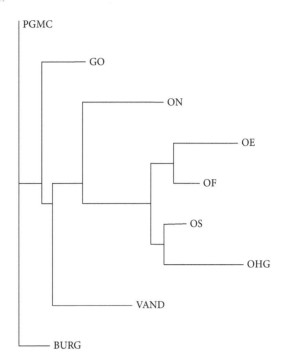

Figure 3.2 Neighbour joining phylogram

of Burgundian, Gothic, and Vandalic. This can be interpreted as a sign of low support for subgrouping in those languages.

UPGMA

The UPGMA (**U**nweighted **P**air **G**roup **M**ethod with **A**rithmetic mean) algorithm was introduced by Sokal and Michener (1958) and produces a rooted tree of the pairwise distances between the taxa. It is important to note that the UPGMA algorithm is *ultrametric*, meaning that the underlying assumption is that the distances from the root to each tip node are equal. Applied to biological or linguistic problems, this requires the assumption of a *strict molecular clock*, that is, the assumption that the rates of change along the branches that lead to the distances in the distance matrix occur at the exact same rate. This results in a tree in which branch length translates to the amount of changes occurring between splits. As the Germanic languages in the dataset were attested at different times with Gothic being significantly older than, for example, the West Germanic languages, the ultrametricity and strict molecular

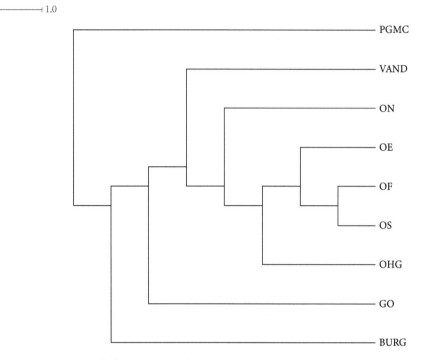

⊢—————⊣ 1.0

Figure 3.3 UPGMA phylogram

clock assumption cannot give reliable results.[2] The following application of UPGMA to the Germanic linguistic data is therefore incorrect on theoretical grounds and is discussed only for illustrative purposes to highlight and discuss the problems of distance-based methods when applied to cladistical problems such as the issue at hand. In Figure 3.3 we see the application of an UPGMA algorithm to the Germanic dataset in which Proto-Germanic was declared the outgroup to have a reference outgroup equal to the root state.[3]

Here we see that, similar to the neighbour joining algorithm, many languages split independently from the phylum with short initial branch lengths. Another decisive disadvantage of UPGMA, that it has in common with other distance-based methods, is the disregard for the cladistic distinction of shared innovations and shared retentions. The distances are computed on both shared innovations and shared retentions with both being weighted equally. This issue can be resolved when the distance matrix is computed by solely incorporating shared innovations. Therefore I compiled a distance matrix on

---

[2] See section 3.1.3 for a detailed discussion of the molecular clock.
[3] Since the UPGMA algorithm is ultrametric, Proto-Germanic is treated as an extant outgroup, yet since this analysis is for illustrative purposes due to the reasons explained above, the results cannot be interpreted in any case.

the basis of shared innovations. The pairwise distances were computed with the following formula:

$$\delta(i, j) = 1 - \frac{I_{ij}}{n_{innov}} \tag{3.1}$$

Therefore, the distance (δ) between languages i and j is computed by dividing the number of shared innovations between the two languages by the total number of *innovations* (i.e. number of innovations undergone in either language). In the equation, I_{ij} is the number of shared innovations between languages i and j. $\frac{I_{ij}}{n_{innov}}$ is thus defined as the ratio of shared innovations to all innovations either language has undergone. Figure 3.4 shows the UPGMA algorithm applied to this innovation-only distance matrix with Proto-Germanic as the outgroup.

In this graph we see that the distances between the splits are very small and the overall ordering of the taxa is compressed at the root. This phylogram demonstrates that, at least for the Germanic dataset, focusing on innovations only when computing a distance matrix does not yield reliable results with the UPGMA algorithm. Although the topology of this tree with regard to the split orderings is not improbable given previous research on the topic, the small branch lengths at the early nodes suggest that individual innovations are given much weight as not many changes are needed to change the topology. Therefore, this approach is not reliably accounting for randomness

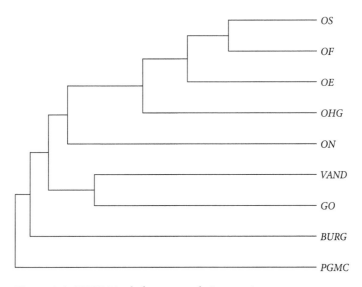

Figure 3.4 UPGMA phylogram, only innovations

Table 3.1 Distance matrix of the
hypothetical languages A, B, and C

	A	B
B	0.1	
C	0.101	0.9

in the process, noise in the data, or statistical association strengths between
taxa.

UPGMA exhibits issues regarding the weighting of individual distances as a
result of disregarding association strengths, common to several distance-based
tree models and briefly discussed before (see section 3.1.1). This is exemplified
by the following example:

Assume the following distance matrix between three languages A, B, and C.

As the matrix in Table 3.1 shows, the three hypothetical languages have differing mutual differences. We see that language A is very close to both B and C
but it is slightly more distant from C by 0.001 units. B and C, however, show a
great distance (relative to the distances of A/B and A/C) of 0.9. The UPGMA
algorithm groups these languages accordingly as displayed in Figure 3.5.

It becomes clear that the algorithm grouped A and B together despite the
great similarity between A and C. Numerically, this is what the algorithm yields
by grouping together the most similar languages first, regardless of the similarity to other languages. By this, A and B become a subgroup solely because
they share the smallest similarity. However, the distance to the next-most
similar language is very small, in fact, it is likely that this distance might have
arisen due to statistical noise or other random processes. UPGMA fails when

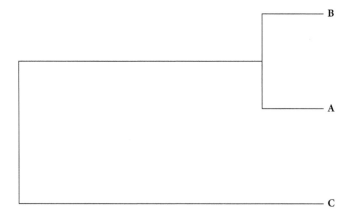

Figure 3.5 UPGMA phylogram, incorrect topology

it assumes triangle inequality (i.e. symmetric relationships between taxa) and instead of representing the groups A and B under the exclusion of C, and A and C under the exclusion of B as equally likely, it opts for the numerically optimal solution, regardless of how slim the margin to the next best grouping is. This means that if, for some reason, the dataset has asymmetric distance relationships between taxa, the model performs badly. This is not to say that this is necessarily commonplace in linguistic datasets but that this is a constraint that has to be taken into account by ensuring that the dataset fulfils the conditions necessary for UPGMA.

NeighborNets

An algorithm that bridges the gap between tree-based linguistic approaches and alternative structures is NeighborNet, first introduced by Bryant and Moulton (2002).[4] The NeighborNet algorithm builds upon the mathematical framework of the neighbour joining clustering method but instead of creating a rooted or unrooted tree, it projects the results as a web of connections that define subgroups by clustering languages more closely to one another (A. McMahon and R. McMahon 2008: 281–284). When applied to the Germanic languages dataset, we observe the following clustering in Figure 3.6:

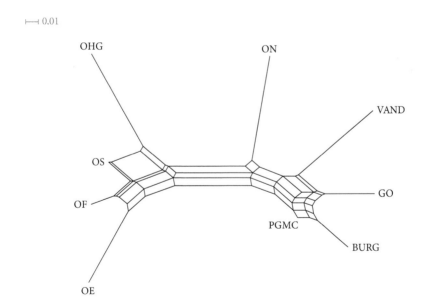

Figure 3.6 NeighborNet clustering

---

[4] For an extensive introduction see Levy and Pachter (2011) who also explore the application of this algorithm to problems of linguistic relatedness.

In this figure, we see two general sides of the net: the left hand side encompasses the West Germanic languages and the right hand side shows Old Norse together with Vandalic, Burgundian, Gothic, and Proto-Germanic. The first observation to make is that if it were not for the external knowledge that the node 'PGMC' encodes the ancestor of all other languages in the network, we would not be able to gather any information about diachronic relatedness from this method. In other words, the network does not show any hierarchical structure based on diachrony. This is, to some degree, by design as the method is such that this model does not seek to emulate tree-like properties. However, due to the lack of hierarchical properties, we are not able to discern innovative from non-innovative groups, a fact pointed out by François (2015: 180). In other words, whether a language dissimilated from its sister languages or vice versa cannot be determined from this net structure. After all, a distance-based approach only displays pairwise distances which lack direction or chronology. From Figure 3.6, we can therefore only deduce that, for example, Old High German has a higher overall distance from the other languages, but not whether it displays more innovative features than the other West Germanic languages or whether Old Saxon, Old Frisian, and Old English have undergone more innovations and have therefore dissimilated from Old High German as a group. Scholars have outlined the advantages of Neighbor-Nets that precisely lie in the absence of defined, hierarchical splits, replacing those tree-like properties with a web-like structure that maps more neatly onto the gradual diversification of languages (cf. François 2015: 173). However, at the same time, the disadvantages we have observed in the analysis above bring to light structural problems that are typical to non-tree projections of phylogeny.

Moreover, as we have seen above, it also inherits certain problems from the general domain of distance-based methods such as the site-independence of distances and the disregard of the different cladistical importance of shared innovations and shared retentions. Despite these issues, at least the latter two points can be overcome by improving upon the data type or the distance-computing algorithm and are therefore not necessarily criticisms of NeighborNet itself. The researcher must merely select and compile the data and the distance calculations carefully to avoid these issues. François (2015: 179), for example, builds his NeighborNet of the northern Vanuatu languages solely on shared innovation data to control for data-related issues. In a similar attempt, the NeighborNet algorithm was applied to the same innovation-only dataset which was used above to create the UPGMA tree in Figure 3.4, the result of which we can observe in Figure 3.7 below.

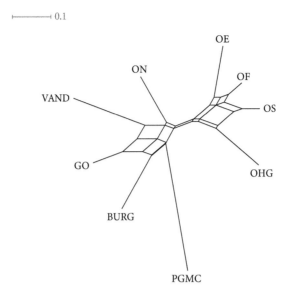

Figure 3.7 NeighborNet clustering, only innovations

This figure demonstrates the application of NeighborNet to an innovation-only dataset. Here we can make the same observations that were made in Figure 3.4, namely that the cluster distances are lower and the overall discriminability of clusters is more ambiguous. For example, the distances between Northwest Germanic and the rest is lower and Old Norse is shifted further to Vandalic, Gothic, and Burgundian than in Figure 3.6. An innovation-weighted approach is therefore less promising for distance matrices when the distances are computed as they are here.

But nevertheless scholars see this method as a promising alternative to tree-based cladistic models. For example Heggarty, Maguire, and A. McMahon (2010) review and discuss NeighborNets for cladistic research in detail. Moreover, many scholars combine phylogenetic inference models with distance-based approaches to explore a problem from different viewpoints (e.g. Bowern 2012).

3.1.2 Bayesian phylogenetic models

Bayesian phylogenetic inference has its roots in bioinformatics and more specifically in the study of the genetic relationship between different organism species. Although a variety of methods is used in this domain,[5] Bayesian

---

[5] See Garamszegi (2014); Ronquist, Mark, and Huelsenbeck (2009) for extensive overviews of different methods and algorithms currently in use in bioinformatics.

inference is often viewed as one of the most powerful tools (cf. Nichols and Warnow 2008; Bowern 2012).

The origins of Bayesian phylogenetics lie in the task of measuring species diversification on the level of molecular genetics. The input data in bioinformatic applications are thus genetic sequence alignments and morphological data (i.e. data that encode observable physiological properties of species as opposed to data obtained from sequencing genomes of organisms). The specific research interest is to estimate the time and sequence of speciation by taking into account molecular evolution speeds and change rates.

The biological goal is similar to that of cladistic questions in linguistics. The linguistic problems are similarly concerned with the time of linguistic diversification, the speed of language change/innovation and the origin times of protolanguages.

The transferability of these biological concepts has been evaluated in various previous studies and theoretical investigations. The general application of biological analogies to linguistic change by no means stand on shaky ground. At least regarding the patterns of transmission and acquisition, the properties of communities with frequent exchanges of linguistic properties are closely related to the analogous processes in evolutionary biology (cf. Labov 2001: 6–14; Walkden 2012). This assumption holds for the abstract scope of linguistic diversification, which is the needed requirement for applying phylogenetic models or, for that matter, other computational methods that involve abstractions to the linguistic change processes. In fact, it has been proposed that phylogenetic models can be used for a variety of cultural evolution problems beyond linguistic aspects alone (Mesoudi, Whiten, and Laland 2004, 2006; Boyd and Richerson 2005; Gray, Bryant, and Greenhill 2010; Gray, Atkinson, et al. 2013).

Atkinson and Gray (2005) find multiple parallels between the evolutionary processes in biology and in linguistics that affect multiple domains of change and pertain to different processes of different scopes. These parallels allow biological methods to be applied to linguistic problems, especially regarding macro-level investigation of linguistic diversification. Not because linguistic change is a biological process, but because both linguistics and genetics evolve under certain conditions that are similar enough for the methods to be shared (see e.g. the extensive discussions of this issue in Croft 2000; Andersen 2006).

Further, we have to bear in mind that in order to use these methods, linguistic change and diversification do not necessarily need to operate exactly in the same ways as their biological counterparts. It is sufficient if the method can serve as a good approximation to the linguistic processes.

Criticisms of phylogenetic models have been voiced criticizing the data sources and applicability to linguistic problems (see e.g. Pereltsvaig and Lewis 2015). In-depth examinations of the criticisms and defenzes of these methods (such as Bowern 2018) have shown that when using problem-appropriate data and specifications, they can yield beneficial insights into language relatedness and ancestral stage dating.

Phylogenetic inference shares several advantages with computational methods in general such as repeatability, interpretability, transparency. This means that it employs statistical and computational tools which operate on all data in the same way. Moreover, it can be applied to a variety of problems (Gray, Greenhill, and Ross 2007). This means that the results obtained from the models can be scrutinized with regard to their set-up and parameters. Errors and issues can be traced back to misspecifications and erroneous basic assumptions. Further, phylogenetic trees are easily communicated and interpreted with little effort since the resulting consensus trees contain the most basic information summary of the model results and the underlying parameters are mathematically defined. The models previously tested for their accuracy are congruent in many aspects with results from the manual comparative method (Greenhill and Gray 2012). As an additional advantage, the models and parameters can be analysed themselves according to stringent procedures to evaluate their fit to the dataset. It is thus possible to explore different parameter settings and model types and determine at the end which models—and in turn which parameters—fit the data best. This method serves as a model-external check that enables the selection of better models and, as a result the interpretation of the parameters in light of these findings. As such analyses can provide a good foundation for model sanity checks, they are frequently used in contemporary studies (e.g. Verkerk 2019).

Several previous studies have employed phylogenetic modelling to estimate the phylogeny and split dates in several language families.

Among the first studies using Bayesian phylogenetic methods in linguistics, Gray and Atkinson (2003) analysed a dataset of Indo-European languages to estimate the age of Proto-Indo-European (PIE). In this investigation, they suggest an older age of the break-up of PIE thus favouring the Anatolian hypothesis. However, their results have drawn criticism from multiple directions. Most prominently, Chang et al. (2015) have employed Bayesian phylogenetics methods in which they find support for the steppe hypothesis by including ancestry constraints on the tree topologies (see section 1.3).

Other scholars have used Bayesian phylogenetics in the past to test previous assumptions about the relatedness of languages in a family, as, for example,

Bowern (2012) has demonstrated for the Tasmanian languages. Further, Bowern and Atkinson (2012) analyse the Pama-Nyungan languages to investigate the major subgroups of this family.

A great number of phylogenetic inference studies focus on lexical data (see discussion in Dunn et al. 2008: 714–718), chief among them studies by Dunn et al. (2008); Greenhill, Gray, et al. (2009); Greenhill, Drummond, and Gray (2010).

The advantages of using Bayesian phylogenetic models for inferring linguistic relations is that they are centred around finding the most probable trees for given data while taking into account the most likely development of each character site instead of applying tree-building tools to single-valued linguistic distance measures. Moreover, the focus of the algorithm is to operate on the data directly and infer the tree structure from the probabilities of every site occurring along the tree. This means that these models reconstruct and infer the possible developments of individual character sites rather than using a global distance metric. This is advantageous insofar as the relationship between the included languages is modelled as a development affecting all features instead of collapsing these features into a single distance value that averages out more intricate character-level developments.

Further, as they take into account change rates and diversification speeds, often branch-specific, which are not uniform (Greenhill, Drummond, and Gray 2010), they are not only more fine-grained and versatile but they also represent an important tool for dating of splits and taxon ages.

It is important to note that during this section, I will predominantly use examples from linguistic phylogenetics, but it needs to be kept in mind that all concepts mentioned here have their original applications in biological phylogenetics.

3.1.3 Core concepts

Bayesian inference

The core element of Bayesian inference in general is the estimation of the probability of a model or model parameters given the data at hand. In general, Bayesian methods model the question 'given the data derived from a real-world process, which parameter values in a certain model are most likely to have produced the data?'. In Bayesian linear regression, for example, the model estimates the probability of a certain regression line given the data, or, more commonly, the probability distribution over all regression lines given the data. In essence this means that Bayesian regression finds those most likely regression lines out of all regression lines that could possibly exist. The results of a Bayesian model are therefore a distribution of those most likely parameters (e.g. slope and intercept of a regression line), and each individual parameter value is a *sample draw*, usually from a sampling algorithm (see below). This distribution is called a *posterior distribution* or just *posterior*. Another crucial element of Bayesian modelling is the existence of priors: parameters that are inferred during model fitting are given prior distributions that are multiplied with the likelihood of the data given the parameter according to Bayes' formula. Those determine the a-priori likelihood of certain parameters and let the researcher discourage the model from making absurd parameter choices.[6] In Bayesian phylogenetics, however, the distributions from which the posterior samples are drawn is not a distribution of parameter values alone but also a distribution over trees. A thorough introduction to Bayesian statistics in the light of Bayesian phylogenetics is presented in Ronquist, Mark, and Huelsenbeck (2009). Before examining the intricate details of Bayesian inference models, it is necessary to outline the notion of probability in the context of linguistic family trees: assume there are three taxa (languages) in the dataset that have undergone different numbers of innovations. Further assume there are four possible innovations in the dataset and language A has undergone innovations in positions 1, 2, and 4, yielding an innovation vector (1, 1, 0, 1). Language B shows innovations 1 and 2 while innovations 1 and 3 are observed in language C.

Figures 3.8 and 3.9 show two potential trees that might be inferred from the data to explain the phylogenetic relationship between languages A, B, and C.

What can be seen here is that the tree topology in Figure 3.8 fits the data better and, in a Bayesian modelling context, this means that the tree in Figure 3.8 is more likely given the data.[7] The tree topologies are generated in a stochastic model which takes as an input all parameters such as root age, branch lengths, and speciation rates and outputs a tree topology based on a specific setting of all parameters. A posterior probability can then be calculated for this tree given the data and by taking into account the model priors: since this analysis is Bayesian, all parameters and topologies have priors which are taken into account for calculating the posterior probability of each tree. The goal of the analysis is thus to find those tree topologies and parameter settings that explain

---

[6] There is much more in the way of theoretical underpinnings to the role of priors in Bayesian modelling, a detailed discussion of which, however, would be beyond the scope of this book. For a detailed introduction, see McElreath (2020: ch. 2).

[7] In both examples, edge lengths can be ignored as these toy examples are illustrative representations of two different topologies, thus lengths are equal for all edges.

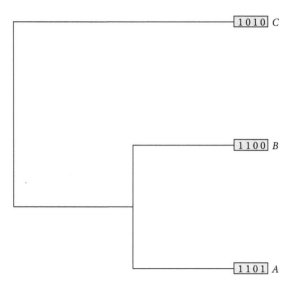

Figure 3.8 A potential tree topology

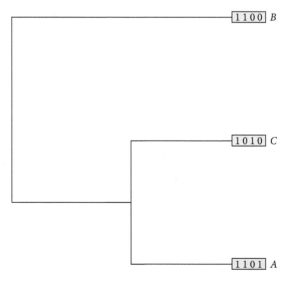

Figure 3.9 A potential tree topology

the data best, or, more accurately, yield the highest posterior probability given the data.

Note that this description of the probability estimation simplifies the matter significantly and must therefore be taken as a coarse outline of the core ideas of tree probabilities. A more detailed presentation of *likelihood* and *probability* in the context of tree topologies is provided in Greenhill, Gray, et al. (2009: 5–10).

The main computational issue with this approach is that the parameter combinations are very large, meaning that even a small number of parameters can lead to a massive inflation of potential trees. Assume we are analysing a dataset using four phylogenetic parameters, each with 100 intervals (e.g. in a parameter between 0 and 1, we are using all parameter settings in steps of 0.01). This would result in 100 million potential trees to be evaluated and with every additional parameter, this number would be multiplied by the number of intervals. It is not uncommon for phylogenetic analyses to have more than forty parameters to be inferred by the model, with most of them having much larger parameter spaces than the four parameters in the example above.

Therefore, it becomes clear that not all possible trees can be evaluated, as doing so would inevitably exceed the computing power even of modern computing architectures. As a result, strategies have been devised to approximate the high-probability tree topologies despite the high-dimensional parameter space.

Fortunately, not all trees that result from these parameter combinations are good fits to the data. In fact, only a small fraction of trees is in the high-probability region. It would therefore suffice to estimate this high-probability region directly without having to evaluate all possible parameter combinations. To achieve this, Bayesian phylogenetic models use Markov-Chain-Monte-Carlo (MCMC) simulations to find and traverse the high-probability regions of the posterior distribution of trees.[8]

In essence, an MCMC simulation traverses the posterior distribution in a guided manner, by a proposal system that uses the posterior probability. In simple terms, the MCMC analysis starts at one point in the parameter space and then moves away from this position by proposing a new location near the starting point. Then, the probability at this new location is evaluated and compared with the probability of the parameter setting at the current location. If the new location has a higher probability, this location is set as the starting point for the next step. If the new location has a smaller probability, then the chain makes the switch to this location with a probability that is proportional to the probability difference between current and new location. This process is repeated multiple times and after a certain number of iterations, the chain arrives at the high-probability space and stays fluctuating in this region.

---

[8] See Ronquist, Mark, and Huelsenbeck (2009) for a concise introduction of MCMC estimation in phylogenetic models.

Afterwards, the samples drawn from this region can be taken as the posterior distribution. This process is akin to a mountaineer ascending to the peak of a mountain by predominantly climbing in directions that are located uphill from their position. The danger of obtaining false results due to the algorithm converging in a local maximum parameter area is mitigated by running more than one chain. If the chains converge in a similar parameter area, the run is regarded as successful and the results can be used. If one chain would remain in a local maximum, the two chains do not converge as they finish their runs in different parameter regions.

This general algorithm that is used in most Bayesian analyses can also be used in phylogenetic models to evaluate posterior trees instead of regression parameters of the type used in Bayesian regression analyses. In essence, it asks the question: 'which tree structures could have yielded the data we see in the daughter languages?'

There are several different types of MCMC algorithms with different efficiencies and applications: the algorithm used in RevBayes is called Metropolis-Hastings.

Substitution models

The substitution model is the part of a phylogenetic model that computes the transitions between the different character states of the phylogenetic data. It essentially models *how* different observed traits in a language (i.e. the *characters* in the data) evolve. The substitution processes in phylogenetic inference are modelled as a continuous time Markov model (CTMC), a transition-based stochastic model of state changes. In molecular genetics, these character states correspond to different nucleotide states in a given nucleotide sequence. The substitution model aims at modelling the state change between any one nucleotide to any other nucleotide. In DNA data, these nucleotide states are C, G, A, and T. The basis of any such substitution model is the *instantaneous-rate matrix* which describes the rate of change between the different possible states. This rate matrix applied to a dataset with three character states A, B, and C would yield the following rate matrix Q:[9]

$$Q = \begin{bmatrix} -\mu_A & \mu_{AB} & \mu_{AC} \\ \mu_{BA} & -\mu_B & \mu_{BC} \\ \mu_{CA} & \mu_{CB} & -\mu_C \end{bmatrix} \tag{3.2}$$

[9] Note that the states here are labelled more universally as A, B, and C instead of the nucleotide names, which is due to the fact that in such substitution matrices, the states can be any discrete labels and not only nucleotide states.

The transition rate between the states, conventionally indicated by μ, thus the transition from state A to state B would be indicated by μ_{AB} in the matrix. In other words, the rate μ_{AB} represents the rate of state A in the data changing to B. This is phylogenetically important to model the state transition rates as different since the branch length estimates and splits can differ under varying transition rates. Concretely this means that when we assume that character state A changes to B twice as often as A changes to C, the resulting tree inferences will be different insofar as they will account for that imbalance in the change pathways of A. For mathematical reasons which can be set aside at this point, the negative diagonal represents the negative sum of all rates in the respective row.

When the substitution models were first proposed in Jukes, Cantor, et al. (1969), these transition rates were held constant and equal such that all nucleotides have the identical global rate of transition to all other nucleotides. What this assumes is that the nucleotides are in fact identical in their probability of changing into any other nucleotide. Applied to linguistics, this means that the transition rates between different character states are set here. In an innovation dataset, this would correspond to the change rate from a 0 ('no innovation') to a 1 ('innovation') and vice versa. The substitution model building on this rate equality is the so-called Jukes-Cantor model which the following matrix visualizes.

$$Q = \begin{bmatrix} -2\mu & \mu & \mu \\ \mu & -2\mu & \mu \\ \mu & \mu & -2\mu \end{bmatrix} \tag{3.3}$$

However, later investigations revealed variation between different nucleotides which prompted researchers to propose modifications of the Jukes-Cantor model in which the transition rates can differ. The resulting models, of which GTR (General time-reversible) models are the most prominent, can therefore account for different transition rates and even infer those rates from the data.

A modification of the original GTR, which builds on unique concepts of genetics (e.g. transitions and transversions), allows for further flexibility regarding transition rates: in the classical GTR model, rates are bidirectional, meaning that the rate of transition from A to B is the same as the rate of transition from B to A. The free transition rate model relaxes this assumption further, giving every transition rate its own value. This allows for asymmetric transitions where directional change is possible.

From a linguistic perspective, these models are difficult to apply insofar as some of them (e.g. GTR (Tavaré et al. 1986) and Hasegawa-Kishino-Yano (HKY) (Hasegawa, Kishino, and Yano 1985)) have strong molecular genetic underpinnings. However, linguistic data still has transitions of states, for example transitions between sounds, cognates, or, in the case of the study at hand, loss and acquisition of innovations. Ultimately, the linguistic problem and the dataset have to be examined to determine which substitution model can apply in the respective context. The Jukes-Cantor model may function as a phylogenetic null model which assumes there to be no differences in the transition rates between all pairs of linguistic states, but there are datasets where this identity of rates is violated. The implications of different substitution models for modelling the Germanic languages are discussed in detail in section 3.2.2.

Characters in linguistics can represent linguistic innovations (such as in this study), or they can represent states of linguistic features (see section 3.1 and the discussion of character states in Ringe, Warnow, and Taylor (2002: 71–78)). Depending on what linguistic data are the basis of a phylogenetic analysis, different transition rates may be needed. Especially for small datasets, inferring the transition rates from the data accurately might not always be possible.

Modelling among-site rate variation

A related concept to substitution models is the among-site rate variation (sometimes called 'cross-character rate heterogeneity') which operates on top of the substitution rates intended to account for different rates of change between different characters in the dataset. In other words, different linguistic features expressed as characters in the dataset may change at different speeds but the substitution model alone estimates one single, albeit directional, change rate for all characters. To account for this problem, the gamma among-site rate variation draws random rate multipliers for each site from a gamma distribution with parameters α and β where $\alpha = \beta$. This yields a distribution that is flat for values of α approaching 1 and increasingly resembles a normal distribution for higher values. Moreover, with increasing values, the standard deviation narrows. Figure 3.10 shows density plots of the gamma distribution at different values of α.

When random variables are drawn from these gamma distributions, the differences between the rate multipliers will be determined by how flat the distribution is. If rate multipliers are drawn from a gamma distribution with $\alpha = 1$, the variations between the rates will differ considerably and will range from close to zero to 6 and beyond. In turn the rates for different sites will be heterogeneous as the base rates are multiplied by a value close to zero for some

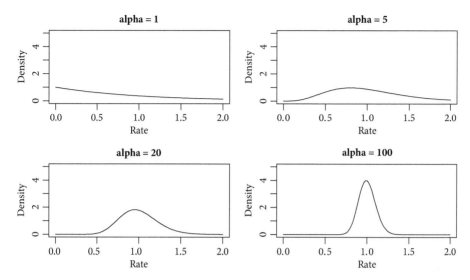

Figure 3.10 Gamma density function

sites and six times higher than the base rate for other sites. If α is very high, the variation between the sites will not differ much as they are multiplied by values close to 1, which de-facto does not change the base rate by much. It is important to note that not every character is assigned its own value of α. Rather, it is drawn randomly for each character anew. This means that the model gauges how much variability in the character states is most compatible with the data. In terms of the Bayesian approach, we could say that the model infers what level of variance in the states we need to explain the data well. If the values for α are small, it means that the sampled tree topologies possess a large variability in their character site rates.

Since α is being estimated during the analysis, the model can, in conjunction with the priors, estimate the value of this variable from the data directly. The implementation of this gamma-rate model in *RevBayes* uses a discretized gamma version (Z. Yang 1994) where the model computes an average of different discretized versions of the gamma distribution (see the discussion in Yanovich 2020: appendix).

Branch rates and the molecular clock

One main element of all tree models is the branch lengths as they determine key findings about phylogenetic relationships. This is different from traditional tree-model depictions as there, branch lengths in most cases do not correspond to any quantitative scale. As we have seen in section 3.1.1, branch lengths were taken as a measure of similarity between clades in distance-based methods. There, the length of the branch represents the distance between two nodes that is computed from the data. In Bayesian phylogenetic inference, branch lengths of clades in a given tree are to be inferred from the data. However in Bayesian phylogenetics, the definition of branch length differs from the interpretation in distance-based methods insofar as the method rests on different base assumptions between the relationship of different taxa. As described above, Bayesian phylogenetics inference does not operate on the premise of distance between taxa expressed by a number computed from an aggregate of the *overall* distance between two datasets behind these taxa. Instead, it computes the most probable ways in which a tree-like split of taxa can account for the data and therefore the minimal unit of computation is characters in one site. In other words, whereas distance methods often express the distance between two datasets as one number, Bayesian inference aims at the differences between these datasets with regard to individual observations (i.e. *sites*). From this, follows a different interpretation of branch length as a function of site changes between two nodes. Longer branch lengths therefore correspond to more changes in individual sites between two nodes. At the same time, branch lengths and transition rates are connected insofar as change rates along branches are assumed to be even faster if they run along the lines of transition rates. That is, if the difference between an ancestor node and a descendant node is mostly in the characters A (ancestor node) > B (descendant node) and if it so happens that the change A > B is overall much more common than vice versa, the branch rates will be assumed to be much higher for this particular edge. These change frequencies between nodes are linked to abstract units of time in which the branch length is equal to the number of changes per one site and therefore the time it takes for these changes to occur. If a branch length is, for example, 1, this branch length denotes that 1 change per one site has occurred along the branch in question and the time this length corresponds to is equal to the time it takes for 1 change per site to occur. This also means that the time does not correspond to absolute or actual time but to the unknown unit of time corresponding to the changes along the branch. This approach therefore is initially not calibrated to actual time, modelling not the actual time but the number of changes per site which correspond to an unknown time frame.

However for some analyses, it may be required to use absolute time as a unit during the analysis. Doing this is important in two scenarios (among others):

(1) The goal of the analysis is to date the age of certain taxa or ancestral states. In this scenario, the actual age of, for example, a protolanguage is to

be inferred. Then, it is necessary to calibrate the model to absolute time in order for the branch lengths, branching times, and ancestral node ages to correspond to years instead of the abstract concept of change rate times. This is the approach used in studies by Chang et al. (2015) and Gray and Atkinson (2003) where one of the research goals is to infer the root age of Proto-Indo-European. A time calibration is usually done by setting observation dates or priors for the tips and the root. This way, the abstract units of time are converted by the model into actual time estimates. For example, if we know that a certain split occurs halfway between node A and node C, and that A and C are approximately 1,000 years apart, we can date the split to 500 years before C occurs.

(2) There are temporal differences between the taxa in the analyses. In cases where not all languages in the dataset are contemporaneous ('extant'), one might want to account for the fact that the innovations and changes present in these languages correspond to different time periods. For example, if one analyses a dataset which contains both modern Swedish and Middle English, the actual time that has passed since their most recent common ancestor is longer for modern Swedish than it is for Middle English. This temporal difference needs to be incorporated in the model because otherwise, the inference might come to incorrect conclusions of the respective phylogeny since it treats both modern Swedish and Middle English as extant. Calibrating this model to absolute time, and giving different attestation ages for both languages, prevents this problem from occurring. Both issues are important for the study at hand as the different occurrence times of the Germanic daughter languages need to be accounted for as well as providing a broad age range for Proto-Germanic.

Up to this point, we have only discussed the importance of absolute-time calibration for different applications of phylogenetic inference. It is therefore important to discuss the mechanisms behind dating and time calibration further in more detail.

The baseline assumption is that over time, changes occur at certain rates which, in a time-calibrated model, correspond to units of absolute time. This results in inferences where it can be estimated that over the course of n years, y number of changes occurred which corresponds to a change rate of $\frac{y}{n}$. The notion of a change rate is expressed in the concept of a *molecular clock* which states that changes occur at a certain rate over the course of time. Conversely, this notion suggests that if the change rate is known or approximated, we can date the divergence times and ages of ancestral nodes. Therefore, time-calibrated models operate under the molecular clock assumption that changes correspond to strict or varying units of absolute time.

This assumption, however, leads to further issues regarding the definition and implementation of the molecular clock into phylogenetic models. The definition of a correspondence between time, and a certain amount of changes, raises the question of how to connect absolute time and change. There are, in general, three major types of modelling the molecular clock: *strict clock*, *relaxed clock*, and *random local clock* models.

Some of the distance-based methods such as the aforementioned UPGMA algorithm as well as certain phylogenetic models operate under the assumption of a strict clock. A strict clock assumes that the change rates of individual sites are constant across the time period in question. This means a global clock with one rate pertaining to all branches of the tree governs the changes. While this approach has the benefit of simplicity, it is often not the tool of choice for many current phylogenetic models. That is, the global uniformity of linguistic change rate is perceived as a problematic assumption (see Bergsland and Vogt 1962; Walkden 2019, for discussion).

The second clock model is the relaxed clock model which, in reality, is an umbrella term for several clock models that, at their core, do not assume a constant global rate of change but instead assign an individual rate to each branch. This results in every branch leading up to a taxon or subclade having their own change rate and allows for clade-specific innovation speeds accounting for more conservative or innovative languages. These rates are not pre-determined but inferred during simulation. A result of rate-specific change estimation is that we are able to gauge the innovation speed of different clades and distinguish between slow-changing and fast-changing languages.

The third type of model is random local clock models which can be seen as a middle ground between strict and relaxed clock models: they modify the strict clock approach insofar as the clock rate is allowed to vary across the investigated time period but the rate is still global, that is, it affects all clades and taxa but varies over time.

As we have seen in this section, Bayesian phylogenetic models can be calibrated to absolute time and, depending on the chosen clock model, infer the rate at which individual languages and subclades undergo innovations.

Speciation and extinction

Two other important parameters in a phylogenetic model are speciation and extinction rates. In essence, both parameters reflect the number of speciation or extinction events per time unit and lineage.

Speciation describes the process under which new lineages are created. A speciation event is thus the phenomenon of one lineage splitting into more than one daughter lineage.[10] For example, North Germanic splitting into Old East Norse and Old West Norse. Essentially, this parameter governs the rate at which new lineages are created.

Extinction is harder to define from a linguistic standpoint. In biological contexts, an extinction event is an event in which a lineage dies out without producing subsequent lineages. Such a lineage extinction may result in a fossil but it might also occur unnoticed since we are only presented with those taxa that either survived or entered the fossil record. Applied to linguistics, this means that an extinction event may either result in a language going extinct of which we have written accounts or of languages we do not know about. In practice, the extinction rate accounts for the possibility that an unknown number of Germanic languages existed without being attested in written form which went extinct due to an unknown cause. Gothic, for example, went extinct insofar as it does not have any present-day descendants. If Gothic had never been recorded, we would be ignorant of its existence. The probability of either known or unknown extinction is modelled by the extinction rate parameter.

Similar to the implementation of branch rates, speciation and extinction rates can be globally *constant* (cf. Nee, May, and Harvey 1994), *episodic* or *branch-specific*. Episodic rates assume that the rate change is due to external, episodic events. In biological applications this can mean mass extinction events or increased speciation due to ecological factors. Branch-specific rates assume that the number of occurring speciation and extinction events is dependent on the branch (cf. Höhna 2014). The biological motivation for this might be that due to factors unique to each branch, speciation and extinction increases or decreases. Examples for this might be increased or decreased reproductive success occurring along a branch or the rate change being associated with environmental factors that apply only to the habitat of the species associated with the lineage in question (see Condamine, Rolland, and Morlon (2013) for environmental factors in biological evolution).

While these different rate models are linked to reasonable real-world phenomena in biology, it is more difficult to determine whether all three models can be used for linguistics. The episodic model might be still applicable as the episodic changes could represent major historical disruptions of the preceding order which leads to an increased likelihood of extinction or the creation of new languages. This is in some regards similar to the notion of 'punctuated equilibrium' proposed by Dixon (1997) in a linguistic context. This concept describes linguistic changes as cumulating in sporadic events that are

---

[10] As most phylogenetic models assume bifurcating trees, a speciation event is one lineage splitting into two descendant lineages.

preceded and followed by long periods of linguistic constancy (see Bowern 2006; Walkden 2019: for discussion).

However, branch-specific rates would require a change in likelihood that is at least somewhat causally linked to the preceding branching event. We would thus find that the rate of diversification in, for example, West Germanic increases as soon as it has diverged from North Germanic and decreases again once it breaks up into multiple languages itself. It is difficult to find theoretical backing for this process and unless there is demonstrable evidence for branch-dependent speciation, at least across a short time period, I will assume a global speciation and extinction rate for this analysis which assumes that lineages split and go extinct at approximately a constant rate. This is further supported by the fact that Germanic is a spatially and temporally small language family where no major disruptions take place locally and only apply to a subset of the lineages.

3.2 The Germanic diversification model

3.2.1 Model specifications

To analyse the Germanic linguistic phylogeny with this Bayesian phyloge-netic model, I set up six differently parametrized models to see how different assumptions influence the phylogeny inferences. These six models differ in both the fossil dating and substitution models, the differences of which will be outlined below.

Firstly, the core elements of all models need to be described to determine and motivate what aspects are chosen to be common across all models. The following sections will examine those elements divided into inferred and fixed parameters. The theoretical underpinnings of the concepts mentioned here are explained in detail in section 3.1.3.

Inferred parameters
The inferred parameters are those parameters in the model that are variable and only assigned priors such that they are inferred by the model during sampling. In contrast to fixed parameters, this leaves the opportunity for the model to come up with the best parameter values directly without them being hard-coded into the model.

The **branch rates** model chosen for these analyses is a relaxed clock with branch-specific substitution rates. This gives the models freedom to let the branch rates vary across clades. Moreover, by doing so, the rates can later be extracted and interpreted. The prior distribution for each branch is drawn according to this hierarchical model:[11]

$$rate_j \sim exponential\left(\frac{1}{m}\right)$$

$$m \sim lognorm(\mu, \sigma)$$

$$\mu \sim norm(-7, 10)$$

$$\sigma \sim exponential(1)$$

Where $1...j$ are the number of branches to be inferred.

This places a prior distribution over each branch rate that is largely uninformative with a wide range from 0 to ∞ with a mean close to zero.[12] The definition of the rate as a function of $\left(\frac{1}{m}\right)$ results in the outcome of the parameter to be a rate multiplier and thus the rate to be interpreted as substitutions per site per time unit. This means that through this setup, m becomes a rate multiplier which can be interpreted more easily.

In conjunction with the rate model operating on the substitution rates, I implemented a **gamma rate among-site variation** model which estimates the variations of rates among different sites. The gamma rate model, including its priors implemented, follows the distribution below.

$$siterates \sim DiscretizedGamma(\alpha, \alpha)$$

$$\alpha \sim lognorm(\ln(5.0), 0.587405)$$

Note that the implementation of the gamma rates in RevBayes is done via a discretized gamma distribution with k categories. For this model, I chose a standard $k = 4$ as the number of categories. This choice is a reasonable balance between a good approximation to the gamma distribution and computational efficiency. The hyperprior (i.e. second-order priors, priors inside of priors) parameters for the lognormal distributions are standard choices for this distribution (see e.g. Höhna, Landis, et al. 2017: 123) and result in an uninformative prior with most of its probability mass under 10. Therefore, this prior a priori favours a low α which is identical with a large among-site variation. Nevertheless the prior is uninformative enough to be overridden by the data.

---

[11] The discussion of the exact prior settings in this and subsequent models is given in section 3.3.
[12] *Informativity* is often used in Bayesian contexts to describe the strength of the prior assumptions. An uninformative prior allows for a large range of parameter values, some of which may be unrealistic or impossible. Informative priors on the other hand encode stronger assumptions about the parameter distribution; they are, however, often better at discouraging unrealistic parameter values and reducing the influence of outliers.

The models also contain parameters for **speciation** (i.e. emergence of a new lineage through a split) and **extinction** (i.e. discontinuation of a lineage). These parameters are set to be global, meaning that they are constant within the time period of each individual tree. This modelling strategy is motivated by the circumstances of the Germanic languages. Linguistically, we cannot demonstrate that in this case, we see a branch-specific speciation or extinction rate. This would entail demonstrating that certain branches possess innate (linguistic or extralinguistic) qualities that make them more likely to produce daughter lineages. The other model is the episodic speciation model which assumes that the rates of speciation and extinction change in episodes due to external factors such as mass extinction and mass speciation events. Over a large time horizon there might be less environmental influence on spread-out language families: one can assume events that could trigger these episodic bursts of speciation or extinction are more localized. Applied to the case of Germanic, however, we do not have the option of assuming that speciation and extinction are not episodic. Rather, Germanic spans roughly 1,500 years from the approximate break-up, in the late Iron Age, of central and northern Europe to the early middle ages where most Germanic daughter languages had become mostly independent. Furthermore we are aware that the migrations and contact situations changed over the course of these 1,500 years. Towards the end of the first half of the first millennium, we find increased linguistic contact situations with Latin speakers and changes to the political landscape due to the weakening of Roman administrative structures in the vicinity of Germanic-speaking communities. This change is exemplified by the migrations of these communities into territories in Europe and northern Africa with predominantly Latin-speaking populations such as the Vandals and Goths. These are changes whose impact on linguistic diversity we cannot determine easily. Moreover, whether or not these circumstances influenced linguistic change and speciation more than in previous periods is unclear. For this reason, we cannot rule out that speciation and extinction rates were episodic. To account for this uncertainty, I re-ran the best performing of the six models at hand after the analysis with episodically determined speciation and extinction rates to estimate the impact of these factors on the outcome. Refer to section 3.2.4 for an analysis of this situation. I did not include the episodic birth–death model into the original model runs as this would have resulted in a doubling in models to compare, and certain models with inherently more variable parameters (e.g. the varying rates and inferred bounds models) would be run with an even greater number of variable parameters.

Table 3.2 Estimates of the existence time of Proto-Germanic

Date	References
Not before 500 BC	Ringe (2017: 241)
Before 500 BC	Lehmann (1961: 73)
500 BC	Grønvik (1998: 145); Mallory (1989: 87)
2,250 BP	Chang et al. (2015: 226)
last centuries BC to first centuries AD	Penzl (1985: 149)
400 BC–50 AD	Voyles (1992: 34)

The model was further calibrated to **absolute time** by means of tip dating and root age priors. The tip dating mechanics are explained later on as they are part of the differences between the individual models. An integral part of absolute time calibration is also a node age prior. This prior sets the time period in which the age of the node is sampled and simultaneously limits the range of hypotheses about the root age considered. Moreover, setting the node age gives the model a calibration point to absolute time. In case of the Germanic node age prior, there are issues to consider regarding dating of the root.

We know that the root node in this phylogenetic model represents the time of divergence of the first clades from the protolanguage, hence the root age for a Germanic dataset represents the time of the first split of a language or clade from Proto-Germanic. The current estimates for the approximate age of Proto-Germanic are summarized in Table 3.2.

This, however, raises the additional question of dating, as the root age estimate of a phylogenetic model is not concerned with the earliest date by which certain defining changes have been completed but the latest date at which the protolanguage split into daughter clades. This poses a problem insofar as the range between the estimates of the inception of a Proto-Germanic language or dialectal area and the time of the break-up might differ considerably. Between the earliest possible date for the late stage of Proto-Germanic and the break-up into a family may lie a time ranging from a few decades to several hundred years. The phylogenetic model, estimating only the date of the Germanic break-up, therefore needs to be calibrated using a sensible prior on the possible age of the root node. I therefore used a weakly informative prior consisting of a truncated normal distribution with a mean of 2.25 and a standard deviation of 0.2, truncated between 1.8 and 3. Figure 3.11 shows this distribution as a density plot. These figures denote the time before present[13] in units

---

[13] Throughout the analysis, the *present* was taken to mean the year 2000 for reasons of convenience.

of 1,000 years. Hence, the distribution could also be described as a normal distribution between the year 1000 BC and 200 AD with a mean at 250 BC and a standard deviation of 200 years. The 'time before present' will henceforth be referred to as the *age* of a tree node. This prior was chosen as most scholars agree on a date around or later than 500 BC and the prior encompasses this temporal space while making dates much earlier than 500 BC more unlikely. It should be noted that the prior impact is small relative to the data observed in the model. In other words, if the data suggested a much earlier date for Proto-Germanic, they would overpower the prior with ease (for age values between 200 AD and 1,000 BC due to the truncated prior). The reason for this is that since the prior is only weakly informative and can thus be easily overpowered by the amount of available data.

As we can see in Figure 3.11, the main centre of the probability mass is between 2.0 and 2.5 with only little mass being allocated towards the outer rims. The goal of this distribution is to encourage root ages between 2.0 and 2.5 but with increasingly discouraging of values younger than 2.0 and older than 2.5. A distribution of this setup accounts for the estimates of the beginning of Proto-Germanic after 500 BC (an age of 2.5) and the earliest textual evidence of Germanic with first individual features of post-Proto-Germanic changes. Setting this prior reasonably is important but the prior choice can easily be overridden by the model as we will see in the later results.

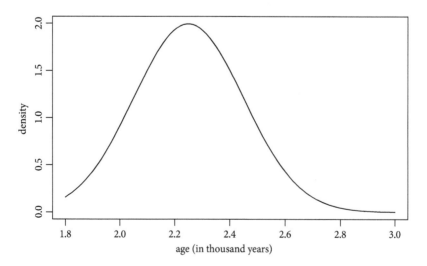

Figure 3.11 Node age prior density

Fixed parameters

The only fixed (i.e. not inferred) parameters used in the models are the tree prior and the root frequencies.

The **root frequencies** are a parameter which governs the state frequencies at the root of the tree. In many applications, the frequency distribution of the individual states in the data is unknown and inferred at the root node. If, for example, a dataset contains three possible character states per site, we could be interested in inferring the frequency at which each character state is represented at the reconstructed root stage. Even if this is not of interest, it might be beneficial to at least model the frequencies to get better estimates of the divergence times and node ages. In the case of this study, the type of dataset demands a fixed setting of root frequencies: the binary innovation data require that the root stage has 0 (the character denoting no innovation at this site) in all sites. Therefore the ratio between character state 0 and character state 1 at the root must be fixed to 1:0. Otherwise, we see an issue called *jogging* that is common to phylogenetic problems where the ancestor state is unknown. Jogging to the root means that between two tip nodes, their most recent common ancestor will likely form an intermediate state between the two tips. This presents an issue in cases where an averaging effect in the ancestor node leads to changes before the ancestor node being attributed to the daughter languages, rather than to the ancestor clade itself. Figures 3.12 and 3.13 show this phenomenon visually.

Suppose there is a clade with three nodes, the tips **A** and **B**, and the root node. Suppose further that A has undergone more changes from the root than B—either because it was observed at a later time or has a higher branch rate than B. Figure 3.12 shows this situation of two tip nodes with four sites of the binary character states **0** and **1**. The root stage is [0, 0, 0, 0] with B having undergone one change and A shows changes in 3 sites.[14]

In the default case without any tip dating or branch rate specifications, the unequal change rates will likely remain undetected and the inference will often resemble the pattern we see in Figure 3.13.

Here, the root stage shows the pattern with state 1 at site positions 2 and 4. The inference here is that the root state is of the type [0, 1, 0, 1] with a change to taxon B of 1 > 0 in position 4 and a change of 0 > 1 in position 1. That is, the changes were partitioned into equal rates along the branches by inferring an intermediate root state. Now, both times there is exactly one change along each

---

[14] Note that in this example, changes 1 > 0 are possible, as innovation deletions cannot always be ruled out as a matter of principle (see discussion in section 3.2.2).

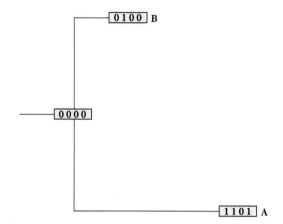

Figure 3.12 Topology with unequal branch rates

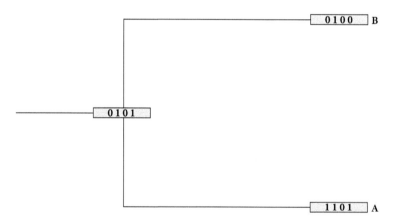

Figure 3.13 Incorrect inference of an underlying topology with unequal branch rates

branch. Yet this situation is less than ideal as the inferences for the times and locations of certain changes is crucial to establishing the correct phylogeny. This problem can be resolved if tip dates and root stages are known.

The concept of jogging was also considered in the ancestry constraints on PIE ancestral states as modelled in Chang et al. (2015). There, it arose due to the incorporation of both ancestral states and daughter languages of the IE family without constraining the ancestral states to be directly preceding the daughter languages. This issue can be addressed by either defining the root stage directly via dummy taxa or, in case of innovation-based datasets, setting the character frequencies, or using known ancestral stages as roots.

In the case of the analysis at hand, this issue was addressed by setting tip dates (see section 3.2.2) and root frequencies. The latter parameter sets the frequency of each character state at the root. For example, a root frequency of [0.3, 0.7] in a binary character dataset represents a situation in which the state 0 occurs in 30 per cent of all sites at the root. The benefit of an innovation-based dataset is that, because this dataset records deviations from the root state, the character state at the root is known. In this case it means that if the root consists exclusively of sites of the character 0 'no innovation', the root frequency can be set to a fixed parameter of [1, 0] as the character state 0 occurs in 100 per cent of the cases. Thereafter, the issue of misattribution of character states to the root is mitigated.

The last fixed parameter common to all models is the **tree prior** (i.e. the model governing the tree topology). The tree prior was selected to be a birth–death[15] prior with fossil taxa similar to the Fossilized-Birth-Death model described in Heath, Huelsenbeck, and Stadler (2014).

As can be seen from the core elements explored above, all aspects of the models are either inferred and therefore not predetermined or task-specific as the fixed parameters are: the root frequencies need to be fixed in order to account for the type of data we are presented with and the birth–death tree prior is a standard choice for models with non-extant lineages and no ancestry constraints (i.e. exclusively historic data which do not include sampled ancestors of certain clades). This means that the core aspects are rather flexible and can be determined mostly from the data rather than from the modelling choices.

Nevertheless, there are certain elements of analysis which need to be predetermined but impact the inferred phylogeny considerably. In this case, this is true for the fossil date priors and the choice of substitution model. For this reason, I chose to split the analysis into six models consisting of combinations of two types of fossil dating priors and three types of substitution models. These six phylogenetic models can later be examined and evaluated for their fit to the data.

3.2.2 Model differences

As mentioned above, the models were run with several different settings concerning the tip dating priors and the site rates. The reason for running different models is that other than the parameters described above, there are several

---

[15] See Höhna (2015) for discussion.

possibilities for setting tip date and site rate priors. In addition, these settings are both crucial to the model outcomes and do not have clear theoretical preferences.

Firstly, the **tip dating**[16] mechanism can be set in two different ways: *hard-bounded* and *inferred*.

The hard-bounded solution is to set a uniform prior on a specific age range for each tip where, as it is implemented in RevBayes, all values within this range have a likelihood of 1 (see Barido-Sottani et al. 2020). This assigns equal probability to ages within a certain range, and zero probability to ages outside of it.

On the other hand, the inferred tip dates set a more informative but less restrictive prior on the age (e.g. a truncated normal distribution). Here, the model infers the age of tip from the data, given that the phylogenetic signal is strong enough to allow for this.

Explaining the advantages and disadvantages of both methods first of all requires a discussion of the meaning of dating in a phylogenetic framework.[17] As it was partially outlined in the discussion of the root age priors, the tip ages in the tree represents the *terminus ante quem* for the occurrence of the respective tip (i.e. the last possible time at which the tip has occurred). This is difficult to apply to languages that are constantly in flux and cannot be easily dated to a single year. Thus, the *terminus ante quem* for each language (each tip) marks the point in time at which the data that are provided to the model have developed. For this analysis it represents the date at which all included innovations have occurred. Moreover, this 'completion' of the innovations does not necessarily correspond to the date of attestation as, by that time, the innovations might have already been completed for a few decades or even centuries.

In this light, hard-bounded and inferred tip date mechanisms have different implications both theoretically and computationally. Hard-bounded priors have the advantage of setting a narrow range of possible occurrence times that can be set according to expert judgement. They imply that there is a plausibility range for the occurrence age of each language which is fixed for each language. The inferred date mechanism gives the model the freedom to determine the tip ages itself. The advantage is that the boundaries of the occurrence times are not fixed but flexible and allow for values outside of a fixed and pre-determined range. However, there are also disadvantages that

---

[16] See Heled and Drummond (2012); Pyron (2011); Ronquist, Klopfstein, et al. (2012); and Warnock et al. (2015) for a discussion of the advantages of fossil calibrations in divergence-time models.

[17] Ho and Phillips (2009) discusses different approaches with regard to their advantages and disadvantages from the modelling perspective.

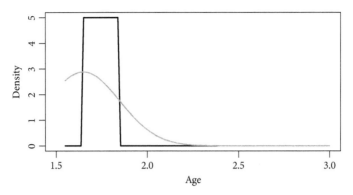

Figure 3.14 Gothic tip date prior

impact the outcome of the analysis both computationally and theoretically. To illustrate one of these issues, Figure 3.14 shows a plot of two prior distributions for the Gothic taxon: one is hard-bounded (*Uniform*(1.65, 1.85), the step function peaking at a density of 5) while the other is soft-bounded (*TruncatedNormal*(1.65, 0.2, 1.55, *root age*), density curve). The uniform prior assumes that at some time between 150 and 350 AD, Gothic reached the point where all innovations had occurred, whereas the normal prior determines the most likely time of this date to be between 150 and 450 with decreasing likelihood towards dates between the root age (up to 1000 BC) and 150 AD.

It becomes clear that the range of values the inferred approach allows increases by more than seven times adding more variability and uncertainty into the system. This is especially a problem for smaller datasets such as the one at hand where the estimates become less accurate. This can lead to an increase in credible intervals of the posterior distribution and even reduce the goodness of fit to the dataset. Moreover, this distribution allocates some probability mass to values greater than 2 (dates older than the year 1 AD) which become increasingly unlikely.

Due to the advantages and disadvantages of each approach, we cannot determine which settings are more adequate for the data. This means that model evaluation techniques need to establish whether adding softer bounds on the tip dates yields a better fit than the hard-bounded model does (see section 3.2.4). In this case, it is not possible to default on the simpler model (i.e. the hard-bounded model) since there is no a priori way to assess whether the bounds we set for the hard-bounded model are adequate. By leaving the model more freedom in determining the tip dates, we leave room for the possibility for softer bounds to be better for this analysis. In this case, the better fit would overpower the increased uncertainty inserted by the flexible bounds. In turn, all models need to be run once with a hard-bounded tip dating mechanism and once with inferred tip dates.

The second parameter that varies across the models is the **substitution model** which governs the site rates. Recall that the site rates represent the rates at which the character states, that make up the dataset, change to a different state. In this particular case, the rate at which 0 changes to 1 and vice versa. There are multiple options to set up the substitution model as outlined above, yet not all of those models and settings are theoretically reasonable. The theoretical basis for setting up sensible substitution models comes from considerations concerning the dataset type. With innovation-based binary character data, there are several possible methods of site rate modelling, three of which were considered for the task at hand.

The first site rate set-up is a *Jukes-Cantor* model which, as described above, sets equal rates across all characters. Under this assumption, innovations and events which delete innovations are equally likely and therefore occur equally often. This presupposes an equilibrium among the innovations which can serve as a model agnostic to the frequency of the character states 0 and 1. The advantage is here that we give all linguistic changes equal weight with regard to their occurrence in the dataset.

While the Jukes-Cantor model seems fairly neutral, there are major issues that are introduced when assuming an equal rate of innovation and non-innovation.[18]

Firstly, the dataset is inherently biased in that it records innovations when they occur and neglects linguistic phenomena where all Germanic daughter languages agree. In other words, while it is intuitive in non-innovation-based binary datasets encoding two exclusive states (e.g. datasets recording the presence or absence of a predetermined list of cognates or exclusive typological properties in certain languages) to assume an equal variation between states, due to the fact that innovation datasets only record a site when one of the languages undergoes an innovation, the states 0 and 1 are no longer independent. Moreover, this leads to a more serious issue of shared retentions versus shared innovations. Since shared innovations have more weight in the establishment of a linguistic subgroup (cf. Campbell 2013: 174–184; and Crowley and Bowern 2010: 108–124). The state 1 should thus have more weight than state 0 in the phylogenetic signal.

---

[18] See section 3.1.3 for discussion of uniformity of rate.

One of the consequences of this model would be to assign a higher rate to state 1, for example to restrict the model from assuming the path 1 > 0 in the data. The corresponding substitution model would place maximum weight on innovations and would therefore represent an **innovation-only** model. Yet this approach itself is not without downsides since it entirely neglects the occurrence of innovation-deleting events. Say, an innovation was jointly acquired in a subgroup but then lost by one of its members. In this case, the innovation-only model would see this as strong evidence against subgrouping. Further, it operates under the strong assumption that every single innovation is equally important for subgrouping and therefore it might underestimate the influence of homoplasies. Therefore, it is important to keep in mind that the innovation-only model as implemented here is *not* the computational equivalent of the traditional cladistical method that strongly prioritizes shared innovations over shared retentions.

The relaxation of the rate change here is intended to reflect the process of innovation obscuring. For example, in a given language with one possible innovation, a *0* in the data can arise in more than one way: either it is a genuine retention or another process has obscured the innovation to such a degree that we cannot observe a *1* in this place anymore. In some instances, intermediate innovations remain unobserved in favour of another innovation. Assume, for example, there are two hypothetical languages that have the reflexes *au* and *a* for earlier *o. If the histories of these languages are not clear, we might assume that the first language exhibits diphthongization/breaking of *o whereas the second shows lowering. The coding for the first language would be (1,0) (= breaking yes, lowering no) and (0,1) (= breaking no, lowering yes) for the second language. If there were, however, an unobserved intermediate stage of language 2 which shows nucleus simplification with a full history *o > *au > *a, we would need to code this as (1,1) (= breaking yes, coda simplification yes). This demonstrates that it cannot be guaranteed that *0* always changes to *1* and never to *0*. This does **not** mean an innovation reversal in the literal sense but an artefact of historical datasets where observing a *0* in one site can mean different things. Another way this can occur is through borrowing from neighbouring variants or languages in places where an innovation would be observed. Specifically, if another variant of a linguistic feature is borrowed which obscures the innovation, we also observe *0* instead of *1* in this position. We thus need a mechanism in the model that can account for this issue.

In conclusion, we want to use a substitution model that regards innovations as more important than retentions but can also account for events that delete an innovation. As a consequence, I used a third substitution model that infers the substitution rates from the data which gives the inference a stable basis to determine the site rates without assuming either an equilibrium or an innovation-only process. Whether or not this inference is successful needs to be tested through model comparison.

Model summary
The following discussion will show a summary of the models run for the phylogenetic inference analysis including the model specifications and a prior summary. Figure 3.15 displays the model graphically whereas Table 3.3 shows a summary table of the priors where the column 'Node' corresponds to the nodes displayed in the graphical model.

Figure 3.15 shows that the inference model consists of four sub-models and a root state setting ρ. The tree model is a time-tree supplied with the root age prior ϕ, a speciation rate λ and an extinction rate ε. Further, the inference model is a relaxed-clock assumption model c. The site rates R are modelled via a gamma distribution and the substitution model Q is, depending on the type of model, as a Jukes-Cantor, an innovation-only or a variable rates model.

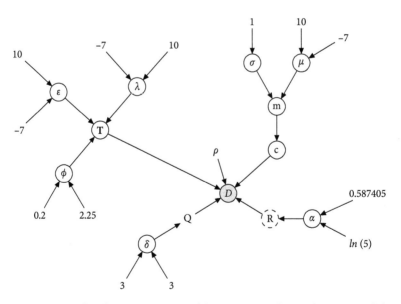

Figure 3.15 Graphical representation of the Germanic diversification model

---

[19] The substitution model displayed here represents the setting for the inferred substitution rates model. The Jukes-Cantor setting is a matrix where the rates are equal while in the innovation-only model, the rate setting is $\delta_{0 \to 1} = 1$.

Table 3.3 Summary of priors

	Node	Prior	Specification
Tree model	ϕ	TruncatedNormal(2.25, 0.2, 1.8, 3)	root age
	ε	LogNormal(-7, 10)	extinction rate
	λ	LogNormal(-7, 10)	speciation rate
Substitution model[19]	Q	$\begin{bmatrix} -\delta_0 & \delta_{0\to1} \\ \delta_{1\to0} & -\delta_1 \end{bmatrix}$	Q-matrix
	$\delta_{0,1}$	Dirichlet(3, 3)	substitution rate
Root frequencies	ρ	$(1, 0)$	
Clock model	c_{branch}	Exponential($\frac{1}{m}$)	branch rates
	m	LogNormal(μ, σ)	branch rates prior
	μ	Normal(-7, 10)	
	σ	Exponential(1)	
Site rate model	R	DiscretizedGamma($\alpha, \alpha, 4$)	site rates
	α	LogNormal($ln(5), 0.587405$)	site rates prior

The prior settings for the substitution, tree, and clock models are explained in the previous section. The priors for the site rate model are standard priors recommended in Höhna, Landis, et al. (2017: 76–78) favouring smaller values of α. Moreover, the extinction and speciation priors are rather flat with a distinct spike at small values between 0 and 0.01. This ensures that the full range of rates up to infinity is possible but very small values are strongly favoured.

The tip dating priors were set according to the estimates of attestation time in previous research. Table 3.4 shows the dates for each language along with sample estimates from previous literature.

It is evident that for all languages, the estimates show relatively long intervals—some spanning several hundred years. This is due to the fact that there is no single attestation point for these languages; rather, the earliest attestations often come from scarce sources such as a small number of inscriptions. This is the case for Old Norse and Old Frisian, for example. In these languages, the first scant attestations predate the larger text corpora by several hundred years.

For the modelling aspect, where dating is important, we are mostly focused on the *terminus ante quem* (see discussion above). In other words, the time period set for the tip dates of the models must coincide with the time period for which we can reasonably well assume all linguistic features to be present. It means that although Old Frisian is attested as early as 800 AD, a great part of

Table 3.4 Attestation time estimates of the Germanic languages

Language	Date	References
Gothic	350	Voyles (1992: 1)
	350–380	Nedoma (2017: 87)
	4th cent.	Robinson (1993: 48)
	Ulfilas' lifetime (4th cent.)	Miller (2019: 7–8)
Old English	mid-5th cent.	Smith (2009: 6)
	700	Lass (1994: 15)
	750/900	Voyles (1992: 2)
	8th cent.	Van Gelderen (2014)
Old Frisian	800–1275	Bussmann (2004: 1) ('Pre-OFris')
	1200	Bremmer (2009: 6)
	1250	Voyles (1992: 2); Versloot (2004: 257)
	13th cent.	Harbert (2007: 18); Robinson (1993: 181)
Old Saxon	700	Lass (1994: 15)
	8th cent.	J. Salmons (2018: 108)
	830	Voyles (1992: 2); Robinson (1993: 110)
	9th cent.	Harbert (2007: 15)
Old High German	600–830	Voyles (1992: 2); Nedoma (2017: 882–883)
	750	Braune and Eggers (1987: 1)
	765	Robinson (1993: 226)
	8th cent.	J. Salmons (2018: 107); Harbert (2007: 15); Sonderegger (2012: 1),
Old Norse	800–1050	Noreen (1923)
	1100	Voyles (1992: 2)
	1150	Haugen (1982: 5)
Burgundian (majority of records)	400–500	Hartmann and Riegger (2022)
Vandalic (majority of records)	400–500	Hartmann (2020: 13); Francovich Onesti (2002: 133–134)

the linguistic innovations we can determine for Old Frisian are attested later. It is therefore important to set a time window for the analysis which is closer to the earliest larger textual attestations but reaches far enough into the earlier times to capture the possibility of innovations being completed earlier.

Concretely this means that while in Old Norse, for example, we find several runic inscriptions showing many features of Old Norse (which would be considered Proto-Norse) from the 9th century on, most information about the language comes from Old Icelandic, and specifically Old Icelandic prose, about

Table 3.5 Hard-bounded tip date priors

Tip	Prior	Corresponding time frame
GO	Uniform(1.6, 1.8)	200–400 AD
ON	Uniform(1.0, 1.2)	800–1000 AD
OE	Uniform(1.1, 1.3)	700–900 AD
OF	Uniform(0.8, 1.0)	1000–1200 AD
OS	Uniform(1.15, 1.35)	650–850 AD
OHG	Uniform(1.15, 1.35)	650–850 AD
VAND	Uniform(1.5, 1.7)	300–500 AD
BURG	Uniform(1.5,1.7)	300–500 AD

Table 3.6 Inferred-tip model tip date priors

Tip	Prior	Corresp. mean date	Corresp. latest date
GO	TruncatedNormal(1.7, 0.2, 1.6, root age)	300 AD	400 AD
ON	TruncatedNormal(1.1, 0.2, 1.0, root age)	900 AD	1000 AD
OE	TruncatedNormal(1.2, 0.2, 1.1, root age)	800 AD	900 AD
OF	TruncatedNormal(0.9, 0.2, 0.8, root age)	1100 AD	1200 AD
OS	TruncatedNormal(1.25, 0.2, 1.15, root age)	750 AD	850 AD
OHG	TruncatedNormal(1.25, 0.2, 1.15, root age)	750 AD	850 AD
VAND	TruncatedNormal(1.6, 0.2, 1.5, root age)	400 AD	500 AD
BURG	TruncatedNormal(1.6, 0.2, 1.5, root age)	400 AD	500 AD

300 years later. For each individual innovation it is difficult to ascertain when exactly it was acquired; thus, in order to capture this uncertainty, we need to set an interval which covers a range of dates leading up to the approximate time of the earliest extensive attestations. For this, I chose uncertainty intervals which span 200 years and end at, or shortly before, the estimated attestations. Table 3.5 shows the tip priors that were set for the hard-bounded models and Table 3.6 shows the priors in the more relaxed tip-inferring model.

3.2.3 Results

This section addresses the results of the phylogenetic inference models. Firstly, I will discuss the consensus trees obtained from the models before analysing the individual parameter estimates and the split frequencies of clades in the posterior distribution. The primary aim of this section will be to outline the results of each model and to discuss how, and with regard to which aspects, the models differ. Afterwards, in section 3.2.4, we will use statistical measures to determine the model with the best fit which will then be discussed in further detail.

All models were run with two chains of 500,000 iterations with a thinning interval of 100. In Bayesian modelling, running two to four chains is the norm. In Bayesian phylogenetics, running two chains is sufficient as convergence can be accurately ascertained. As a result, the posterior distribution contains 2,500 samples per chain after the first 50 per cent of iterations were removed as a burn-in.

The convergence of the models was checked using the Gelman-Rubin convergence diagnostic as implemented in the R-package *coda* (Plummer et al. 2006).

Consensus trees

Among the central tools in phylogenetic posterior analysis is the graphical display of the consensus trees. Consensus trees are a type of summary tree from all trees in the posterior distribution which depicts the most common structure in the posterior distribution. It shows those clades that exhibit a support of greater than 0.5. In phylogenetic inference, *support* denotes the frequency of the occurrence of a given clade relative to the total number of posterior samples. Thus, a support of 0.7 indicates that 70 per cent of all posterior samples show this clade. In this study, I will take a support value of greater than 0.9 is as the cutoff point to safely assume a clade is supported by the data. All splits with support of lower than 0.9 are taken to be insufficiently supported by the data and therefore need to be discussed with caution if not discarded entirely. This value is essentially a credible interval cutoff point that in Bayesian contexts can vary between 0.89 and 0.95 (McElreath 2020: 56). A credible interval is the value range which contains the unobserved ('true') parameter with a probability of 89 or 95 per cent, depending on the interval size.

The following plots show the consensus trees for all six models, the first of which to be investigated is the Hardbounded-JC model with uniform tip date priors and a Jukes-Cantor substitution model. The tree in Figure 3.16 shows this consensus tree. All consensus trees discussed in this section show the following properties:

1. **Grey transparent bars** on splits denote the posterior split/node age 0.95-credible intervals.
2. **Numbers** on branches denote the posterior support of the respective clade. As consensus trees only depict clades with a support of > 0.5, the numbers only range from 0.5 to 1.

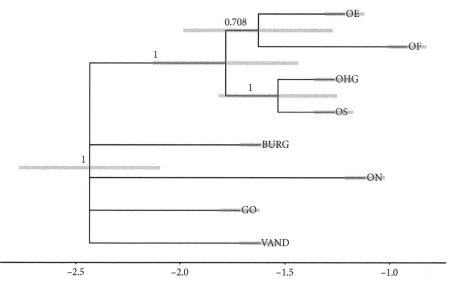

Figure 3.16 Consensus tree of model *Hardbounded-JC*

3. **Multifurcating** clades are shown in the consensus tree when its member taxa do not belong to any clade with support > 0.5. It needs to be kept in mind that the phylogenetic model *always* assumes bifurcating splits in individually sampled trees and the multifurcating consensus thus represents a graphical display of insufficient clade support even though each individual posterior tree is strictly bifurcating.

4. The **scale** shown on the bottom of each tree gives the absolute time the model was calibrated to in thousands of years. The negative values on the scale indicate that the values represent years *before present* with the present being 0 on the scale.

In this tree we can observe that Burgundian, Gothic, Old Norse, and Vandalic are not represented in any clade whereas West Germanic surfaces with full support. Further, Old High German and Old Saxon are grouped together in a clade with full support whereas Old English and Old Frisian, although they are represented in a clade, do not exhibit support beyond 0.9.

The consensus tree of the Hardbounded-InnovOnly model (Figure 3.17) is considerably different from the previous tree in Figure 3.16. Here we see that, although clades containing Burgundian, Gothic, and Vandalic are still not represented by a majority of posterior samples, we see full support for West Germanic and Ingvaeonic. Moreover, Northwest Germanic has become a clade, even if the grouping is not supported above the 0.9 threshold.

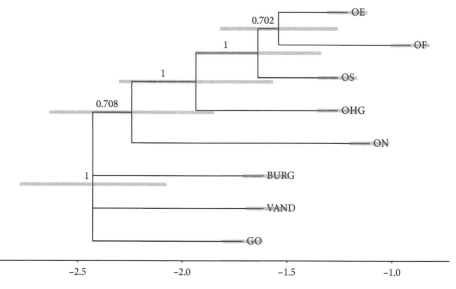

Figure 3.17 Consensus tree of model *Hardbounded-InnovOnly*

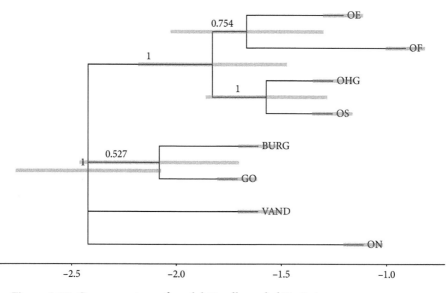

Figure 3.18 Consensus tree of model *Hardbounded-VarRates*

The results in Figure 3.18 are close to those of the corresponding Jukes-Cantor model with one exception: here, Burgundian and Gothic form a clade that is barely above the consensus tree support threshold but far from being well-supported.

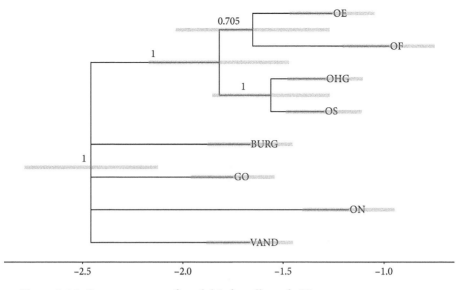

Figure 3.19 Consensus tree of model *Inferredbounds-JC*

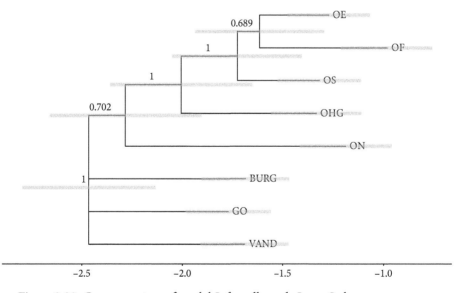

Figure 3.20 Consensus tree of model *Inferredbounds-InnovOnly*

In comparison with Figure 3.16, the inferred-bounds model in Figure 3.19 does not show any notable differences in its results except the larger intervals of the tip and node ages.

The same is true for Figure 3.20 which now additionally shows an unsupported Gotho-Burgundian clade in contrast to the model in Figure 3.19.

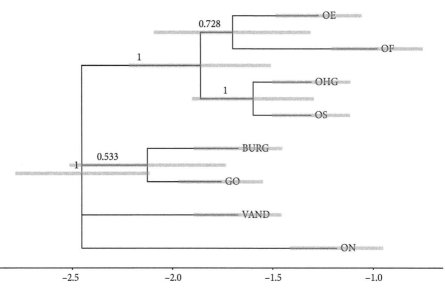

Figure 3.21 Consensus tree of model *Inferredbounds-VarRates*

The model in Figure 3.21 changes notably from the model in Figure 3.18 when the tip dates are added since the Old Saxon–Old High German clade is unsupported in this model. Moreover, Northwest Germanic and Gotho-Burgundian pass the threshold by a slim margin.

Parameter estimates

This section investigates and compares the posterior estimates of the model parameters across the six different models (see Table 3.7 for a summary of the posterior estimates).

The α parameter governing the among-site variation is estimated between 12 and 48 across all models with a relatively coherent mean between 28 and 31. The fact that the models do not differ notably regarding this parameter shows that the among-site variation is not significantly affected by either the substitution model or the tip date inference. The divergences we do see among the models are likely to be due to random noise. This does also imply that between the different types of innovations (phonological, morphological, syntactic, and lexical), there were no detectable differences in the rate of change. In other words, with regard to this dataset and analysis, changes in, for example, the domain of syntax and phonology behave similarly in their change rates—an observation that parallels the research in, for example, Longobardi and Guardiano (2009) which finds that the informativity of syntactic changes regarding the phylogenetic signal is comparable to changes in other domains.

Table 3.7 Posterior estimates of model parameters

Parameter	Model	Mean	Point. estimate	Lower-89CI	Higher-89CI
alpha	Hardbounded-JC	29.02	26.44	12.11	44.05
	Hardbounded-InnovOnly	30.52	27.74	13.38	47.58
	Hardbounded-VarRates	30.11	27.59	13.37	46.70
	Inferred-JC	28.72	26.31	13.24	43.99
	Inferred-InnovOnly	30.13	27.80	14.16	46.33
	Inferred-VarRates	29.98	27.42	13.29	45.12
extinction-rate	Hardbounded-JC	0.01	0.00	0.00	0.01
	Hardbounded-InnovOnly	0.01	0.00	0.00	0.01
	Hardbounded-VarRates	0.01	0.00	0.00	0.01
	Inferred-JC	0.01	0.00	0.00	0.01
	Inferred-InnovOnly	0.01	0.00	0.00	0.01
	Inferred-VarRates	0.01	0.00	0.00	0.01
origin-time	Hardbounded-JC	2.42	2.42	2.15	2.71
	Hardbounded-InnovOnly	2.42	2.41	2.11	2.70
	Hardbounded-VarRates	2.42	2.41	2.12	2.69
	Inferred-JC	2.46	2.46	2.18	2.73
	Inferred-InnovOnly	2.46	2.46	2.19	2.75
	Inferred-VarRates	2.45	2.45	2.17	2.73
speciation-rate	Hardbounded-JC	0.37	0.34	0.12	0.58
	Hardbounded-InnovOnly	0.36	0.34	0.12	0.57
	Hardbounded-VarRates	0.37	0.34	0.13	0.58
	Inferred-JC	0.36	0.34	0.12	0.58
	Inferred-InnovOnly	0.35	0.33	0.12	0.56
	Inferred-VarRates	0.36	0.33	0.12	0.56
change rate 0 → 1	Hardbounded-VarRates	0.69	0.69	0.63	0.75
	Inferred-VarRates	0.69	0.69	0.62	0.75
change rate 1 → 0	Hardbounded-VarRates	0.31	0.31	0.25	0.37
	Inferred-VarRates	0.31	0.31	0.25	0.38

Speciation and *extinction* rate are equally uniformly coherent across the models. The speciation rate implies that on average 0.3 speciation events occur per lineage and per 1,000 years. The low extinction rate across the models suggests that extinction events are a negligible factor turning the phylogenetic inference models into nearly pure Yule (birth-only) models.

The root age parameter is centred around 2.45 and essentially equal across the models. This is especially surprising given that the models inferring the tip dates operated under considerably more relaxed time calibrations. As a result, we are given a relatively secure estimate for the *termini ante quem* and *post*

quem for the break-up of the Germanic languages. According to the phylogenetic models, the break-up occurred in the time frame between 750 and 100
BC with an approximate most likely (maximum likelihood) date of 450 BC.
While the issue of dating is analysed in-depth in section 3.2.2, it is important
to note that the phylogenetic evidence projects Proto-Germanic unity to be
older than 150 BC.

For the rate matrix parameters used in the variable rates models, we find that
the change $0 \to 1$ is always notably higher than the change from $1 \to 0$ in both
models. The inferred-age model, however, shows a change rate for $0 \to 1$ that
is approximately equally high as its hard-bounded counterpart. The values for
the change rates call for comment: the rates indicate a change $1 \to 0$ occurs in
30 per cent of the cases which suggests that 1 in 3 changes is obscured or not
recoverable. Recall that innovation deletion can arise through different mechanisms and does not indicate, in this case, an actual innovation reversal. Since
the Dirichlet(3,3) prior on the rate matrix is weakly informative and centred,
it could be the case that this figure of 30 per cent deletions is too high. This
issue is investigated in section 3.2.4.

The posterior estimates (see summary in Table 3.8) for the tip dates between
the hard-bounded and the inferred tip models are not considerably different. We see that most estimates of the inferred models are very close to their
hard-bounded counterparts. This could be indicative of the fact that the more
flexibly calibrated models arrive at a similar posterior distribution to that of the
hard-bounded models because the flexibility does not add notable information
to the model. Whether this flexibility yields a better fit to the data, however,
needs to be explored (see section 3.2.4).

Split frequencies

Split frequencies in a phylogenetic model denote the proportion of samples in
which a certain split or, in this case, clade occurs in the posterior distribution.
Important clades (i.e. support > 0.5) are represented in consensus trees which
can be observed in Figures 3.16 to 3.21. Further, one can extract split frequencies and node ages of specific clades that are not represented in a consensus
tree and analyse those across the models.

Table 3.9 shows the summary of eight potential clades and their support and age across different models. Some clades are subgroups that were
established or hypothesized to exist in previous research and some, such as
NWGmc-Vandalic, are previously never suggested clades that were included
for purposes of reference.

As the summary contains *splits* of clades, the ages given in these tables refer to the break-up times of these clades. Therefore, an age of 1.5 would represent a clade splitting into two daughter clades 1,500 years before present.

From the tables, we can gather that the only clade with full support in all models is West Germanic with an estimated break-up time between 300 BC and 500 AD. These large credible intervals indicate great uncertainty in the data about the actual time of the split.

The innovation-only models differ considerably in their split support strengths from the other models. There we see that Northwest Germanic and Ingvaeonic are supported with high support values, while in other models this is not the case. This raises the question of what this implies about the dichotomy of the innovation-only models and the variable rates models. On

Table 3.8 Posterior estimates of tip ages

Parameter	Model	Mean	Point. estimate	Lower-89CI	Higher-89CI
BURG-age	Hardbounded-JC	1.60	1.60	1.50	1.68
	Hardbounded-InnovOnly	1.60	1.60	1.52	1.70
	Hardbounded-VarRates	1.60	1.60	1.52	1.69
	Inferred-JC	1.69	1.67	1.50	1.86
	Inferred-InnovOnly	1.69	1.68	1.50	1.87
	Inferred-VarRates	1.69	1.67	1.50	1.87
GO-age	Hardbounded-JC	1.70	1.70	1.60	1.78
	Hardbounded-InnovOnly	1.70	1.70	1.60	1.78
	Hardbounded-VarRates	1.70	1.70	1.61	1.79
	Inferred-JC	1.78	1.76	1.60	1.95
	Inferred-InnovOnly	1.78	1.76	1.60	1.95
	Inferred-VarRates	1.78	1.76	1.60	1.95
OE-age	Hardbounded-JC	1.20	1.20	1.10	1.28
	Hardbounded-InnovOnly	1.20	1.20	1.11	1.29
	Hardbounded-VarRates	1.20	1.20	1.11	1.29
	Inferred-JC	1.28	1.26	1.10	1.45
	Inferred-InnovOnly	1.28	1.26	1.10	1.44
	Inferred-VarRates	1.29	1.27	1.10	1.46
OF-age	Hardbounded-JC	0.90	0.90	0.82	1.00
	Hardbounded-InnovOnly	0.90	0.90	0.82	1.00
	Hardbounded-VarRates	0.90	0.90	0.82	1.00
	Inferred-JC	1.00	0.98	0.80	1.18
	Inferred-InnovOnly	1.00	0.98	0.80	1.18
	Inferred-VarRates	1.00	0.98	0.80	1.18

Table 3.8   (cont.)

Parameter	Model	Mean	Point. estimate	Lower-89CI	Higher-89CI
OHG-age	Hardbounded-JC	1.25	1.25	1.16	1.34
	Hardbounded-InnovOnly	1.25	1.25	1.17	1.34
	Hardbounded-VarRates	1.25	1.25	1.15	1.33
	Inferred-JC	1.31	1.30	1.15	1.46
	Inferred-InnovOnly	1.35	1.32	1.15	1.53
	Inferred-VarRates	1.32	1.31	1.15	1.47
ON-age	Hardbounded-JC	1.10	1.10	1.00	1.18
	Hardbounded-InnovOnly	1.10	1.10	1.01	1.19
	Hardbounded-VarRates	1.10	1.10	1.02	1.19
	Inferred-JC	1.20	1.18	1.00	1.38
	Inferred-InnovOnly	1.20	1.18	1.00	1.38
	Inferred-VarRates	1.20	1.18	1.00	1.39
OS-age	Hardbounded-JC	1.25	1.25	1.15	1.33
	Hardbounded-InnovOnly	1.25	1.25	1.15	1.33
	Hardbounded-VarRates	1.25	1.25	1.15	1.33
	Inferred-JC	1.32	1.30	1.15	1.47
	Inferred-InnovOnly	1.33	1.31	1.15	1.50
	Inferred-VarRates	1.33	1.31	1.15	1.48
VAND-age	Hardbounded-JC	1.60	1.60	1.52	1.70
	Hardbounded-InnovOnly	1.60	1.60	1.50	1.68
	Hardbounded-VarRates	1.60	1.60	1.51	1.69
	Inferred-JC	1.69	1.67	1.50	1.87
	Inferred-InnovOnly	1.70	1.68	1.50	1.87
	Inferred-VarRates	1.69	1.67	1.50	1.87

the one hand, we might expect to see a lower level of innovation deletions than inferred in the variable rates models; however, on the other hand, variable rates models are more robust as they account for variance in the observation of the individual characters. The innovation-only models mainly assume that every innovation is observed with full accuracy without errors and without missing any intermediate steps.

Here the shared innovations are more strongly represented which means that those proposed clades such as Ingvaeonic and Northwest Germanic that exhibit strong support in innovation-only models but little support in others tend to be established on grounds of only a few innovations. In other words, Ingvaeonic is only a reliably inferred subgroup on the basis of a small number of innovations in innovation-only models. In the other models, this does not suffice to establish a reliable subgroup.

Table 3.9 Support and posterior estimates of age of specific clades across different models

Clade	Model	Support	Age mean	Age median	Age lower-89CI	Age upper-89CI
Anglo-Frisian	Hardbounded-JC	0.71	1.62	1.61	1.34	1.93
	Hardbounded-InnovOnly	0.70	1.55	1.53	1.29	1.76
	Hardbounded-VarRates	0.75	1.67	1.65	1.37	1.97
	Inferred-JC	0.70	1.66	1.66	1.35	1.98
	Inferred-InnovOnly	0.69	1.62	1.61	1.37	1.89
	Inferred-VarRates	0.73	1.71	1.70	1.38	2.02
East Germanic	Hardbounded-JC	0.23	2.24	2.24	1.93	2.55
	Hardbounded-InnovOnly	0.30	2.29	2.28	1.96	2.59
	Hardbounded-VarRates	0.21	2.27	2.27	1.94	2.57
	Inferred-JC	0.21	2.30	2.30	2.00	2.61
	Inferred-InnovOnly	0.29	2.34	2.34	2.01	2.63
	Inferred-VarRates	0.20	2.31	2.31	1.99	2.60
Gotho-Burgundian	Hardbounded-JC	0.47	2.07	2.05	1.78	2.40
	Hardbounded-InnovOnly	0.47	2.08	2.06	1.73	2.36
	Hardbounded-VarRates	0.53	2.09	2.07	1.77	2.40
	Inferred-JC	0.49	2.12	2.11	1.79	2.46
	Inferred-InnovOnly	0.49	2.14	2.13	1.78	2.46
	Inferred-VarRates	0.53	2.13	2.12	1.78	2.45
Gotho-Nordic	Hardbounded-JC	0.04	2.17	2.17	1.84	2.54
	Hardbounded-InnovOnly	0.01	2.16	2.14	1.86	2.45
	Hardbounded-VarRates	0.03	2.16	2.13	1.90	2.53
	Inferred-JC	0.04	2.18	2.17	1.88	2.53
	Inferred-InnovOnly	0.02	2.22	2.24	1.95	2.51
	Inferred-VarRates	0.04	2.23	2.21	1.90	2.56

Table 3.9 (cont.) Support and posterior estimates of age of specific clades across different models

Clade	Model	Support	Age mean	Age median	Age lower-89CI	Age upper-89CI
Ingvaeonic	Hardbounded-JC	0.00	–	–	–	–
	Hardbounded-InnovOnly	**1.00**	1.64	1.63	1.39	1.89
	Hardbounded-VarRates	0.00	–	–	–	–
	Inferred-JC	0.00	–	–	–	–
	Inferred-InnovOnly	**1.00**	1.73	1.72	1.47	2.00
	Inferred-VarRates	0.00	–	–	–	–
Northwest Germanic	Hardbounded-JC	0.34	2.21	2.20	1.86	2.53
	Hardbounded-InnovOnly	0.71	2.22	2.23	1.88	2.53
	Hardbounded-VarRates	0.37	2.23	2.23	1.91	2.56
	Inferred-JC	0.34	2.25	2.25	1.91	2.57
	Inferred-InnovOnly	0.70	2.28	2.27	1.99	2.61
	Inferred-VarRates	0.37	2.26	2.27	1.94	2.58
NWGmc-Vandalic	Hardbounded-JC	0.26	2.29	2.29	1.99	2.57
	Hardbounded-InnovOnly	0.19	2.32	2.32	2.02	2.63
	Hardbounded-VarRates	0.28	2.31	2.31	2.01	2.61
	Inferred-JC	0.27	2.34	2.34	2.05	2.64
	Inferred-InnovOnly	0.21	2.37	2.36	2.09	2.66
	Inferred-VarRates	0.28	2.35	2.34	2.07	2.65
West Germanic	Hardbounded-JC	**1.00**	1.78	1.77	1.49	2.06
	Hardbounded-InnovOnly	**1.00**	1.93	1.92	1.61	2.21
	Hardbounded-VarRates	**1.00**	1.83	1.82	1.54	2.12
	Inferred-JC	**1.00**	1.83	1.83	1.54	2.12
	Inferred-InnovOnly	**1.00**	2.00	2.00	1.71	2.29
	Inferred-VarRates	**1.00**	1.87	1.86	1.56	2.15

Other subgroups that were proposed in the past such as East Germanic, Gotho-Nordic, and Anglo-Frisian were inferred with less support. However, of those three clades mentioned, Anglo-Frisian was inferred with much higher support than East Germanic or Gotho-Nordic.

Further, it is necessary to examine the posterior branch lengths across the different models (see Table 3.10). Branch lengths are defined as the distance between two consecutive splits in a tree; in an absolute time-calibrated model they represent the time between a clade being created by a splitting event and the break-up of the clade in subclades or taxa. Investigating the inferred branch lengths for clades yields linguistic insights into the time during which a clade was extant. In other words, the inferred branch lengths give the time duration a clade such as West Germanic existed before it split into multiple daughter clades or taxa.

It is salient that the branch lengths are positively correlated with the tree support (correlation coefficient: 0.70) as most proposed clades with low support values likewise exhibit very small lower credible interval values. The reason for this is that both low support and short branch lengths are the result of an unclear topology in a tree. If the distinguishing innovations are few and uncertainty is high, two clades will often switch positions in the ordering of the clades having only small branch lengths. Thus short branch length estimates are the result of low phylogenetic credibility in a tree and therefore need to be analysed with caution.

The posterior estimates for the clade with the highest support, West Germanic, show a relatively long branch length on the absolute scale around 0.4 (i.e. 400 years), with the exception of the innovation-only model. Most other proposed clades have significantly shorter branch lengths, partially due to their low support as outlined above. For example, the mean branch length for Northwest Germanic is approximately 0.13 (i.e. 130 years) which is at least half the time that can be inferred for West Germanic.

3.2.4 Model comparison

Up to this point, the different models were treated as equal and their outputs compared. However, certain models—especially the innovation-only models—yielded results that are notably different from the other models. In order to determine which model yields the best fit to the data, we need to employ quantitative tests to gauge each model's relative fit in comparison with the other models.

Two of the recommended methods that are already implemented in *RevBayes* are the *stepping-stone sampling* algorithm and the *path sampling*

Table 3.10 Support and posterior estimates of branch lengths of specific clades across different models

Clade	Support	Support	Brlen mean	Brlen median	Brlen lower.89CI	Brlen upper.89CI
	Hardbounded-JC	0.71	0.15	0.11	0.00	0.35
	Hardbounded-InnovOnly	0.70	0.10	0.07	0.00	0.23
Anglo-Frisian	Hardbounded-VarRates	0.75	0.16	0.11	0.00	0.36
	Inferred-JC	0.70	0.17	0.12	0.00	0.39
	Inferred-InnovOnly	0.69	0.11	0.08	0.00	0.26
	Inferred-VarRates	0.73	0.16	0.11	0.00	0.38
	Hardbounded-JC	0.23	0.16	0.12	0.00	0.36
	Hardbounded-InnovOnly	0.30	0.14	0.09	0.00	0.33
East Germanic	Hardbounded-VarRates	0.21	0.15	0.10	0.00	0.34
	Inferred-JC	0.21	0.15	0.11	0.00	0.36
	Inferred-InnovOnly	0.29	0.12	0.08	0.00	0.29
	Inferred-VarRates	0.20	0.14	0.09	0.00	0.31
	Hardbounded-JC	0.47	0.28	0.25	0.01	0.54
	Hardbounded-InnovOnly	0.47	0.27	0.22	0.00	0.54
Gotho-Burgundian	Hardbounded-VarRates	0.53	0.27	0.24	0.00	0.54
	Inferred-JC	0.49	0.27	0.23	0.00	0.56
	Inferred-InnovOnly	0.49	0.26	0.21	0.00	0.52
	Inferred-VarRates	0.53	0.26	0.22	0.00	0.55
	Hardbounded-JC	0.04	0.14	0.09	0.00	0.35
	Hardbounded-InnovOnly	0.01	0.14	0.07	0.00	0.36
Gotho-Nordic	Hardbounded-VarRates	0.03	0.17	0.12	0.00	0.40
	Inferred-JC	0.04	0.19	0.15	0.00	0.43
	Inferred-InnovOnly	0.02	0.15	0.11	0.00	0.44
	Inferred-VarRates	0.04	0.14	0.09	0.00	0.33

Table 3.10 (cont.) Support and posterior estimates of branch lengths of specific clades across different models

Clade	Support	Support	Brlen mean	Brlen median	Brlen lower.89CI	Brlen upper.89CI
Ingvaeonic	Hardbounded-JC	0.00	–	–	–	–
	Hardbounded-InnovOnly	1.00	0.28	0.26	0.06	0.48
	Hardbounded-VarRates	0.00	–	–	–	–
	Inferred-JC	0.00	–	–	–	–
	Inferred-InnovOnly	1.00	0.28	0.25	0.07	0.48
	Inferred-VarRates	0.00	–	–	–	–
Northwest Germanic	Hardbounded-JC	0.34	0.16	0.12	0.00	0.32
	Hardbounded-InnovOnly	0.71	0.14	0.11	0.00	0.29
	Hardbounded-VarRates	0.37	0.14	0.11	0.00	0.29
	Inferred-JC	0.34	0.16	0.12	0.00	0.33
	Inferred-InnovOnly	0.70	0.14	0.11	0.00	0.28
	Inferred-VarRates	0.37	0.14	0.11	0.00	0.29
NWGmc–Vandalic	Hardbounded-JC	0.26	0.11	0.08	0.00	0.24
	Hardbounded-InnovOnly	0.19	0.09	0.06	0.00	0.22
	Hardbounded-VarRates	0.28	0.10	0.07	0.00	0.22
	Inferred-JC	0.27	0.11	0.08	0.00	0.22
	Inferred-InnovOnly	0.21	0.08	0.05	0.00	0.19
	Inferred-VarRates	0.28	0.09	0.07	0.00	0.21
West Germanic	Hardbounded-JC	1.00	0.49	0.48	0.19	0.76
	Hardbounded-InnovOnly	1.00	0.32	0.30	0.09	0.53
	Hardbounded-VarRates	1.00	0.45	0.44	0.17	0.70
	Inferred-JC	1.00	0.48	0.46	0.20	0.77
	Inferred-InnovOnly	1.00	0.30	0.28	0.08	0.50
	Inferred-VarRates	1.00	0.45	0.43	0.16	0.69

algorithm (Xie et al. 2011). Both are used to approximate the *marginal like-lihood* of the models which can then be compared with one another. The marginal likelihood is defined as the probability of the data given a certain model averaged over all parameters this model contains. As a result, the marginal likelihood estimate disadvantages models with many parameters, each of which does not contribute much to the fit, as well as models that are severely underspecified and therefore yield a subpar fit. In other words, the marginal likelihood estimation aims for a balance between model complexity and model specificity.[20] Stepping-stone sampling and path sampling are algorithms to estimate the marginal likelihood in phylogenetic models that run several iterations of the model, each time raising the likelihood by a discrete value. The result of both algorithms is the logarithm of the respective model's marginal likelihood estimate that can then be compared to the other models. In Table 3.11, we see the marginal likelihoods of each model once for the stepping-stone sampling (SS) and the path sampling (PS) algorithms. Afterwards, a base (or null) model (M_0) is selected, *Hardbounded-JC* in this case,[21] from which value all other model's likelihood values are subtracted. As a result, the difference between each individual non-null model and the null model $\Delta(M_0, M_i)$ can be further interpreted.

There are no fixed thresholds or cutoff points at which the models are deemed significantly different; however, a recommended non-significance interval is between -1 and 1. If the likelihood differences fall in this range, the models are not notably different. If values are < -1, the alternative model is preferred whereas for values > 1, the null model is preferred (cf. Höhna, Landis, et al. 2017).

The likelihood comparison summary in Table 3.11 shows that the best model is model *Hardbounded-VarRates* (hard-bounded tip dates with an inferred site change rate) with the second-best model being *Hardbounded-InnovOnly* (hard-bounded tip dates with a fixed site rate that only allows for innovations) However, the difference between all models is strong, therefore *Hardbounded-VarRates* is preferred.

Further, in Table 3.11, all inferred-bound models perform worse than their hard-bounded counterparts. This indicates that the flexibility given to the tip dates does not benefit the inference. This does not mean, however, that hard-coded constraints are better in all cases. It is an observation that arises when comparing relaxed tip date priors and more constrained priors, namely that

[20] For a concise overview along with example references see Höhna, Landis, et al. (2017: 86–89).

[21] The choice of the M_0 model is arbitrary, I selected this model at this point since it is the model with the fewest parameters and the strongest assumptions.

Table 3.11 Marginal log-likelihoods of the phylogenetic models under the stepping-stone sampling (SS) and path sampling (PS) algorithms along with their differences to the model *Hardbounded-JC*

Model	SS	$\Delta_{SS}(M_0, M_i)$	PS	$\Delta_{PS}(M_0, M_i)$
Hardbounded-JC	−1527.182	0	−1526.877	0
Inferred-JC	−1539.954	12.772	−1539.004	12.127
Hardbounded-VarRates	−1517.159	−10.023	−1516.922	−9.955
Inferred-VarRates	−1527.377	0.195	−1527.083	0.206
Hardbounded-InnovOnly	−1525.075	−2.107	−1525.095	−1.782
Inferred-InnovOnly	−1538.119	10.937	−1538.258	11.381

added flexibility does not improve inference in this particular case. Thus, the hard-coded constraints are set well enough to provide a better fit to the data.

Episodic model

As discussed in section 3.1.3, some phylogenetic models allow for the temporal flexibility of speciation and extinction rates by means of using an episodic rate change model. I decided to test this approach on the best model among those previously run. If the speciation rates change considerably over time, the models above would need to be re-evaluated under the episodic paradigm. The episodic speciation and extinction model, however, was found to be inappropriate for this task. To test the influence of episodic changes on the model parameters, I set up a model with the same architecture as the *Hardbounded-VarRates* model under an episodic extinction and speciation rate.[22] The rates themselves received the same priors as before, the episodic model was given ten rate change events uniformly distributed over the entire age of the tree. In other words, instead of drawing one global extinction and speciation rate, the model draws ten different rates for ten equally long time periods from the sampled root to the sampled tips. As the rates are recorded, they can later be analysed as to their impact on the inference. If in most posterior samples, the rates at the root of the tree are considerably lower than at the tips, this means that there is a significant rate increase over the course of the time the tree covers. Figure 3.22 shows the output of this analysis.[23]

---

[22] As the fossil-only tip dating priors and the episodic speciation/extinction model were incompatible in the inference framework RevBayes, I set the youngest taxon (*Old Frisian*) as extant and its tip nodes at 0.8 which means that in Figure 3.22, the time axis needs to be interpreted as 'thousand years before 1200 AD'.

[23] The plot was created using the R package *RevGadgets* (Höhna and Freyman 2016).

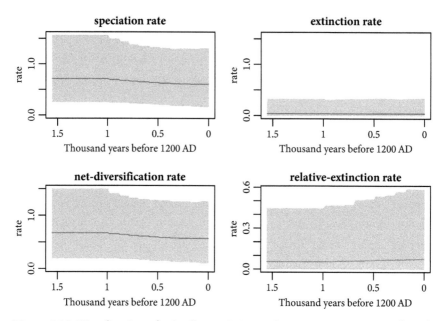

Figure 3.22 Visualization of episodic speciation and extinction rates over inferred time

As we can observe, the credible interval for speciation rate is large and the mean speciation rate almost constant over time. Equally, the extinction rate is estimated as being constant. The narrowing of the credible intervals of the speciation rate is not indicative of a rate change but represents the slim reduction in uncertainty regarding this parameter. In other words, the credible intervals are compatible with either a strong increase or decrease in speciation rate but that, in general, there is little evidence for either in the data. As a result, we have to conclude that for this dataset and problem, allowing speciation and extinction rates to vary does not help the model to explain the data better.

Informative rate model

The rate matrix estimates presented in section 3.2.3, specifically the high rate of $1 \rightarrow 0$, might be due to the weakly informative prior on the rate matrix. To investigate this issue and to ascertain what effect a stronger prior on the rate matrix has, the Hardbounded-VarRates model was re-run with a prior of Dirichlet(5, 1) which disproportionally favours changes from 0 to 1. This prior has a median of 0.13 for the rate $1 \rightarrow 0$ and a mean of 0.17, meaning half of the samples drawn from the prior will have a value lower than 0.13. However, the results show that the chains converge at the interval [0.23, 0.35] with a mean of 0.3, which is equal to the estimates of the Hardbounded-VarRates. In other words, the evidence from the data overpowers the prior settings. This does not mean that a rate 1 → 0 has to be taken at face value, it merely means that even when the model is strongly biased against higher values for 1 → 0, convergence is still reached at the level of the original prior.

3.2.5 Discussion of findings

This section will predominantly involve a summary and discussion of the findings obtained using the phylogenetic models with regard to model-internal issues. Most of the interpretation of these findings in light of previous research and the findings of the agent-based model will be discussed in the sections pertaining to the individual issues of Germanic phylogeny (see sections 5.1 to 5.6).

The main finding of this analysis is that there is very limited support for most potential subgroups. Except two clades, there is not much phylogenetic signal in the data to support strong subgrouping between the Germanic daughter languages. The consensus tree of the preferred model (Figure 3.23) shows this issue clearly.

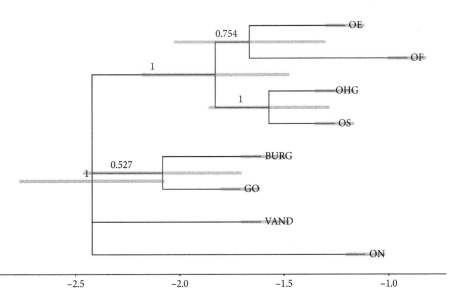

Figure 3.23 Consensus tree of the preferred model *Hardbound-VarRates*

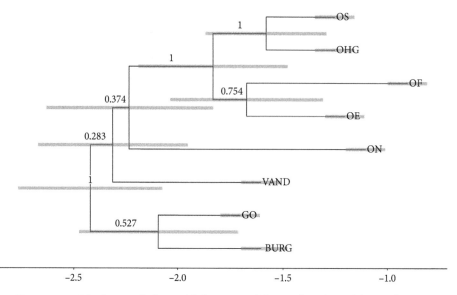

Figure 3.24 Maximum clade credibility tree of the preferred model *Hardbound-VarRates*

The main clades that are supported are West Germanic and Old High German–Old Saxon. All other clades exhibit low support, considerably below the cutoff point value of 0.9. This leaves the subgrouping of Old English, Old Frisian, Burgundian, Gothic, Old Norse, and Vandalic unaccounted for. It is clear that both Old Frisian and Old English are West Germanic; however, it is unclear if they split from West Germanic as a subgroup or individually.

Figure 3.24 illustrates the issue of low clade credibility further. It shows the, by definition bifurcating, maximum clade credibility (MCC) tree which is complementary to a consensus tree, in that it shows the tree having the highest overall clade support of all sampled trees summed across all clades. In essence, it shows the single most credible tree in all posterior samples. Such an MCC tree does not aim to replace consensus trees as it shows a different aspect of the posterior trees. In this example, it can serve as an illustration of the posterior tree with the highest total support of all its clades. The individual clade probabilities do not change in this tree; only the groupings themselves are different from a consensus tree.

In the MCC tree at hand we see the low-credibility clades Anglo-Frisian and Northwest Germanic as coherent subgroups. Notably in this tree, Vandalic is grouped together with Northwest Germanic as a single clade.

Similar to the low split support, we find strongly inflated age intervals for the individual splits. These intervals span 500 years and more. While this issue is partially due to the uncertainty in the tip dates, a variance this extreme is also due to apparent uncertainty in the data. The tip dates themselves are very well calibrated as they are, since a more strongly inferential tip date approach did not yield considerable improvements on the outcome. As a result, the time windows for the origin dates of the taxa are compatible with the data.

The analysis of the models has shown that a balanced approach towards substitution models is preferable. This means that for this innovation dataset, we cannot assume either an equilibrium in the change rates nor can we only assume innovations being obtained without processes that interfere with this direction. However, model comparison has also shown that the second best model in fact was the innovation-only model which suggests that the innovations have more weight than the deletion of innovations. This was also inferred by the preferred *Hardbound-VarRates* model which gives the acquisition of innovations a rate of 0.69. As a tentative interpretation of these values we can state that this is the expected outcome in a dataset that focuses on innovations along the tree. Applying an innovation-only model comes with the disadvantage of not accounting for innovations being lost which has an impact on the inference: the innovation-only models show consensus trees where certain subgroups are notably more securely inferred than in the other models. Moreover, even strong priors favouring a change from 0 to 1 are overpowered by the signal in the data and, in addition to the previous considerations, the innovation-only models are therefore computationally disfavoured. This approach, however, is not without merit insofar as the innovation-only model performed second-best and shows that the subgroups we find under this model tend to be present in the data. When the more balanced approach of the inferred rates model adds more uncertainty to these innovations and the support for these clades diminishes, it is an indication that only few innovations are responsible for the subgrouping which might be too sensitive to fluctuations. This implies about Germanic that the subgroups for which we find strong support in the innovation-only models, most notably Ingvaeonic and Anglo-Frisian, rely on few innovations with high uncertainty given that the clade credibility diminishes once the parameters of the substitution rates are changed.

Further, the extinction rate in this dataset is near zero which means that, in this time frame, extinction rates cannot be determined accurately or are negligible. Equally, changes in speciation and extinction along the tree were not detectable via an episodic rate change model. A global speciation setting is sufficient to account for the data. This does not mean that, in reality, there were no changes in the rate of speciation and extinction. On the contrary, one might hypothesize that during late antiquity, where population movements occurred that might or might not have been unusually large, we might see an increase in speciation (i.e. more languages breaking away from larger linguistic units) at least regarding those languages that were spoken in migrating communities such as Gothic, Vandalic, and Burgundian. In this analysis, however, these potential changes in speciation rates are not detectable because they are likely too minor to be visible in a dataset of this size and scope.

The coherence of the dataset with regard to the individual substitution rates across different sites is rather homogeneous with a mean α value of 30. As a result, we can assume that the rate difference per site is not flat but rather has most of the probability mass at around 1. It is, however, not strong either as would be the case for values of $\alpha > 100$. We can therefore conclude that the substitution rates differ across sites but not by large values which means in effect that the underlying changes occur at similar rates.

Lastly, the inferred dates for the root age and the sufficiently supported splits indicate an early date of the entire tree. Whereas the root age interval is sampled to be between 2.15 and 2.7 (between 700 and 150 BC), the mean and median ages at approximately 2.45 (450 BC) are on the early end of most previous estimations pointing to a date later than 500 BC for the break-up of Proto-Germanic. Similarly, the splitting of the West Germanic languages is estimated by the model to have occurred between 170 BC and 370 AD, which is early compared with most previous estimates.

3.3 Beyond phylogenetic tree inference

The insights gained from the phylogenetic models have shown a rather inconclusive picture regarding subgrouping in the Germanic language family. This is not unprecedented as previous phylogenetic inference studies have also encountered similar problems. It becomes clear that the possible subgroups in Germanic do not exhibit sufficient differentiation with regard to the underlying data. This issue therefore needs to be taken as the basis of further investigation as we have seen that phylogenetic analysis alone does not yield reliable results for Germanic. The current phylogenetic models may therefore be complemented by focusing on certain aspects where alternative models can yield further insights.

A spatial component, although newer approaches incorporate geospatial elements in their models (see Ree et al. 2005; Landis et al. 2013), would improve the subgrouping insofar as geographic distance and subgrouping is likely to be correlated to some degree.[24] That is, distant speech communities are less likely to undergo common changes and some type of changes such as areal spreading affects far-apart communities less by definition.[25] However, accounting for this distance was not incorporated in the Bayesian phylogenetic model at hand which is agnostic of geographic distribution. It is worth noting that this aspect is not a criticism of the model per se, as in some cases it might be advantageous to leave out the geographic component to investigate the relationship estimates that were inferred independently of geographic proximity. It is advisable to consider comparing a geospatially agnostic model with spatial models in any analyses to investigate the effect of geographic parameters themselves.

Nevertheless, geographical distance further is a factor in the emergence of new subgroups beyond the pure processes of innovation spreading but isolation of linguistic communities—whether due to migration, geographic barriers, or even social processes—likewise contributes to this issue.

Furthermore, Bayesian phylogenetics assumes 'hard' splits in every individual tree as do all tree-based models, the practice of which has been criticized in light of the debate around the adequacy of the tree model (see section 1.4). The split time intervals can be interpreted as a 'softer' diversification process, yet the underlying mechanic assumes trees that assume clear, sudden splits for the clades. Assuming a hard-splitting tree model as a necessary abstraction from the real-world process is legitimate, however, yet certain conditions have to apply in this case. Specifically, if languages diversify in such a way that the diversification process is short enough that, out of this gradual diversification, no significant innovations arise that obscure the genetic relationships in a tree-based inference model, then a hard split is a good model for this process.

Adjacent to this issue is the assumption of bifurcating splits in these models. Rapid consecutive splits may be interpreted as a simultaneous diversification process but again, the models themselves only assume bifurcation.[26]

---

[24] Bouckaert et al. (2012) use phylogenetic models with a geographic component directly to quantitatively investigate current theories concerning the Indo-European homeland.

[25] This is not to say that geographically close languages are necessarily linguistically close but that under certain circumstances (e.g. in a dialect continuum) the spread of linguistic change is dependent on geographical variables of which distance is one. Thus, in studies such as François (2015: 179) it is the case that geographically close members of a language family tend to show lower linguistic distance.

[26] That the consensus trees as the outputs of such models are not necessarily binary-branching is not a violation of this assumption as each individual tree sampled by the model is binary branching.

Resulting from these assumptions at the basis of phylogenetic models is the conceptual difficulty in capturing linguistic processes that violate these assumptions. Phenomena such as dialect continua are real entities but in the results of phylogenetic models they appear mostly as the absence of phylogenetic support. In other words, when a certain subclade shows daughter taxa and clades with low support, one possible interpretation is a dialect continuum. This is the case for Germanic where West Germanic itself is inferred as a clearly distinct clade but Old English and Old Frisian show low grouping support, which suggests that these languages exhibit too few clearly distinct innovations that warrant further subgrouping. This particular property of Germanic is not surprising, as it has surfaced before in phylogenetic studies on this family (see e.g. Verkerk 2019). The alternative of subgrouping might therefore be the assumption of a dialect continuum that has brought forth these languages. In this interpretation, the degree of horizontal transmission, areal changes, and linguistic contact have yielded a diversification process for these languages that is incompatible with rigid tree-like structures, or at least not captured by them.[27]

It would therefore be a further complement of the existing methods to apply a model to the Germanic dataset which specifically models geospatial relationships and dialect continua. The building of such a model and the requirements for implementing an algorithm will be addressed in the following chapter.

Only when clade support is low, consensus trees *display* these clades as multifurcating. Thus, this is a way to depict strong uncertainty in bifurcating sub-branches.

[27] For an extensive discussion of the interplay between language contact, language change, and language relatedness see Aikhenvald (2007); Hickey (2020); Heine, and Kuteva (2020); Grant (2020).

4

A wave model implementation

A wave model can be computationally implemented in multiple ways; the modelling method I chose in this approach is to simulate the areal spreads and horizontal transmission of changes in a geographical setting as part of an agent-based model (ABM). Agent-based models are a type of model that simulates virtual entities, 'agents', which interact with one another along the parameters and rules of the simulation. Their interactions and the simulation outcomes can give insights into the trajectories of patterns and behaviour of the modelled entities. The following sections explain the concept of ABM simulations further.

The simulation of a wave model would thus entail simulating speech communities acquiring and transmitting innovations that can overlap and create new speech communities as a result. This model therefore could account for phenomena such as vertical transmission, simultaneous linguistic dissimilation of groups of speakers, and a more gradual development of languages from a common protolanguage.

Thus, the aim of this model is to simulate waves of innovations in a confined geographical space where each innovation spreads through a part of a community. There, spatial factors such as geographical barriers as well as linguistic factors can be simulated in the same model.

After the simulation of a variety of innovation scenarios, the models which approximate the innovations best are chosen to be analysed further. In addition to the gradual change processes which are captured by this ABM, it yields the advantage of granularity: it can build on the notion that parameters such as site rate, speciation, and change rates are branch-dependent or episodic in phylogenetic models and assume parameters to be flexible on an even more fine-grained level. In turn, the parameters do not necessarily need to be set globally or language-dependent in ABMs, but individual for every simulated agent. In the subsequent analysis, linguistic areas can be probed for what range of parameter values is present in the agents that make up the simulated community and whether spatial patterns can be found.

In short, the ABM used in this study is an approximation of the real-world diversification processes in the Germanic languages by simulating the

Germanic Phylogeny. Frederik Hartmann, Oxford University Press. © Frederik Hartmann (2023).
DOI: 10.1093/oso/9780198872733.003.0004

diversification process with virtual agents under different parameter settings. The simulation can afterwards be analysed to determine which parameter values and diversification pathways approximate the data best in order to draw conclusions about the actual process.

This chapter is structured as follows: first, it gives a general overview of agent-based models in section 4.1 before the core assumptions are outlined that are required to model language differentiation in an ABM simulation. The core mechanisms of the ABM used in this study are presented in sections 4.4 to 4.5, before section 4.7 goe into detail about how the individual mechanisms presented before are computationally implemented in the model. To show the general workings of the ABM, a test model is run on a toy dataset in section 4.8. Sections 4.9 and 4.10 summarize the model and its priors before, finally, section 4.11 examines the results of the main ABM simulation.

4.1 On agent-based models

Agent-based models were first used in physics, biology, and social sciences as a means to simulate processes that involve a heterogeneous mass of simulated entities. The method came into being at the time standard quantitative models were assumed to be inadequate for some problems in especially computational social science and biology.[1] Agent-based models are often used to simulate complex dynamics in populations, processes, and systems comprised of individual sub-units. They can thus be used to model and analyse a wide variety of problems from population dynamics, molecular evolution, epidemiology, and social interactions.

Agent-based models are therefore best described by outlining the differences from other quantitative models: the heart of agent-based models is simulating a number of entities (so-called agents) in a defined space according to defined parameters. The agents in this simulated space usually have a clearly defined spatial location and can possess different features that govern their properties, interactions, and behaviour. Since agent-based models are usually very task-specific, whether or not the individual agents possess features that are distinct from one another is mostly defined by the type of task itself. For example, behavioural simulations of emergency evacuations of buildings can be conducted without agent-specific properties (see e.g. Ren, C. Yang, and Jin 2009). In this case, the agents are all equal and their actions are only governed

---

[1] For a general introduction see Railsback and Grimm (2019).

by the global (applying to all agents equally) property of wanting to escape the simulated room through the nearest exit.

Global parameters are different from the individual properties of agents in an ABM. For this reason, one has to distinguish between the two: global parameters are sets of parameters which define the basic structure of the actions of, and interactions between, individual agents. Global parameters can be, for example, birth/death probabilities of agents, speed of movement or frequency of interaction. Of course, these parameters can also be properties of the agents; the decision about what parameters to include as global parameters or properties of individual agents depends on the task at hand. To illustrate the usual procedure of conducting an agent-based simulation, I will briefly outline the steps in the process: first, one has to decide on the design of the study. How meaningful the results of a simulation are depends heavily on what the aim of the study is. The parameters are subsequently chosen and it is decided which parameters are to be set as global parameters. Thereafter, the simulation is run: a simulation is commonly divided into runs and ticks. A *run* refers to one simulation pass with a given set of parameters and consists of a certain number of ticks. A tick is one iteration loop of the simulation in which all or a subset of agents are updated. Usually, a run, while representing an entire simulation from beginning to end, is not exhaustive. The global parameters are fixed for each run which requires simulating multiple runs to be able to compare the results with the parameters of each run. This procedure is also called a parameter sweep in which many different permutations of parameter combinations are tested to evaluate the effects of the different parameters on the simulation outcomes.

4.2 Agent-based models to model language differentiation

Both in the field of language change research as well as in studies on language differentiation, agent-based models have been used on multiple occasions.

Sóskuthy (2015) who models sound change emergence though agent-based models where the agents are subject to different phonological pressures can be taken as an example for such studies. Other studies such as Winter and Wedel (2016) use agent-based approaches to study agent interactions and the effect on sound change and changes in the sound inventory. These represent a plethora of research into intra-population changes and the emergence of different varieties. They are not necessarily directly comparable to the more geospatial models of language evolution. Geospatial models include simulations of agents that are not rooted in abstract agent communities but attempt to account for geographical distributions of agents in inter-agent interactions. Such applications are used in sociology (e.g. Weidmann and Salehyan 2013; Bhavnani et al. 2014) or cultural evolution (e.g. Turchin et al. 2013). As agent-based approaches are suited for simulating speech communities, they are used as methods for the development of languages. Among the first, Steels (2011) investigates language evolution by tying it to models of cultural evolution. Furthermore, Gong, Minett, and Wang (2006) show the emergence of a common language through communication. Several studies investigate language emergence from a single starting language into multiple languages over time reviewed in Wichmann (2008: 451). In such studies, emphasis is placed on understanding the main driving factors of differentiation. Schulze, Stauffer, and Wichmann (2007) review the effects of geographical distance and natural barriers on language development and differentiation.

Probably the most important difference between ABMs and other methods in computational cladistics is that ABMs are *simulation-based*, contrary to descriptive or analytical approaches such as phylogenetic modelling or statistical analyses. That is, they aim at approximating a real-world process *generatively* through simulations rather than analytically describing or analysing observed data.

This property of ABMs comes with certain benefits concerning modelling of the differentiation of languages. The approach is inherently bottom-up (Lekvam, Gambäck, and Bungum 2014: 50). The entire notion rests on the attempt to recreate the processes in the real world in a simulated rule-governed space. Complex simulations can still encompass randomness, but in essence, they are strictly rule driven. These rules in the form of interactions and parametrized events taking place in the simulated space can be altered, removed, and added while monitoring their effect on the outcomes. In comparison with more inferential methods, this approach yields the advantage of not needing to infer processes based on data but to observe the fundamental and complex linkages between factors, parameters, and events. In other words, the researcher can observe the behaviour of a system under varying conditions rather than deducing the process from observed data only.

It has to be noted that one of the additional differences between ABM approaches and inferential methods is that the different outcomes and the interactions between parameters are observed in a wide possibility space. With external factors involved such as geographical data (in geospatial models), we can observe high-dimensional interactions between the parameters themselves and external settings of the simulation. In this case, high-dimensional interactions are parameter interactions that contain a high number of variables. In low-dimensional interactions, two or three variables interact (i.e. exhibit inter-dependencies with regard to some outcome variable), whereas high-dimensional interactions can have interactions between more than three variables. In inferential methods, we are used to thinking in a data-driven way, that is, we observe data directly and infer the immediate processes that might have given rise to these data. In Germanic cladistics it is particularly salient that purely analytical tools are limited since we do not have much diachronic coverage of the processes. Between the proposed protolanguage and the attestations of the individual languages, we have no records of the developments that took place in between these two points in time. Therefore, as already discussed in previous chapters, we are faced with a centuries-spanning black box where we can only infer the processes that have taken place. An agent-based model of this problem can help by recreating the most important processes that were present in the beginning of the development to investigate which factors have contributed to yielding which outcome. However, it is not given that all ABMs can be employed to model these processes we observe in Germanic cladistics. An ABM that provides a good fit has to be individually crafted to suit the requirements that this specific problem entails. ABMs which are primarily used for simple problems are not ideal for this task since they do not provide sufficient flexibility to approximate the real-world processes. That is, simple ABMs that model diversification using only a low number of parameters might not capture crucial patterns in the real-world process. With an ABM specifically fit to the problem of Germanic linguistics, we can, however, recreate the processes at hand in this very instance to observe the effects and to understand which trajectories of movement and interactions might approximate the data best. The specific model type that was used here shall be further described in section 4.3.

4.2.1 ABMs as process simulations

As already mentioned, ABMs are *simulations* and not statistical or computational inference models. Therefore, they are best suited to investigating dynamic processes which are sparsely documented. The basic notions behind the simulation of individual aspects are outlined in the following sections.

General dynamics
ABMs exhibit great flexibility and fluidity in all facets of the architecture. Having this built-in dynamic structure means that processes are neither discrete nor fully hard-coded but repeatable and gradient. It is generally

advantageous to not need to assume fixed terms for processes such as migration speed since such a factor is not just decided once but can change in frequency of occurrence and impact strength over the course of a simulation. The ability of the simulated system to change on its own on the basis of inherent factors and interactions makes it more flexible in terms of capability to approximate real-world processes. This flexibility and ability to self-develop is then found in all sub-processes in the model. This is not to say that more flexible parameters are always better in any case. In certain cases, they merely increase random noise or the likelihood of overfitting. For this reason, to make use of the flexibility of agent-based models to the full extent, one must also add sensible model parameter spaces and fit diagnostics.

Innovation dynamics

The dynamics of innovation in language can be modelled as conditional probabilistic processes that occur as events of varying and individual frequency. This means that innovations in language do not need to be predefined or deterministic but can be modelled as fluctuating events. In particular, the innovation of a certain linguistic feature can be modelled as an event that occurs with a certain (globally or agent-specific) probability. This probability can be globally fixed or change based on certain conditions during the course of a simulation.

Contact dynamics

Language contact effects can also be dynamically modelled in an ABM simulation. These contact effects are mainly modelled as interactions between agents where one agent transfers certain features of its language to another. It is also important to note that this is not done at predetermined points in time, but rather governed by simulation-internal factors. Thus, we can generate spreading of language properties that comes close to how innovations spread in a wave-model. Innovations can spread and be overlaid with other innovations during the simulation. Thus, contact can be modelled more fluidly and with smooth transitions between the speech communities.

Migration dynamics

Migration dynamics as such are mainly based on how frequently a community changes its position in the simulation space. Migrations in an ABM can be modelled as a confluence of many individual actions of the agents. It is possible to approximate a 'relaxed' migration model insofar as individual agents can migrate to a neighbouring location or larger groups of agents can migrate together. The decision to migrate, however, can be set as an individual decision of an agent itself. Thus, large migration movements would emerge when an areal group of agents exhibits similarly high migration probabilities.

4.3 Agent-based models with Bayesian assumptions

Bayesian probability is, in the broadest sense, a probability concept which represents a specific interpretation of probability.[2] Whereas the frequentist interpretation of probability assumes probability to be equal to the relative frequency of occurrence of an event after many trials, inherent to Bayesian probability is the notion that probability can best be approximated by a probability distribution while at the same time this distribution contains the key concept of uncertainty: the probability of an event is not a fixed value but distributed around a mean value with a certain standard deviation. This concept is best exemplified using the example of a fair coin toss. We assume, a fair coin exhibits, theoretically, the probability of $\frac{1}{2}$ for the event 'heads' when tossed. However, as soon as the coin is tossed ten times, the relative frequency of 'heads' might not be exactly $\frac{1}{2}$. If this experiment is repeated twenty times, we can observe twenty different proportions of the event 'heads' after ten tosses. The density of these twenty observations might peak at $\frac{1}{2}$, but adjacent values will also be likely to have given rise to the data. In the Bayesian sense, we want to infer the probability of 'heads' from the available data, that is, to estimate the (posterior) probability of certain probabilities for 'heads' *given* the data.

The most important notion at this point is that events, even with theoretical fixed probabilities, can, when tested, exhibit some degree of uncertainty. This uncertainty is assumed to be inherent to our knowledge of the events, which is a crucial assumption as it describes quantifiable events as at least partially influenced by other factors and chance. The Bayesian approach, which is relevant for the type of ABM described in the following sections, will also draw on this principle of uncertainty, prior, and posterior distributions. The central point of a Bayesian approach is the question of which events (and with which probability) have most likely given rise to the data we observe.

I will briefly illustrate this notion using the example of a hypothetical 'innovation' parameter which determines the occurrence of a linguistic innovation in the (non-deterministic) ABM simulation. In a fixed-value approach, the parameter could be set to a specific value, for example 0.3, which would result

---

[2] In recent years Bayesian statistics was popularized again by influential works such as McElreath (2020); Gelman et al. (2013).

in a probability of 30 per cent for the occurrence of a linguistic innovation at each time step. This would inevitably result in the assumption that this probability is **always** and **exactly** 0.3. However, if the simulation were re-run with the same value, it might produce a slightly different outcome since this time, other agents interact and other conditions and situations arise. This means that different final states of the simulations are compatible with the same parameter value. Or, vice versa, a specific situation in the real-world could be compatible with different parameter values in the simulation. As a result, we have to simulate a large range of parameter values to gauge the different possible outcomes.

A way in which this can be done is that for every run of the simulation, a new value is drawn from a prior distribution, resulting in different values each time with every parameter value having its own prior probability. This means that if a rather flat distribution is assumed, the range of possible values increases, virtually representing a situation in which this parameter varies much from time step to time step. On the other hand, an underlying probability distribution with a small standard deviation will yield values that are similar to one another. This approximates a situation in which a particular area in the parameter space is designated for this parameter. After the simulation has been run multiple times, we can filter out those results that do not approximate the observed data well and we obtain a posterior distribution.[3]

This has implications for the interpretation of a simulation result: both the flat and a narrow posterior probability distribution for an individual parameter need to be interpreted differently. If the posterior parameter probability distribution is flat (i.e. approximates a uniform distribution), we can interpret this as this parameter setting being not very influential for the simulation outcome. If there were simulation-internal drivers demanding a certain parameter setting space from this parameter, the parameter would adjust accordingly and hence develop a more narrow probability distribution.

To summarize, the Bayesian approach enables exactly these insights into the mechanics of the ABM simulation: (1) it assumes a prior probability distribution for the inferred parameters, and (2) it can, in the posterior, show both flat distributions, and a very narrow distribution approximating a fixed value. The latter benefit of obtaining a posterior distribution for parameters is that the shape of the posterior can indicate whether a parameter has an impact on the outcome. If, for example, the *migration* parameter approximated a uniform distribution in the posterior runs, this would indicate that a large variety of

---

[3] For more detail see section 4.6.1.

migration values are compatible with the data, or, in other words, the parameter *migration* is negligible in its impact on the simulation outcome. If, on the other hand, this parameter showed a very narrow posterior distribution around the value 0.5, it would indicate that only a small range of values around 0.5 yielded a good fit to the data. Therefore, the flexibility in the parameters is of crucial importance to the interpretation of the simulation results.

4.4 The setting and purpose of the Germanic diversification model

As has been touched on in previous sections, the aim of this endeavour is to devise an agent-based model that simulates the diversification of the Germanic languages by modelling the process of innovation, innovation spread, and population migration. The result is thus a model that computationally reconstructs the historical events by drawing mainly on a wave-like horizontal process.

The environment to which the model is applied is an approximation of late Bronze Age and early Iron Age northern central Europe. This approximation is represented as a grid (i.e. a map) with representations of three terrain types: *inhabitable land*, *sea*, and *river*. The map is subdivided into smaller pieces of terrain (henceforth: *tiles*) which the simulated entities (henceforth: *agents*) are positioned. Figure 4.1 shows a zoomed part of the simulation surface to illustrate the individual terrain types.

The agents in this model represent individual speech communities and function as the smallest simulated units. Each agent is positioned on an inhabitable tile and can border a river tile, a free (inhabitable) tile, an occupied (inhabitable) tile, and a non-inhabitable tile.

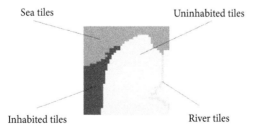

Sea tiles   Uninhabited tiles

Inhabited tiles   River tiles

Figure 4.1 Zoom of the simulation surface showing the three terrain types including inhabited tiles that are occupied by agents

Each agent possesses: (1) A unique position on the map; (2) a linguistic vector of innovations; and (3) an individual set of parameter settings. Each agent's **feature vector** is a innovation-based binary feature vector (e.g. (0, 0, 1, 0) for a vector with four positions) where the positions represent individual innovations that can be observed in any of the Germanic daughter languages. This means the initial stage (Proto-Germanic) is an all-zero vector since no innovations have occurred yet. Note that this is the raw setting and the individual mechanics and details of the model are presented in the following sections.

4.5 Parameters of the model

This section aims at explaining the individual actions each agent can take during the simulation. This will be done by isolating each action and displaying its effect on the course of the simulation in detail.

Every time unit (*tick*) a given agent executes the following actions based on their probability (see Table 4.1).

It has to be noted that *spreading* is an outward force, radiating from an agent, while *aligning* is an inward force, making the agent adapt another state of its

Table 4.1 Agent action overview chart

Linguistic	Innovation	The agent's feature vector undergoes an innovation by changing a 0 in the grammar vector to 1.
	Spreading	The agent transfers an innovation to one or more (depending on *spreading vulnerability*) neighbouring agent's feature vector.
	Spreading (river)	The agent transfers an innovation to one or more agent's feature vector across river tiles.
	Spreading (sea)	The agent transfers an innovation to one or more agent's feature vector across sea tiles.
	Aligning	An agent removes an innovation in a position where a neighbouring agent's grammar does not exhibit an innovation.
Non-linguistic	Migration	An agent changes its position by moving to a neighbouring free tile.
	Migration (river)	An agent changes its position by moving to a neighbouring free tile across river tiles.
	Birth	Another agent on a neighbouring tile is spawned and inherits both the original agent's feature vector and parameter settings.

neighbour. Here, the *spreading* of innovation and its antagonist *aligning* operate on different states: a zero state does not spread outward and an innovation
state cannot be obtained through aligning. This is a necessary compromise
in order for the model to fit the binary innovation data type. If aligning and
spreading applied universally, 0 and 1 would be grammar types and behave
like two competing innovation forms rather than 0 being the previous state
while 1 is the innovation whose diffusion through the speech community is to
be investigated. As discussed in detail in section 3.2.2, the change from 1 to 0
does not mean a reversal to the previous state. By *alignment*, the agent acquires
a trait that obscures the previously acquired innovation (see also section 4.5.2
for further discussion of this parameter).

4.5.1 Migration and birth

The parameter migration governs the spreading of the Germanic-speaking
communities from the initial starting positions. A higher parameter value thus
means faster spread. Since spreading can lead to a situation in which multiple
individual agents become isolated from the rest of the area, an increase in the
number of agents needs to account for an increase in population as a result of
eastward migration.

To illustrate the migration mechanic in the context of this ABM, I set up a
simple example ABM whose output can be observed In Figure 4.2. This ABM is
set on a surface of 20 × 20 tiles, one of which is occupied by a single agent. This
agent only possesses the ability to move to an adjacent tile with a certain globally determined probability. In this case, the migration of this agent proceeds
as follows: each tick an agent is selected, two random values are drawn, one
from a uniform distribution between 0 and 1 and one from a truncated normal
distribution *TruncatedNormal*(0.5, 0.1) the latter of which shall represent the
agent's probability of migrating (*migration rate*). If the value drawn from the
normal distribution is higher, the migration triggers and the agent moves to

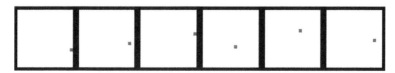

Figure 4.2 Example ABM migration: snapshots at ticks 0, 20, 40, 60, 80,
100

a randomly chosen adjacent tile. This action repeats 100 times which gives a simulation with 100 ticks. The output in Figure 4.2 records the agent's position at tick 0, 20, 40, 60, 80, 100.

From this figure, we can deduce that over the course of 100 ticks, the agent randomly moves through space but as there is no predetermined direction and each adjacent tile has the same chance of being selected as a new location, the agent approximately stays within the same right half of the simulation.

If we apply this simple migration mechanic to larger populations of agents, we see a certain behaviour that can be seen in Figure 4.3. This simulation starts on a 50 × 50 tile surface with agents occupying the first five rows of the surface.

As we can see here, some agents start to move far away from the rest of the agents as time increases. Given enough ticks, the agents would eventually space themselves out evenly across the surface. This is a problem insofar as such a migration system would eventually yield a large majority of the agents being detached from every other agent. To counter this, I imposed a migration restriction according to which an agent can only migrate to a free tile provided that it initially was adjacent to at least one other agent. This prevents individual agents from moving off into the space of the surface, requiring them to stay in groups for a longer time. Figure 4.4 is the output of such a migration system. When comparing Figures 4.3 and 4.4, we can observe that although the restricted migration over time out of the agents, in this scenario, there is some group coherence observable.

After having investigated the migration mechanic, the second action that an agent can take is that of *birth*. It is not technically an action but a mechanic that is tied to each agent. In this example simulation, each time

Figure 4.3 Example ABM migration with multiple agents: snapshots at ticks 0, 20, 40, 60, 80, 100

Figure 4.4 Example ABM migration with multiple agents and migration restrictions: snapshots at ticks 0, 20, 40, 60, 80, 100

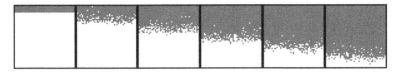

Figure 4.5 Example ABM migration and birth with multiple agents and migration restrictions: snapshots at ticks 0, 20, 40, 60, 80, 100

an agent is selected, a random value is drawn from a normal distribution *TruncatedNormal*(0.1, 0.1) to determine the probability of the action *birth* firing. If this is true, another agent is spawned on an adjacent free tile. This yields an output such as Figure 4.5.

Here, we see that not only are the agents migrating, the gaps are filled with new agents with the probability of around 0.1 (mean value) each time an agent is selected.

It is worth noting that computationally, both mechanics interact insofar as when there are more agents in simulated space, more agents are free to migrate again if they were previously bound by the migration restriction (see above). This means that *birth* has an enhancing effect on *migration*.

4.5.2 Innovation spreading and aligning

The linguistic change innovation and transmission complex of mechanics is more detailed and has more considerations tied to it.

The first mechanic is the simple innovation mechanic. As an example, I demonstrate this mechanic using a simulation of multiple agents on a 50 × 50 tile surface. Every agent has an *innovation vector* consisting of one binary value with 0 meaning that the agent has not undergone an innovation and 1 representing the agent having undergone an innovation. On this 50 × 50 example surface, all but one agent have undergone no innovation. Every time an agent that has undergone an innovation is selected during the simulation process, a probability value is drawn from a normal distribution *TruncatedNormal*(0.1, 0.1) and if this value is higher than a randomly drawn value from a uniform distribution between 0 and 1, the agent spreads its innovation to a randomly selected neighbouring agent. Figure 4.6 shows the model output of this example simulation.

Here we see that after 100 ticks, in a large portion of the agents in the upper left quadrant the innovation has spread. However, if a model incorporates more than one innovation, it is necessary to investigate the behaviour of the

Figure 4.6 Example ABM innovation with one starting agent: snapshots at ticks 0, 20, 40, 60, 80, 100

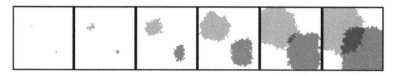

Figure 4.7 Example ABM innovation with two starting agents and two possible innovations: snapshots at ticks 0, 20, 40, 60, 80, 100

simulation with two innovations. To achieve this, I set up the same basic setting as before; however, this time there are two innovations present and the spreading probability of each variant is described by *TruncatedNormal*(0.15, 0.1). This means that each agent has an innovation vector consisting of two positions for the two innovations. Thus there are four possible types of this innovation vector: [0, 0], [0, 1], [1, 0], and [1, 1]. Agents can undergo no innovation, only one of two or both. Thus we will find that over time there will develop four linguistic communities. Figure 4.7 shows the output of this simulation.

The four different shades indicate the different stages. The darker grey area in the intersection of the two spreading innovations shows the emergence of the fourth variety through the intersection of two innovations.

For this innovation mechanic, it is also necessary to implement a counterbalance mechanic that makes an agent lose the innovation if a neighbouring agent does not possess the innovation. This serves two purposes: on the one hand it provides a necessary counterweight to the innovation, which would otherwise sweep through the simulation space radially. On the other hand, it is an implementation of inter-speaker (or speech community for that matter) assimilation as discussed previously in works such as Giles, Coupland, and Coupland (1991) or Pickering and Garrod (2004).

To demonstrate this, we implement an aligning parameter with a probability drawn from *TruncatedNormal*(0.05, 0.1). Each time an agent that possesses at least one of the two innovations is selected during the simulation, it adapts the neighbouring earlier state with a certain probability. Figure 4.8 shows this situation:

Figure 4.8 Example ABM innovation with two starting agents and two possible innovations including alignment: snapshots at ticks 0, 20, 40, 60, 80, 100

Here we can see that the spreading does not proceed as smoothly as in Figure 4.7 but rather the innovations start forming smaller enclaves. Note that this simulation was run using the same seed value as the simulation displayed in Figure 4.7. This means that the two runs would have proceeded identically if it were not for the newly implemented aligning mechanism. We have to keep in mind that the mechanics *innovation spreading* and *aligning* do not necessarily denote two different real-world processes. One could argue that *aligning* refers to the spreading of a different linguistic variant. However, in this innovation-based setting where the linguistic properties of an agent are represented as binary vectors denoting the presence or absence of a certain innovation, *aligning* is always the spreading of the 0-class. Thus we cannot interpret both mechanics separately. Rather we have to see them in relation to each other as they interact substantially: if one of the two parameters is higher than the other, that variant will spread faster and eventually overtake the other. If they are equal, the variants will be in an equilibrium. This specific property can be explored using a second simulation where the alignment parameter is activated after tick 60 but then equally strong as the spreading parameter (both *TruncatedNormal*(0.2, 0.1) in this case). Figure 4.9 shows the output of this simulation.

Here we can see that up until tick 80, the two innovations spread evenly, but after this tick, the progress is small. This is the near-equilibrium created by the aligning mechanism. Because the values are drawn from relatively flat normal

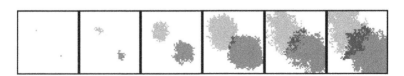

Figure 4.9 Example ABM innovation with two starting agents and two possible innovations including strong alignment after 60 ticks: snapshots at ticks 0, 20, 40, 60, 80, 100

distributions, one of the variants still increases in spread in this simulation; however, the last two states captured in Figure 4.9 show no fast expansion as was the case in the snapshots before.

Another component is a modification of the spreading parameter that tries to overcome two different problems: (1) multidirectional spreading and (2) distance-based constraints.

(1) is defined as the possibility of one agent spreading its innovation to more than one other agent. In the simulations so far, the agents equally spread their innovation to one other agent. This might not make an impact in an example simulation such as those here, but for more complicated simulations where agents differ in their spreading parameter, it is important to allow individual agents to spread an innovation to more than one other agent community.

(2) This spreading to more than one community can be biased for distance meaning that if an agent spreads the innovation, it spreads it first to other agents that are more similar before spreading it to other agents that are more different. The way this can be implemented is by setting a parameter value *spread vulnerability* that is equal to the percentage of adjacent agents to which to spread the innovation. Hence a *spread vulnerability* value of 0.5 would mean that the agents spread their innovation to half of the adjacent agents that do not have this innovation. Further it can be implemented that more similar agents are favoured. For example, if there are four surrounding agents, one of them being more similar to the agent in question, the innovation would then be spread to the more similar agent and one of the more different agents.[4]

This can be demonstrated in an example simulation. Here, I set the *spread vulnerability* to be fixed to two agents for simplicity reasons. Further I determine that the agents favour spreading to agents that do not have any innovation before spreading to agents that already possess one other innovation, thus simulating different distances between agents. Figure 4.10 shows the output of this model. Note that this model is otherwise identical to the model shown in Figure 4.7.

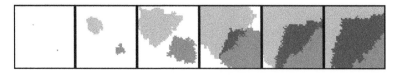

Figure 4.10 Example ABM innovation with two starting agents and two possible innovations: snapshots at ticks 0, 20, 40, 60, 80, 100

---

[4] For the real-world analogue of this mechanism, see the discussion in Bowern (2013).

In this figure, when the two innovations meet (between the 40th and 60th tick), the innovations spread to the other agents that have already undergone an innovation more slowly. We see that once the two innovations meet, the fast spreading continues towards the upper right and lower left corners whereas it is slowed down towards the upper left and lower right corners.

4.5.3 Geospatial parameters

In the example simulations that were shown in the previous sections, the agents were located on a symmetric plane surface whereas in real-world applications, it is, depending on the problem, often not desired to simulate agents on a plain two-dimensional surface. Especially when moving or spreading actions are involved, certain surfaces may want to be designed in such a way that makes it more difficult for agents to perform these actions across certain areas. More concretely, if an actual geographical space is the setting for the simulation, the researcher might want to implement areas such as rivers or large bodies of water that exhibit a lower rate of movement as it may tend to be more difficult to move across these spaces.

To explain this concept using an example simulation, I adapted the migration model displayed in Figure 4.5 and added an obstacle which is intended to slow down the migration of a certain part of the agents on the surface. Figure 4.11 shows the output of this example simulation. Here, I inserted a barrier (dark bar) on the mid-right hand side of the surface.

We can see in this example that the agents move from top to bottom relatively equally as the simulation displayed in Figure 4.5 has shown. However, once the agents approach the barrier, there is a very small probability (distributed as $TruncatedNormal(0, 0.05)$) to cross this barrier. A few agents succeed in crossing the barrier (seen on the lower part of the surface at tick 80). From there on they continue migrating as normal. It needs to be stressed that whether or not the obstacle is a hindrance to movement or spread

Figure 4.11 Example ABM migration with multiple starting agents and a partial barrier: snapshots at ticks 0, 20, 40, 60, 80, 100

depends on the parameter that governs the movement across the obstacle. We also might think of a scenario in which an obstacle propels migration or spread forward. Computationally, this occurs when the parameter governing spread/migration across the obstacle is higher than the parameter for regular spread/migration.

A particular property of these barriers is that they act as a filter where only a small variety of agents succeed in crossing the obstacle. This can lead to founder effects on the other side of the obstacle. A founder effect, the observation that if a given scenario—ABM simulations in this case—contains a filter which only a few agents can pass, then these agents will propagate their properties in this new region. This can lead to (1) the variety of different properties being greatly reduced after the filter than before and (2) certain properties dominating the entire post-filter area depending on what properties the agents that first crossed had. To investigate these founder effects further, I devised a simulation building on the framework assumed in the simulation depicted in Figure 4.7. Assume that in this simulation, there are two innovations on one side of a very selective barrier. The output of this model can be seen in Figure 4.12.

This simulation is worth dissecting in detail. We see that up until tick 40, the two innovations spread approximately equally fast in the top half of the surface. Shortly before tick 40, the innovation indicated by a light grey colour crosses the barrier twice. At tick 60, we can see that this innovation spreads rapidly whereas the other innovation just had a crossing event. At tick 80 we see that, save the upper right quadrant of the post-barrier area, the area is predominantly occupied by agents with one innovation. This is in stark contrast to the pre-barrier where at this tick all agents exhibit both innovations. Eventually, the second innovation spreads in the post-barrier region as well; however, since the first innovation was first to pass the filter, it was to dominate the post-barrier region for most of the second half of the simulation. This phenomenon thus is a demonstration of a founder effect.

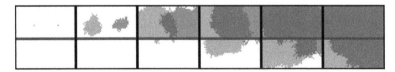

Figure 4.12 Example ABM innovation with two starting agents and two possible innovations: snapshots at ticks 0, 20, 40, 60, 80, 100

4.5.4 The innovation mechanism

In the previous sections we have seen how the agents in the model spread innovations and migrate to neighbouring unoccupied tiles. What is so far still missing is the mechanism of how innovations occur in an agent. The most simplistic case is to set an innovation parameter *innovation* to a value which corresponds to the probability for each agent to develop an innovation at that particular tick. If this is the only mechanism implemented, we effectively assume everything else to be random. This includes the time and order of the innovations occurring. To investigate the effects this particular set-up has on the simulation, I compiled an example simulation based on the simulation shown in Figure 4.12. The only adjustments regarding this simulation were that the spread probability was set to 0.05 and the probability of spread across the barrier was set to 0.01. The important parameter for this run is the innovation parameter since, in contrast to the simulation shown in Figure 4.12, this example does not assume two starting innovations. Rather, each time an agent is selected there is a chance that this agent will develop a random innovation. For simplicity reasons, I fixed the maximum number of innovations to 2 for each agent which means each agent has an innovation vector consisting of two positions. Therefore, the agents' vectors can be of the following types [0, 0], [0, 1], [1, 0], and [1, 1]. To demonstrate the impact of this basic innovation mechanism, I set the innovation parameter to 0.005, the decision about which agent undergoes an innovation and which innovation is being undergone is random. Figure 4.13 shows the output of this model.

What we can see here is that very soon many areas of innovation are formed until by tick 80, most of the agents possess both innovations. The simulation shows that the same innovation is innovated independently multiple times. This is due to the fact that, each tick, each agent has a chance of 0.005 to undergo an innovation. This means that there is a potential for an average of

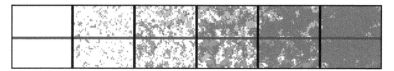

Figure 4.13 Example ABM innovation mechanism with two possible innovations and random innovation occurrence: snapshots at ticks 0, 20, 40, 60, 80, 100

1,104 innovation events in a single simulation with 100 ticks and 2,208 agents. Further it means that each of the two innovations can be independently inno-vated on average 552 times over the course of 100 ticks. It is established that there are homoplastic events that can occur in the real world, whereas the chance for real-world homoplasy is likely to be more infrequent. Especially when each tick is fitted to correspond to one year, we do not expect homo-plastic events to occur and to spread on average five times per year for a given feature. However, this needs to be investigated further and ideally determined by the model itself. For this reason and in order to make sure that homoplasy can still occur, the probability for homoplasy was added as a separate parame-ter in the main model. The innovation mechanism was implemented such that the quantity of parallel innovations can be controlled. In a model in which new innovations are picked at random, we can see a scenario where a single inno-vation can occur up to five times in parallel. To discourage random parallel innovations in which the same innovation independently occurs up to sev-eral hundred times during a simulation run, parallel innovations are governed by a separate parameter. This parameter represents a probability with which each tick one of the previously occurred innovations can be innovated again. Concretely this means that every innovation can occur only once but that, with a certain probability, some innovations can be innovated again. It needs to be emphasized that this mechanism is not implemented as an analogue to a real-world force but rather as a way to control and monitor the occur-rence of homoplasy. In essence, this is a requirement of the computational process.

To prevent the model from spawning this high number of innovations dur-ing the same run, I fixed the number of innovations to two. This means that once an innovation occurred, it can only spread but it cannot be re-innovated again. The result of this implementation can be seen in Figure 4.14. Note that, since this is an example simulation, homoplasies were prevented entirely for reasons of simplicity. In the main model of this study, a homoplasy parameter was implemented that governs how frequently homoplasies can occur. There, homoplasies do occur and their frequency is inferred through a parameter.

Figure 4.14 Example ABM innovation mechanism with two unique possible innovations: snapshots at ticks 0, 20, 40, 60, 80, 100

4.5.5 Hierarchical modelling

After having illustrated the principal notions behind Bayesian-type ABMs, another aspect of Bayesian modelling is important to introduce, as it builds on the core assumptions and extends these. Hierarchical Bayesian models are a part of Bayesian data analysis in which the posterior distribution of a given parameter is estimated hierarchically, meaning that the parameters that are used to determine the distribution of the model prior at the lowest level are themselves modelled as a probability distribution. The intuition behind this is to model varying parameter behaviour at multiple levels. Concerning terminology, higher-order priors (i.e. any parameter higher than the base-level) is called a *hyperprior*.

The hierarchical approach can be utilized for Bayesian ABM simulations to allocate more freedom to develop agent-specific traits. To illustrate this, assume an ABM simulation with an agent A and a migration parameter M. Under the assumption that M is a local parameter, the probability distribution of M develops over time. We can assume that

$$P_i(M_A) \sim TruncatedNormal(0, 1) \tag{4.1}$$

with i being the initial state. This denotes a relatively flat initial prior distribution of the probability for M.

The parameters of the underlying distribution that are updated allow for the development of this agent's individual parameter distribution. To modify the distribution, one has to subtract from, or add a certain value to, the parameters of the distribution.

$$P_{i+1}(M_A) \sim TruncatedNormal(0 + x, 1 + y) \tag{4.2}$$

Here, x and y are the values that are used to modify the distribution of $P_i(M)$. One could set x and y to a fixed global value which would result in $P(M)$ of all agents being updated with the same value each update.

$$P_n(M_A) \sim TruncatedNormal(\alpha_n, \beta_n)$$

$$\alpha_n = \alpha_{n-1} + x$$

$$\beta_n = \beta_{n-1} + y$$

α and β denote the parameters of the truncated normal distribution after the preceding update. Setting x and y to a fixed value would result in a

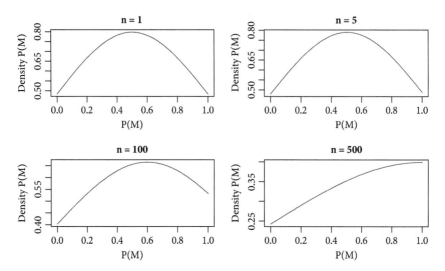

Figure 4.15 Fixed-value update of α and β by 1 per time step

linear growth of α and β. After $n = 500$ updates, the distribution $P_n(M_A) \sim$ *TruncatedNormal*$(\alpha_{500}, \beta_{500})$ would approximate a probability distribution with a large standard deviation. This is illustrated in Figure 4.15 where the development of the probability distribution of M_A is shown. There, the normal distribution parameters α and β were increased by 0.01 at each update.

What we can observe is that the more updating $P(M)$ undergoes, the wider the distribution becomes and the more the mean approaches 1. This issue can be resolved when a hierarchical model is introduced in which the update values are also drawn from a probability distribution. This hierarchical model can be described as follows:

$$P_n(M_A) \sim TruncatedNormal(\alpha_n, \beta_n)$$

$$\alpha_n = \alpha_{n-1} + \gamma$$

$$\beta_n = \beta_{n-1} + \rho$$

$$\gamma \sim norm(\mu_1, \sigma_1)$$

$$\rho \sim norm(\mu_2, \sigma_2)$$

The parameter values μ_1, μ_2, σ_1 and σ_2 are fixed values which are predetermined. What can be observed in this model is that the updating values γ and ρ are no longer fixed values but are themselves sampled from a underlying distribution instead that can itself be updated. This has the advantage that

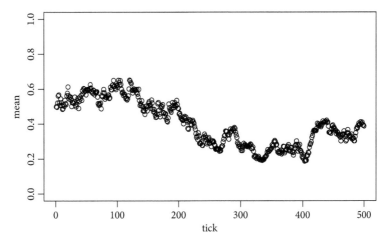

Figure 4.16 Change of mean under a random normal-valued update process

the updates of an agent's parameters are variable and draw from a parameter space defined by fixed global hyperparameters. The interpretation of such hierarchical ABMs is different from non-hierarchical agent-based models. A hierarchical model assumes not only that the main model parameters are variable to a certain degree, but also that the parameters defining those are variable. This two-level hierarchical system can be interpreted as individual populations having unique internally variable preferences but they draw from the same global pool of hyperparameters to update these preferences.

As explained above, normal-valued updates lead to a fluctuation in the mean of an agent's value. If the hyperparameter is drawn from a normal distribution $Normal(0, 0.01)$, we see a single agent's mean value fluctuate over time as we expect there to be similarly many positive as negative updates. Figure 4.16 shows a trace plot of a single agent's mean value development over 500 ticks.

This development is one of many possible developments of different agents with the same update mechanism. When we plot the development of multiple agents at a time, we can observe the effect of this updating process in more detail. Figure 4.17 shows this plot.

Here we can see that different patterns emerge and that, after a certain number of ticks, we see agents developing their individual properties. These differences in the mean value occur randomly but generally follow an observable parameter value. As different agents develop individual patterns, it is possible to have different scenarios arising that can be evaluated against an empirical data baseline. For example, if we had empirical data that suggests

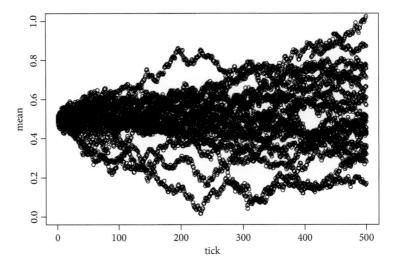

Figure 4.17 Trace plot of mean development for twenty agents under a random normal-valued update process

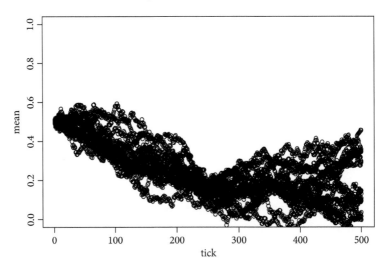

Figure 4.18 Change of mean under a random normal-valued update process with values < 0.2 at tick 250

that the mean value at tick 250 is unlikely to be above 0.2, we can filter out all runs that do not meet this criterion. Figure 4.18 shows twenty runs that exhibit a value of less than 0.2 at tick 250.

From this plot we can deduce that under the current parameters, the most likely runs follow approximately this pattern. Ideally, these simulations return the most likely traces that are possible given the data and the parameters.

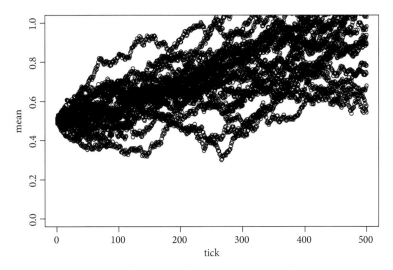

Figure 4.19 Change of mean under a random normal-valued update process with *update ~ Normal*(0.001, 0.1)

It is further possible to alter the parameters such that the normal distribution underlying the updating has a slightly positive or negative mean. This will produce the output that the agent's values tend to develop positively over time. Figure 4.19 shows the output of the same principle as displayed in 4.17 with the exception that the underlying normal distribution was assigned a mean of 0.001.

As we can see in this example, most agents' values tend to develop positively. This shows us that this approach can not only simulate various patterns of agents' value development but also take into account situations in which we see a steady increase in this parameter globally.

It has to be kept in mind that this architecture of building an agent-based model draws its core principles from Bayesian hierarchical modelling; it is not to be confused with an actual Bayesian hierarchical model. This term commonly refers to a specific Bayesian type of data analysis only in which the data are approximated using a hierarchical model architecture.

4.6 The evaluation of the model

So far we have only discussed the individual parameters and how a simulation run proceeds. In a single simulation run with randomly chosen parameters, the run would proceed according to the parameter settings and produce an outcome. This is therefore just a *generative model*, a computational simulation that takes parameter settings as inputs and produces an output. This in itself models *one* possible way in which the Germanic languages could have diversified but the task of the study is rather to *infer* the most likely diversification processes from the data. Therefore, an integral part of the model is the method in which the simulations are run and how we determine which of those runs are indicative of the real process of Germanic diversification.

This is done with a so-called *Approximate Bayesian computation* approach. The general aim is to systematically simulate different diversification processes and to determine which runs among the total number of simulated processes reflect the data best. Afterwards, we can analyse these best-fitting runs to gain insights into what common properties the runs share. These observations about the simulations can then be transferred to gain insights about the real-world process.

4.6.1 The concept of Approximate Bayesian computation

A crucial step in determining the working mechanics of an agent-based model is to choose the best evaluation method. After set-up, the model runs for a predetermined number of ticks until it produces an output. This output is usually the final state of the model which is expressed as a single performance metric, or more than one. These metrics are used to determine whether a certain run was successful when compared against a fixed baseline or which output it produced. However, the form in which a simulation is evaluated heavily depends on the data and the research question. There are three main different modelling approaches:

- Initial stage known—outcome to be simulated.
- Outcome known—initial stage to be simulated.
- Initial stage and outcome known—process to be simulated.

These three types operate on different premises and different types of available data. The first task can be described as a modelling environment in which the model is tasked with exploring a simulation space anchored to a specific initial stage. Here, the initial stage is defined in advance and a set of parameters is selected. The simulated development thus resembles the behaviour of the agents under different parameter settings. In such studies, the model is used for observing the impact of different parameters on the agents' behaviour.

The outcome itself is not fixed or predetermined as the sole interest of the researcher lies in investigating the parameters and their contribution to certain aspects of the simulation.

The second type of model is in some respects the inverse of the previous model type. In this case, not the outcome but the initial stage is simulated. Such approaches aim to determine the most likely initial stage given a certain outcome state and certain parameters.

The third type is a combination of the previous two approaches: it assumes a known initial stage and a known outcome. The simulated space is the process inbetween both stages. The particular interest is in the pathways that the agents took during the process. The present study uses this third approach since the data structure and our knowledge of the Germanic situation warrants such an approach. The initial stage, in this case Proto-Germanic, is the known initial stage from which the Germanic languages developed, thus building on the comparative method which provides the means to infer the properties of this initial stage. Moreover, the known outcome is the linguistic situation and geographic distribution of the Germanic daughter languages. The research goal is therefore clearly defined as finding patterns in the agent's pathways between Proto-Germanic and the daughter languages.

However, as a next step, it is necessary to define the means of evaluating the runs. Because the initial stage is known, the model can simulate possible development pathways into several daughter languages. The model itself is capable of simulating a vast variety of different scenarios especially since there is randomness implemented in the model. Yet these scenarios do not need to reflect what we observe in the Germanic linguistic data. In fact, the vast majority of those runs will not approximate the data. Thus out of all possible runs, we want to keep and evaluate those runs that actually reflect the data best. In this case, the data are the linguistic innovations of the daughter languages which are encoded in feature vectors (see section 4.4). Afterwards, we want to examine the 'successful' runs to determine whether there these runs have dominant patterns in common. This approach resembles the notion of *Approximate Bayesian computation*.

Approximate Bayesian computation (ABC) is a prominent analytical technique from the domain of Bayesian modelling. In short, ABC draws upon a generative function which generates data according to a stochastic process. The different outcomes of this function are determined by the input variables. After generating a large number of outcomes, only those runs are accepted as 'successful' which approximate the data best. To illustrate this notion, a simple univariate ABC model will be set up in the following section. Let L

be a language which has undergone n = 40 innovations over the course of t = 200 years. Now we want to estimate the average innovation probability each year which is simultaneously the rate of innovation. According to Frequentist statistics, the average probability is

$$\bar{p}(innovation) = \frac{n}{t}$$

Which equates to:

$$\bar{p}(innovation) = \frac{40}{200}$$

and gives an average innovation probability of 0.2. However, since we know that such processes are subject to random variance, we can approximate the problem using an ABC model. In this model, the occurrence of innovations over 200 years is simulated under the influence of different p. Every run i, the generative function F draws a value p_i from a prior distribution of p and simulates how many changes L would undergo if it had an average innovation probability of p_i. Having run the model for 100,000 iterations, the model has simulated a variety of hypothetical innovations given various values for $p(innovation)$. As we know that in reality L has undergone exactly forty innovations, we can discard all runs which yielded outcomes different from n = 40. If we plot the remaining $p(innovation)$, we see the frequency distribution of all values for $p(innovation)$ which yielded exactly forty changes. Figure 4.20 shows this plot; Figure 4.21 displays the same data with adjusted x-axis. The

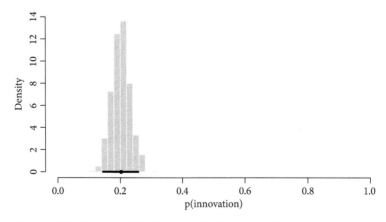

Figure 4.20 Posterior distribution of p(innovation)

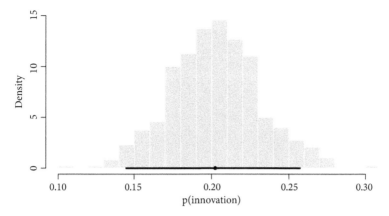

Figure 4.21 Posterior distribution of p(innovation), adjusted x-axis

black line segment indicates the 89 per cent HDI[5] credible interval which lies between 0.16 and 0.25 with the black dot representing the distribution mean. The prior distribution selected for this task was a uniform prior *uniform(0, 1)*.

From these plots we can deduce that values of *p(innovation)* between the credible intervals 0.16 and 0.25 can likely have yielded the number of innovations we observe in the data. The important property of such ABC models is that they simulate a variety of different scenarios, in the above case the outcomes under various *p(innovation)* values, and after examining those runs which yielded the actual data, we find patterns in those runs that give insight into the factors that might likely have given rise to the actual data. After running the above ABC model we can say with relative certainty that the average innovation rate of *L* was between 0.16 and 0.25.

In many ABC models, especially in more complex multivariate tasks, the simulated data rarely or never match the observed data *exactly*. Thus, such models introduce a tolerance value which determines how much runs are allowed to deviate from the actual data in order to still be accepted as 'successful'. To demonstrate this using the above task, let the tolerance value be $\varepsilon = 5$. This means that after every run, the algorithm compares the outcome to the observed data. If, as a result, the distance between outcome and observed data is smaller or equal to ε, the run is accepted. For the example above this means that runs are accepted when they produce numbers of innovations between

---

[5] Recall that HDI (*Highest density interval*) is a summary measure that gives the value range encompassing a set percentage (89% in this case) of the overall density of a distribution (i.e. the most probable interval).

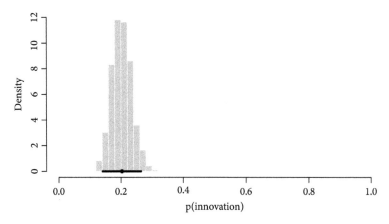

Figure 4.22 Posterior distribution of p(innovation) of the ABC with error included

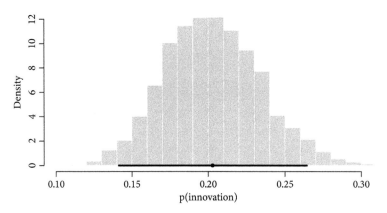

Figure 4.23 Posterior distribution of p(innovation) of the ABC with error included, adjusted x-axis

thirty-five and forty-five. The results of the model with tolerance term introduced are plotted in Figures 4.22 and 4.23 whereas the latter represents the frequency distribution with adjusted x-axis.

The 89 per cent HDI credible interval of this model lies between 0.15 and 0.25. We can observe that introducing the tolerance term does not affect the outcome statistic much in this example but it might provide important room for accepting runs to make the tasks more efficient for cases in which the event of an exact match is very rare.

At this point, it is important to note that the main diversification model in this chapter is *not* a pure ABC model. It is a simulation-based inference ABM that borrows core concepts from ABC methods but adapts and transforms them to a large degree. This means that the references to ABCs here and henceforth are mainly mentioned to illustrate the theoretical underpinnings of a part of the core mechanics of the model on which the model builds but adapts to fit the requirements of the research question. It must, however, be kept in mind that the final model is itself not an ABC model.

4.6.2 The spatial component

So far we have only discussed the spatial actions of agents in the abstract by only referring to the setting of the simulation as *simulation surface*. However, the spatial component is an integral part of the simulation as linguistic continua are to a large extent dependent on the spatial situation meaning what varieties are geographically close and how strong their mutual influence is.

The anchoring of the simulation in the geographical region of northern Europe was achieved by letting the simulation run on a surface based on the geographical shape of the region. Figure 4.24 shows the map that was the basis of the simulation. The map is derived from a sketch map of the region.[6]

The map in Figure 4.25 shows northern Europe with four differently shaded regions: light grey represents the sea (passable), dark grey shows inhabited terrain, and white shows terrain that is not inhabited by any Germanic-speaking community. Black shows impassable terrain where agents cannot

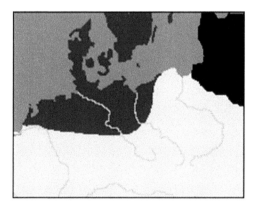

Figure 4.24 Simulation surface map of northern Europe

---

[6] Source: https://upload.wikimedia.org/wikipedia/commons/c/c5/Pre-roman_iron_age_%28map%29.PNG, accessed 27.5.2021.

migrate. Further, the rivers (passable) are indicated on the map as well. As dis-cussed above, both the sea and rivers are natural barriers that can be passed but doing so is governed by a different set of parameters. The inhabited terrain represents the starting position of all agents in the simulation.

A second set of maps was used to aid in the evaluation of the runs (see Figures 4.25 to 4.30). Whether or not a simulation provides a good fit is depen-dent on how well the simulated agents approximate the language in a particular area. For example, we want to evaluate how well those agents that are located in Scandinavia approximate Old Norse. In order to do this, the areas have to be pre-defined for every observed language. The areas were created using the geographical approximations in Mallory (1989: 87); W. König (2007: 46, 56, 58, 66); and Fortson (2010: 352).

Figure 4.25 Evaluation space of Old English

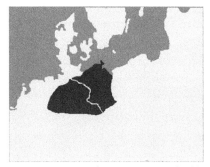

Figure 4.26 Evaluation space of Old Saxon

Figure 4.27 Evaluation space of Old High German

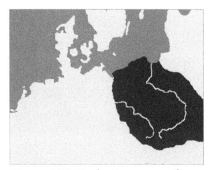

Figure 4.28 Evaluation space of Gothic, Burgundian, and Vandalic

Figure 4.29 Evaluation space of Old Frisian

Figure 4.30 Evaluation space of Old Norse

Note that the maps shown here are only meant to indicate the *approximate* location of a given language. As languages do not neatly follow these borders, they are just a rough area used to evaluate the simulations and to ensure that certain languages are simulated in approximately the correct area. These areas—although they mostly are—do not need to be mutually exclusive. There can be some overlap in regions where there is some uncertainty about where the approximate border of two regions is.

This is especially true for languages in the east, where multiple languages (i.e. Gothic, Vandalic, and Burgundian) are evaluated but the demarcations of the areas are unknown. In other words, since we do not know the geographical spread of these three languages, we assume a common area for all of them and see the simulations treat this area with similar properties. Doing this also entails that the three languages need to be evaluated differently. Instead of using the mean of the fit of all agents in this area, the agent with the least-best fit will be selected as the fit measure instead. This will result in an overall worse fit for Burgundian, Gothic, and Vandalic than for other languages since we do not use the mean of all agents but the worst-fitting agent, but it will provide the following two benefits:

The approximation to the language will be location-independent, meaning that the fit to Vandalic, for example, does not depend on a predetermined region but evaluates if there is *any* agent with a relatively good fit to Vandalic. Moreover, it will ensure that the area as a whole moves towards a better fit to either of the languages.

This means, however, that when evaluating the results, one needs to take into account that the languages Vandalic, Gothic, and Burgundian will exhibit a worse fit relative to the other languages.

Furthermore, the geographical position of Old English calls for comment. Old English is evaluated in what is today southern Denmark and northern Germany. This corresponds approximately to the position in the dialect continuum before the migration to the British isles. In reality, however, the linguistic ancestors who spoke a language that would later become Old English came from the coastal area of the North Sea coast and were not necessarily confined to the historical region of Anglia on the Cimbrian Peninsula. In this computational model, however, one has to set a region more clearly. Moreover, the model assumes that by the time the simulation is evaluated, the Old English features were already mostly present before the migration to the British Isles. Although this is in line with previous research (see esp. section 5.5.2), it is a limitation of the geospatial model that, in this case, it cannot easily display abrupt migrations to a place off the map. Therefore, this limitation has to be taken into account.

After the decline of the Germanic-speaking population in east-central Europe after the westward migrations (cf. W. König 2007: 58), there were no speech communities in the east that could have participated in shared changes. However, in a model whose time frame encompasses this period, a mechanism needs to account for the fact that after the westward migrations, no considerable contact took place between east-central and west-central Europe. For this reason, an area was defined beforehand where agents were incrementally removed to achieve a more realistic linguistic situation in this area after the migrations. This was achieved by gradually removing agents from the area in question from the year 500 AD onwards.

4.6.3 The temporal component

Bayesian phylogenetic models can account for uncertainty and differences in the data record (i.e. attestation times) as to when the ancestor language started diversifying and when the innovations in the daughter languages were completed. This creates the temporal dimension in the scenario that needs to be accounted for in an ABM setting as well. There is the possibility of setting the simulation time to a fixed number of ticks, which would mean that one has to determine an exact and fixed time span between the start of the diversification and the completion of innovations for individual daughter languages. This, however, would mean that strong assumptions would be required for the simulation. There is another possibility that can be adopted from Bayesian phylogenetics: taxon and root age uncertainty. The mechanics of this are comparable to the same functions in Bayesian models. In every simulation, an origin time is sampled from the prior along with the attestation times of individual taxa. Then, the simulation is run and the taxa are evaluated at the times sampled for each taxon.

For example, let A and B be taxa and O the starting time of the diversification. Let us further assume that the ages of these linguistic entities are sampled to be A: 1.5, B: 1.7, and O: 2.2 on the scale of 1,000 year-steps. A tick in this hypothetical simulation represents two years. Thus, after the simulation is started, it runs for $\frac{O-B}{2}$ ticks until taxon B is evaluated. Thereafter it continues to run for another $\frac{B-A}{2}$ ticks when taxon A is evaluated and the simulation ends. The relative temporal distance between the taxa and the root and between each of the taxa therefore matters for the simulation and can be sampled as ages for the taxa and the root. For example, if the simulation only yields a good fit to the data when taxon A is evaluated 200 ticks after taxon B and taxon B is evaluated 400 ticks after the simulation started, then we can determine the relative temporal distance of the taxa. These relative dates can be made absolute by setting absolute, hard-bounded priors on the dates.

It is important to note at this point that the taxa dates are not intended to be inferred in the model. They are mainly used to calibrate the model to actual time and to facilitate inferring the root age. The estimation of the process becomes more accurate when the model is given information about the relative temporal attestation distances between individual taxa.

Table 4.2 shows the priors used on the origin and the taxa (in 1,000 years). These priors are, with the exception of the prior on the origin, equal to the priors used in the Bayesian phylogenetic model (see Table 3.5).

Table 4.2 Origin and tip date priors

	Prior
Origin	Uniform(1.9, 2.8)
GO	Uniform(1.6, 1.8)
ON	Uniform(1.0, 1.2)
OE	Uniform(1.1, 1.3)
OF	Uniform(0.8, 1.0)
OS	Uniform(1.15, 1.35)
OHG	Uniform(1.15, 1.35)
VAND	Uniform(1.5, 1.7)
BURG	Uniform(1.5, 1.7)

4.6.4 Optimization of runs

As described previously, ABC approaches are very resource intensive. This is the case because they are, in some ways, an alternative to grid approximations where the parameter space is searched according to a predefined grid. This grid consists of multiple different parameter combinations which are all evaluated. However, this approach cannot be used for this particular investigation as the parameter space is too large to iterate over each possible combination of values. An ABC approach solves this problem by running the simulation many times, each time using a randomly selected parameter set drawn from a prior distribution. It increases in accuracy by increasing the number of evaluations. However, this approach is still inefficient as the number of runs needed is high. Additionally, the random sampling represents a random walk through the parameter space with some parameter combinations not being explored.

Bayesian statistical inference has faced this problem early in the 1950s in problems for which the likelihood space could not be evaluated efficiently with random walk approximations. The solution to this problem came with the advent of greater computational power: algorithms that make it possible to explore the posterior distribution more efficiently. The most basic algorithm, which is sometimes used as a shorthand for the entire group of algorithms, Markov-Chain Monte Carlo (MCMC) (see discussion in section 3.1.3).

While the ABM used in this study falls into this category, it is distinct from many statistical Bayesian models in two main aspects:

(1) In Bayesian phylogenetics, for example, there is a likelihood function applied to the data during model fitting to calculate the likelihood of the data given the parameters. The model at hand does not possess a likelihood function as the discrepancy between observed and simulated languages is determined through means of a distance function. Section 4.6.5 provides more information on the distance measure and the loss function derived from it.

(2) The model is evaluated one step at a time with the amount of data increasing during simulation, whereas in most statistical analyses, the data is present *before* the analysis. Thus we do not find a pre-defined set of datapoints which are to be evaluated but the number of available datapoints increases while simulating.

However, as classical MCMC methods are problematic to apply in this instance and sampling is too inefficient without any sampling technique, an algorithm needs to be applied that handles points (1) and (2) while still increasing sampling efficiency. This algorithm must be able to operate on output values that do not need to resemble a likelihood function. Secondly, the algorithm must be able to explore the parameter space with little data at first and increasingly optimize the sampling strategy when more data are available. Therefore I used a hybrid system between ABC and a Gaussian Process Regressor (GPR) as sampling optimizer. A Gaussian Process Regression is a Bayesian technique of fitting curves to data. This enables the regression model to fit a nonlinear curve to a set of datapoints rather than a regression line.[7] Gaussian processes work under the assumption that nearby datapoints can be interpolated to estimate the unobserved transition areas between two points. Applied to the problem at hand, the GPR can fit a regression curve to the loss metrics of the previous runs.

This means in effect that for the first run, a GPR optimizer selects parameter points from a search space defined as a prior distribution and evaluates these points by running the model. The output of this model is then fed back to the regression model where a GPR calculates the global minimum of the parameter space given the available data. Afterwards, a point from the estimated global minimum is selected as a 'best guess' to be evaluated next. After the evaluation of this point, the result is fed back to the GPR again where the regression is fitted anew. After a number of iterations exploring the search space, the GPR optimizer will select parameter values predominantly from the parameter region around the global minimum. This means that after a certain period of iterations, the algorithm will converge to a certain minimal point which ideally coincides with the global minimum.

Such GPR optimization approaches are currently used in high-dimensional hyperparameter tuning problems in machine learning. There, this method is one of the tools used for obtaining the best model and hyperparameter set-up of a machine learning task. Borrowing this method from machine learning is a reasonable approach since, in many machine learning settings, we do find multi-parameter models which run one at a time and whose output performance cannot likewise be evaluated using a likelihood function.

For the application in this specific task, this procedure presents a hybrid method between MCMC-based methods and Approximate Bayesian Computation: the simulations proceed in a *guided* walk through the parameter space instead of being randomly evaluated as in ABC applications and without following an MCMC chain. To ensure that the minimum found by the GPR optimizer is not just one of many possible local minimums, several instances of such a GPR optimizer are run for multiple iterations. The final results encompass all runs of all GPR instances and the best 5 per cent of runs are selected.

---

[7] For a discussion of GP optimization methods see e.g. Shahriari et al. (2016).

The particular optimization algorithm that was used was the Python module *Hyperopt* (Bergstra, Yamins, and Cox 2013).

To summarize, traditional ABC procedures are too resource-intensive and unspecific to run on a problem with this size of parameter spaces. Thus, the GPR algorithm specifically designed to optimize high-dimensional problems. Implementing the GPR does not change anything in the models directly but it merely has the effect that the ABM simulations reach the well-fitting parameter space faster.

4.6.5 The evaluation process

Distance function

As already touched on above, the simulations aim at modelling language diversification processes and henceforth to analyse those runs that best approximate the observed real-world data. However, in order to be able to analyse the simulations that come closest to the observed reality, a function needs to be devised that calculates the difference between the observed features and the simulated features.

The distance function used to calculate this difference is a modified Hamming distance. This modified Hamming distance was devised to account for the fact that the features and the absence of innovations are unequally distributed. For example, let A_1 be the binary feature vector of a language and A_2 be the simulated language vector. Assume further that

$$A_1 = [0, 1, 1, 0, 0, 0]$$

The regular Hamming distance gives the proportion of positions which differ between A_1 and A_2. Thus, if we assume that

$$A_2 = [1, 1, 1, 0, 0, 0]$$

we have one position where A_2 differs from A_1 which would give a Hamming distance of 0.167 which results from $\frac{1}{6}$. However, assume that

$$A_2 = [0, 0, 0, 0, 0, 0]$$

we see that the calculated Hamming distance would be 0.334 resulting from $\frac{2}{6}$. However, this means that if, in a particular simulation, the simulated language does not undergo any innovations, the distance would be only twice the distance of the simulation where only one innovation was incorrect. As this example shows, when there is an imbalance in the number of innovations vs. non-innovations, which is the case for the data at hand, we find that regular Hamming distance poorly resembles the goodness of a simulation: we find that the more the imbalance is in favour of one character, the better simulation runs are rated that resemble the majority character. In other words, if this Hamming distance were used to assess the ABM's simulations, those runs that do not simulate any innovations at all would always be favoured over those that simulate an accurate number of innovations, albeit in the wrong places.

To combat this problem, the Hamming distance metric was replaced with the *Matthews correlation coefficient* (MCC). The MCC score is a metric which gives equal weight to the accuracies of *0* and *1* in a binary dataset. As a result we can punish over- and undershooting the number of innovations.

As the original MCC ranges from −1 to 1, where 1 represents a perfect fit but the loss metric for the ABC process requires a distance from 0 to 1 (see below), the raw MCC score was altered according to the following formula:

$$1 - \frac{MCC + 1}{2}$$

where *MCC* is the MCC score between −1 and 1. This formula changes the MCC score to be in range 0 to 1 with 0 representing a perfect fit. This results in a metric that is essentially a weighted Hamming distance.

In this calculation, missing values were dropped and only complete cases were considered in the calculation. This introduced volatility in those languages with many missing values but as the simulation is run a large number of times, this will solely result in higher uncertainty in the results for those particular languages rather than introduce a systematic bias.

At the end of the simulation, or, more, precisely, at the inferred observation date of a language, the distance from the observed data is calculated for every agent independently. The overall fit to that language is taken to be the mean fit of all agents in that region. It needs to be stressed that the mean distance per language is only used for the optimization, the results are calculated on the agents themselves.

Loss function

The weighted Hamming distance as described above is not sufficient to calculate the goodness of the simulation. If one were to simply calculate the mean or the sum of the distances between the observed innovation vector for each language and the simulated innovation vector for each language, it could distort the results.

Suppose we have three languages A, B, and C. Let there be two simulations, I and II, in which all three languages were approximated with certain distances.

Simulation I: A = 0.3, B = 0.3, C = 0.3
Simulation II: A = 0.1, B = 0.1, C = 0.5

If we take the mean distance or the sum of the distances, we would see that simulation II is always better than simulation I. However, the accuracy is in both cases differently distributed: simulation I has an evenly distributed distance across A, B, and C whereas simulation II approximates A and B very well and C is approximated worse than it is in simulation I. Accepting simulation I as a good fit would mean sacrificing the bad approximation of one language for the good approximation of other languages. This effect is even more pronounced when there is a larger number of languages to be simulated since this shrinks the weight of the accuracy that every language contributes to the sum. Thus it is even more probable for a good simulation run to have one very badly approximated language.

To counterbalance this phenomenon, a method needs to be implemented that punishes a bad approximation more than it rewards a good approximation. For this reason I implemented a loss function that is calculated on every weighted Hamming distance. The function is calculated as follows:

$$\sum_{L=1}^{n} -\ln(1 - d_L)\,\text{with}\; \{d \in \mathbb{R} \mid 0 < d < 0.9999\}$$

Here, L stands for a single language and d stands for the weighted Hamming distance of the simulated and observed innovation vectors. As for values of d_L approximating 1 the function approximates infinity, I capped the function to be only calculated on values of d_L smaller than 0.9999. For values larger than 0.9999, I assigned a constant value of 12 in place of $-\ln(1 - d_L)$. The value of 12 is approximately equal to a fit 0.99999 and prevents the loss function from approaching infinity in case of fits worse than 0.99999. Figure 4.31 shows the function in a plot. The x-axis represents the Hamming distance and the y-axis is the resulting loss. This means that a Hamming distance of 0.5 would result in a loss of 0.69 whereas a distance of 0.1 results in a loss of 0.105. This shows that the higher the distance, the more this distance is pronounced.

Such logarithmic loss functions are widely used in machine learning research (e.g. Bishop 2006: 206). Applied to the above example this means that the loss function discourages sacrificing one language accuracy for another. This way, the gap between simulation I and simulation II is narrowed.

A second issue for these simulations is specificity—meaning how well a certain region represents the data for that language and *not* any other region.

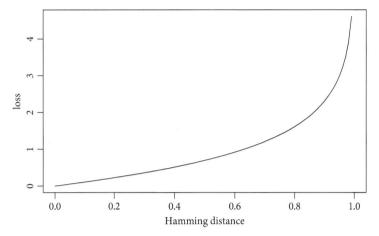

Figure 4.31 Logarithmic loss function

It was observed in preliminary analyses that certain regions tended to yield a better fit for the language of another region. For example, in some runs, the geographical area of observed language A was better approximated by language B. This cannot be entirely avoided, as there is some variation in how good the fit to a certain language is and it should not be avoided as this yields insights into the relationship of the regions in question. Nevertheless, to disfavour the better fit of a region to languages of other regions, a *specificity* term was added to the optimization function:

$$\sum_{L=1}^{n} -\ln(1 - ((d_N + 1)/2)) \quad \text{with} \quad \{d \in \mathbb{R} \mid 0 < d < 0.9999\}$$

This represents the distance between the fit for the language in question (e.g. simulated language A in observed region A) and the fit of the best-fitting other language in this region (e.g. simulated language B in observed region A). Taken together as a joint loss, both functions assure that the simulated outcomes both fit well to their observed region *and* yield the best possible fit among the other languages in that observed region.

4.7 The modules of the ABM

After we have seen which parameters govern the simulations and how agents interact with one another, the next step is to determine how innovations that are spread among agents are innovated and how the parameters are updated over the course of a simulation. Figure 4.32 shows the different modules

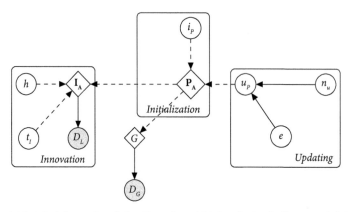

Figure 4.32 Model graph of the Bayesian ABM only including model-internal nodes

This graph (and all subsequent ABM model graphs) differs in graph element definitions from classical Bayesian graphical networks for which reason the elements are explained below:

1) diamond-shaped nodes denote agent-based model parts, i.e. parts which do not represent stochastic processes themselves.
2) grey nodes represent observed variables.
3) colourless nodes represent stochastic nodes, i.e. distributions from which random numbers are drawn.
4) dashed circles represent stochastic nodes which are model-external processes belonging to the sampling algorithm.
5) solid arrows represent stochastic paths where random numbers are drawn or inferred.
6) dashed arrows represent non-stochastic paths where two nodes are directionally linked through an ABM-related action.
7) non-circled variables represent constants fed to stochastic nodes as priors.
8) nodes with subscripts represent nodes that stand for a repeated action on the element specified in the subscript.
9) Greek-letter parameters denote model-external parameters whereas model-internal parameters are indicated by Latin letters.

governing these processes in a graphical model. The model thus consists of three modules *Innovation*, *Initialization*, and *Updating*. The modules *Innovation* and *Updating* govern the development of parameters and agents *during* a simulation whereas *Initialization* is the module dedicated for inferring the initial state of the agents. The modules themselves are described in more detail below and, for a big-picture overview of all model parts, see section 4.9.

4.7.1 The updating module

Whether or not an agent executes an action is determined by its individual parameters. These, however, are not fixed but follow a probability distribution, in this case a truncated normal distribution between 0 and 1. The agent's parameters therefore do not define the probability itself but the parameters of the probability distribution. This is the hierarchical modelling approach used in this ABM (see section 4.5.5) in which agents' parameters both have a mean and a variance and are drawn from hyperparameter distributions.

The use of normal distributions for these contexts calls for comment. Using normal distributions does not, paradoxically, imply that the underlying process is normally distributed. Normal distributions can arise as snapshots of fluctuating processes for which, due to measurement error or a large number of smaller, but unobserved or even unobservable factors, this fluctuation will have no innate direction. In other words, in order for a process to be both stable or consistent and fluctuating, the fluctuations will occupy a certain range around the position in which the process is stable. The fluctuations then will diminish with increased distance from this stable region. When summarized, the density of these fluctuations will approximate a normal distribution with the stable region being around the mean and the degree of fluctuation will be represented by the standard deviation of the distribution. There are, without question, non-normally distributed processes in real-world applications; these are often the result of different forces applying to different regions of the parameter space. The innate property of normal distributions of representing a fluctuating but stable and unbiased process makes them ideal for modelling purposes under certain conditions. They can be a source of randomness in simulation systems such as the one in this study and they can function as unbiased estimates for priors and micro-level fluctuations.

What is specifically *not* assumed is that the real-world processes are indeed normally distributed but that they are the most neutral distribution to choose in a variable space where there are assumed to be stable or high-probability regions that also include fluctuation. An excellent discussion of the topic of why normal distributions are an unbiased modelling choice rather than a statement of the actual state of a system is provided by McElreath (2020: 72–76).

Each tick, every agent's parameters are updated by adding (or subtracting in case of negative values) a value from a normal distribution. This means how far an agent's parameter moves in the probability space is ultimately dependent on a normal distribution where large jumps are unlikely but small, incremental steps are common. In order for the agents to not execute a random walk in the parameter space detached from neighbouring communities, there is an ε value which governs how similar the particular agent stays with each update towards its neighbours. If the value is high, the agents' parameters perform mostly independent random walks through the parameter space; if the value is low, agents will stay very similar to their neighbours regarding their parameter settings.

Each tick, every agent's individual parameter settings are updated according to the following Bayesian model:

$$P_n(ParamA) = e(\mu_{n,t-1} + \gamma) + (1 - e)\bar{\mu}_{env}$$

$$\gamma \sim norm(\mu, \sigma)$$

$$\mu \sim inferred$$

$$\sigma \sim inferred$$

In this model, μ and σ constitute hyperpriors. A hypothetical update at the transition from timestep t-1 to t of an agent n's parameter $ParamA$ could run as follows:

Let the hyperprior settings follow a standard normal distribution ($norm(0,1)$) and the regularizing factor e be 0.6. The parameter would update according to this formula:

$$P_n(ParamA) = 0.6(\mu_{n,t-1} + \gamma) + 0.4\bar{\mu}_{env}$$

$$\gamma \sim norm(0, 1)$$

Initially, the parameter changes μ and σ are drawn from normal distributions during the optimization process. They indicate values for how much the agent's parameters change. Now, let μ be 0.5. This means that, without further processing, the parameter values of Agent n would change by 0.5. The regularizing term e makes sure that the mean parameter setting of the environment $\bar{\mu}_{env}$ regularizes the change. Extreme changes can therefore be prevented if the environment has different values on average.

$$P_n(ParamA) = 0.6(\mu_{n,t-1} + 0.5) + 0.4\bar{\mu}_{env} \tag{4.3}$$

If we assume that $\bar{\mu}_{env}$ has the value of 0.2, we get the following formula:

$$P_n(ParamA) = 0.6(\mu_{n,t-1} + 0.5) + 0.08 \tag{4.4}$$

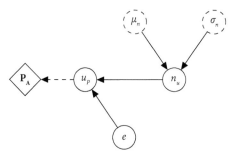

Figure 4.33 Graphical representation of the updating module

If we further assume that the previous parameter value of agent n was $\mu_{n,t-1} = 0.4$, we get the following new parameter value:

$$P_n(ParamA) = 0.62 \qquad\qquad (4.5)$$

This means that the new parameter value of agent n after the update is 0.62.

Note that since these values are essentially *probabilities*, their range is constrained to values between 0 and 1 by the model. If, during a run, an agent would receive an update that would raise the new value above 1 or lower below 0, the new value is set to either 1 or 0.

The updating module therefore can be summarized with the graphical model in Figure 4.33 below.[8]

A parameter P of the agent A is updated by the update function u_P for the parameter P. It takes as input two values e and n_u. e is a 0 to 1 bounded value representing the ratio of global environmental independence. n_u is the updating distribution from which the base updating value is drawn. The shape parameters for n_u are drawn from prior distributions in the optimization function μ_n and σ_n.

4.7.2 The innovation module

The innovation module governs the process by which agents undergo, spread, and lose innovations. Figure 4.34 displays this module.

The innovations are, as described above, mostly determined by the interactions between agents and the agents' parameters (P_A), but two variables influence the innovations: occurrence time and homoplasy rate.

Occurrence time (t_I) is a parameter applied to each innovation and is global (i.e. constant during the run of one simulation). It determines from what point

---

[8] Note that μ and σ in the above equations are denoted μ_n and σ_n in this graphical model.

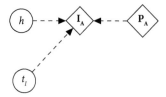

Figure 4.34 Graphical representation of the innovation module

in time onwards an innovation can occur (the actual occurrence is determined by other parameters). The motivation behind this occurrence time mechanism is that this enables the model to infer the time an innovation occurs for the first time. There is, of course, no real-world process that prevents a certain innovation from occurring at a certain time; the implementation here is solely for the purpose of tracking and inferring the occurrence time of individual innovations. Concretely, this mechanism allows the model to directly infer the approximate date (and thus in some cases also the order) of individual innovations. As *priors* for each innovation, I use the relative frequency of the innovation across the languages as a proxy for time of innovation. This means that if an innovation is present in, for example, 4 out of n languages, the mean of the prior will be located at $1 - \frac{4}{n}$ relative to the entire number of ticks. Thus the starting prior mean of 0.25 in a simulation with 500 ticks would correspond to an earliest innovation starting time of tick 125 for this innovation. This modelling strategy follows the logic that innovations that are later developments in individual languages are less likely to be found in a large number of neighbouring languages. This mechanic can be applied because other confounding effects such as occurring homoplasy are accounted for by other means (see below). It needs to be kept in mind that these prior specifications are solely the initial settings for the simulation and therefore global. The posterior distribution of runs will be able to move away from these settings if the data require it.

The second element in the innovation module is the homoplasy rate (h) which determines the global probability of an innovation being innovated a second time. In practice, if the requirements are fulfilled, an existing innovation is deleted from the record of past innovations so that it occurs again.

4.7.3 Initialization and region-specific updating parameters

At the start of each simulation run, all agents' parameters are initialized randomly between the interval of 0–0.7 which allows for great variation but disfavours extremely high values.

As the model stands so far, all agents would be subject to the same global updating process. The result would be that although agents develop their own parameter settings over time, this process is very indirect as it does not make the geographical differences observable in the model. For this reason, all model hyperpriors with regard to updating were made specific to the individual regions outlined in section 4.6.2. This means that instead of one global updating hyperprior for all agents, every region now has its own updating hyperprior that is sampled from the optimization process. Afterwards, we can more directly infer the different levels of hyperprior distribution between different regions. In other words, we assume the parameter changes to vary by region; for example some regions might have a higher *migration rate* value than others which can be inferred due to this mechanism. This is similar in concept to a Bayesian varying slope model.

Wherever an agent does not belong to a specified region, it receives a standard normal updating hyperprior defined as *norm*(0, 1).

4.8 Putting the model approach to the test

Undoubtedly, the real-world application of this model is vastly more complicated than all the simplified demonstrations can account for.

Therefore it is important to demonstrate the goal and the working of the model in an example simulation where the purposes of the approach can be demonstrated in a simplified task. The goal of this demonstration will be the question, can this method approximate the conditions of a simple ABM? For this, I adapted the simulation displayed in Figure 4.12 and set up an example scenario with three population-level parameters and an innovation mechanic as explained in 4.7.2. What follows is a test and an illustrative example of how the mechanisms explained in the previous sections work. However, this example is a *toy* model with fewer parameters and a simple, abstract simulation surface. Due to this fact, all prior settings used here are solely specific to this toy example. Ideally, this demonstration can practically explain in a simplified scenario some of the mechanics of and the core notions behind the main diversification model.

The parameters of this demonstration model are:

(1) **Innovation**: Innovations occur at a specific rate.
(2) **Spreading**: Innovations spread to an adjacent agent.
(3) **Obstacle spreading**: Innovations spread to an agent on the other side of the obstacle.

Figure 4.35 Example ABM run with two possible innovations: snapshots at ticks 0, 20, 40, 60, 80, 100

The procedure is as follows: I set up an innovation spreading model with fixed parameters. Thereafter, the model is run and the final output is stored to serve as the model which is to be evaluated.

The parameters I chose for this simulation are the following:

Innovation: 0.00005
Spreading: 0.15
Obstacle spreading: 0.005

I further assume that Innovation 2 occurs before Innovation 1. It has to be noted that the parameters in this example are fixed values. Recall that, in the main simulation, all variables are given in the form of normal distributions to account for inherent variability of observation. This example simulation is intended to show the possibilities of interpreting an ABM that generates the data in this way.

Figure 4.35 shows the model output of this model that was run with the parameters shown before. In the following section we will assume we know neither the parameters this model was given, nor the intermediate steps. All we have as a given are the parameters themselves and the final state which is seen in Figure 4.35 in the rightmost frame.

The next step is setting up the agent-based model as it is used in the main simulation. This involves creating a distance function for evaluating each run and setting up the optimizer and its priors.

Distance function:

As a distance function I use the same function that I use in the main simulation which evaluates the weighted Hamming distance of each agent to the data in the final tick. It has to be noted that, in the main simulation, I only compare individual areas to the data. However, in this example, I will use all agents for evaluation as in this example we are given the entire picture; in the original data, we only have a few regions where we know the state of the innovations. The distance function then operates as follows: after each run it iterates over each agent and compares the simulated innovation vectors to the observed simulation vectors. Then it calculates the ratio of incorrect positions in the vector for each agent. For example if one agent is simulated to have the innovation vector [0, 1] but the observed vector for this agent is [1, 1] then the function assigns a Hamming distance of 0.5 to this agent. The aggregated Hamming distance is then used as the accuracy of this run. Since the highest possible aggregated distance is 2,208, the optimizer will then try to minimize this distance through best-possible prior setting. Note that I use the simple Hamming distance for this task as the weighted Hamming distance can only be applied if the data show large innovation vectors with an imbalance in frequency between zeros and ones.

Innovation timing:
On top of the basic innovation parameter, a second parameter was constructed that globally handles the timing of the innovations. While the innovation parameter itself only determines if a given agent undergoes an innovation, the timing mechanism determines which innovation is allowed to occur at which tick. For this, a single parameter is assigned to every innovation that determines the tick after which the innovation can occur. This parameter represents the time as a percentage relative to the total number of ticks. A parameter value of 0.5, thus, indicates that the innovation occurs after half of the total ticks. Implementing this system gives the simulation the possibility to spread out or cluster the occurrence of innovations. Without this timing mechanism, the innovations would occur approximately evenly spread out depending on the spreading probability.

Optimizer and priors:
The optimizer is the same optimizer used in the main simulation (see section 4.6.4). To demonstrate the influence of sensible prior setting for optimization, I ran this simulation process twice. The first time, I assigned flat uniform priors to all parameters to demonstrate the role of search space specification. In a second run, I specified the search space using the following priors:

$$Spreading \sim Normal(0.25, 0.3)$$

$$Innovation \sim Normal(0, 0.001)$$

$$Obstacle.spreading \sim Normal(0.1, 0.2)$$

$$Innov.1 \sim Normal(0.5, 0.1)$$

$$Innov.2 \sim Normal(0.5, 0.1)$$

The spreading prior was chosen as a weakly informative prior with the mean of 0.25. This prior choice arises from the observation that large values of

Spreading probability are unlikely whereas small values are also more unlikely, but more likely than extremely high values. To reflect this reasoning, the chosen prior gives more weight to *Spreading* values in the first half of the spectrum.

Innovation was given an informative prior centred around 0 that makes large values implausible. The standard deviation of 0.001 is even less informative than it could be. This prior setting is based on the notion that with an innovation probability of 0.1, for example, there is a 10 per cent chance of every agent undergoing an *Innovation* each tick. This would result in 22,080 expected innovations during one simulation run.

The prior for *Obstacle spreading* was chosen to be similarly informative to the spreading prior; however, we might conclude that spreading across an obstacle is less likely to occur. However, it cannot be ruled out that it might be propelling spreading forward. Thus the mean of the prior is lower than for normal spreading; the standard deviations, however, allow for *Obstacle spreading* to be higher than regular spreading.

The priors for the two possible innovations (*Innov. 1* and *Innov. 2*) are centred around 0.5 which allocates less probability value to the innovations occurring very late or very early. This is a reasonable assumption as the model will determine the timing of individual innovations internally.

All simulations were run with 400 evaluation runs over eight initializations of the optimization algorithm which gives a total of 3,200 evaluated runs. The goodness of prediction for each run was determined as a Hamming distance from the observed innovation distributions. It was detected that disproportionally many runs achieve an accuracy of 419. Such 'pockets of high accuracy' arise when there is an imbalance of innovations in the outcome space. This means concretely that there will be several runs where runs achieve higher accuracy by making every agent adopt every innovation. If, in the outcome situation, more innovations are favoured, the runs filling the space with innovations will be rated higher. However, this is not informative as filling the space can arise due to various different parameter settings. Therefore, these runs were excluded from the model. Note that in more complicated models, these 'pockets of high accuracy' are unlikely to arise as the outcome space is too complex to allow for these errors.

4.8.1 The results of the example simulation test

For the evaluation, the top 5 per cent of runs with the highest accuracy were selected and evaluated further below.

It has to be noted that, over a long enough time scale, the number of runs in the better accuracy region would eventually reach the same level as the model with stronger priors.

General parameter estimates

The posterior parameter estimates obtained from this simulation can be summarized graphically with distribution plots. The plots shown in this section all contain the same elements. The histogram represents the posterior distribution of the parameter in question whereas the dashed curve indicates the prior for this particular parameter. The *line segment* below the histogram marks the 89 per cent highest density interval of the posterior distribution and the *black dot* indicates the mean of the posterior distribution.

The spreading parameter (Figure 4.36) was evaluated as very similar in the uniform and the normal model. However, the normal model exhibits narrower credible intervals.

Table 4.3 shows a summary of the posterior simulation estimates. The information provided here about each posterior distribution is the credible intervals, the mean and the maximum likelihood estimate (**MLE**).

It can be observed that, in most cases, the more informative normal prior yielded better results. In the case of *Innovation* and *Obstacle spreading* (Figures 4.37 and 4.38), the flat prior was especially disadvantageous as the posterior distributions very much cover more than two thirds of the outcome space. This result is due to the fact that these two parameters are both highly dependent on other parameters and less significant for the outcome. For

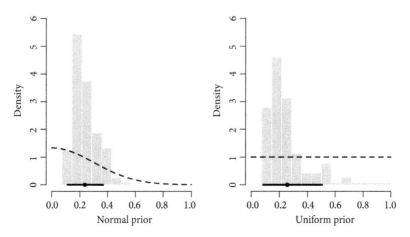

Figure 4.36 Posterior distribution plot of *Spreading*

Table 4.3 Posterior estimates of simulation parameters

Parameter	89-CI Normal	89-CI Uniform	Mean Normal	Mean Uniform	MLE Normal	MLE Uniform	Orig. value
Spreading	0.11 – 0.37	0.08 – 0.51	0.236	0.255	0.197	0.168	0.15
Innovation	0.03 – 1.00	0.14 – 0.96	0.410	0.462	0.356	0.336	0.00005
Obstacle spreading	0.00 – 0.33	0.00 – 0.72	0.078	0.424	0.000	0.490	0.005
Innov. 1	0.51 – 1.00	0.46 – 1.00	0.763	0.746	0.990	0.841	0.41
Innov. 2	0.00 – 0.48	0.00 – 0.69	0.168	0.361	0.009	0.187	0.34

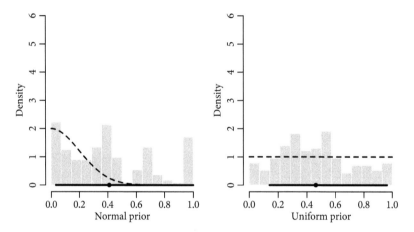

Figure 4.37 Posterior distribution plot of *Innovation*

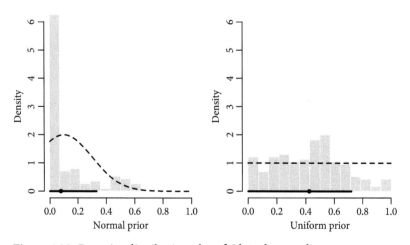

Figure 4.38 Posterior distribution plot of *Obstacle spreading*

example, *Obstacle spreading* is dependent on *Spreading* as only if this parameter is above a certain level, can *Obstacle spreading* take full effect. If *Spreading* is low, there might not be an influence of *Obstacle spreading* as there are fewer agents in the vicinity of the obstacle to be able to cross it. Therefore, the significance of the *Obstacle spreading* parameter increases with higher *Spreading* values. Moreover, we find that *Innovation* is dependent on the two innovation timing parameters. For very high values of *Innovation*, the weight of the significance is entirely shifted towards the timing parameters. The reason for this, is that, when the *Innovation* parameter is high, the simulation gets many potential innovations each tick. However, an innovation only occurs if the current tick has surpassed the timing of one of the innovations. This is true for smaller models with fewer innovations; however, in the main model where we find several hundred innovations, the significance of the innovation parameter is larger. The innovations, however, were not very precisely estimated in both normal and uniform models. The reason for this is that the parameters for *Innov. 1* and *Innov. 2* (Figures 4.39 and 4.40) are highly dependent on the particular setting of *Spreading* and *Innovation*. A higher spreading value may yield a faster spread of late innovations. This means that the posterior estimates of this simulation are not necessarily the optimal solution for analysing the results. This is because there is a number of different interactions between different parameters that need to be analysed in detail. It is therefore clear that the parameters, although informative about the general parameters, cannot be analysed independently of one another but need to be seen as highly covariant.

For this reason, a more in-depth analysis will be conducted using linear regression models. The dataset for this subsequent analysis is the posteriors

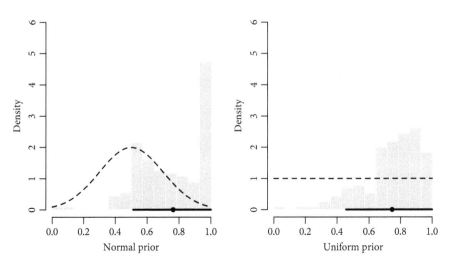

Figure 4.39 Posterior distribution plot of *Innov. 1*

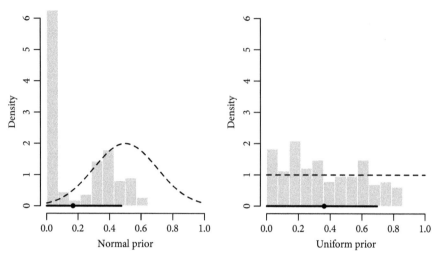

Figure 4.40 Posterior distribution plot of *Innov. 2*

obtained using informative priors. For the Bayesian linear regression models, I used the R-package *brms* (Bürkner 2017). In the linear analysis, I aim at exploring the correlations between the *Spread* parameter and the other parameters including their interactions. Although the parameters are logically independent, their correlation patterns indicate which combinations of parameters are more frequently present in the posterior sample of the simulations. This can reveal potential co-dependencies between the parameters.

Bayesian regression models are similar to frequentist regression analysis insofar as both fit functions (e.g. lines, polynomials, or splines) to data to estimate regression coefficients. The model was fit using the model formula below. Note that, before running the linear model, all parameters were centred and z-scaled.[9]

$$R_i \sim Student(\nu, \mu_i, \sigma)$$

$$\mu_i = \alpha + \beta_1 P_n + \beta_2 P_{n+1} + \beta_3 P_n \times P_{n+1}$$

$$\alpha \sim Normal(0, 1)$$

$$\beta_n \sim Normal(0, 1)$$

$$\sigma \sim Exponential(1)$$

$$\nu \sim Gamma(2, 0.1)$$

[9] Centring and z-scaling is a technique to standardize values of a variable. The standardization is achieved by subtracting the variable mean from every value before dividing the values by the standard deviation of the variable. The result is a variable with mean of 0 and a standard deviation of 1 which can be more easily interpreted in many cases, especially in cases where multiple variables have different and/or abstract scales.

Table 4.4 Summary of posterior coefficients

	Estimate	Est.Error	l–89% CI	u–89% CI
Intercept	−0.12	0.06	−0.22	−0.02
Innovation_rate	−0.12	0.06	−0.21	−0.02
Obstacle_spread	−0.17	0.06	−0.26	−0.08
Innov1	0.19	0.06	0.10	0.28
Innov2	0.57	0.06	0.47	0.67
Innovation_rate:Obstacle_spread	−0.14	0.08	−0.27	−0.02
Innovation_rate:Innov1	−0.00	0.07	−0.11	0.11
Innovation_rate:Innov2	0.01	0.08	−0.12	0.13
Obstacle_spread:Innov1	−0.06	0.06	−0.16	0.04
Obstacle_spread:Innov2	0.06	0.08	−0.06	0.19
Innov1:Innov2	0.27	0.07	0.16	0.38
sigma	0.58	0.05	0.50	0.65
nu	14.94	10.11	5.10	34.01

In this formula, R represents the outcome variable, the *Spread* parameter in this case whereas P_n stands for a predictor variable. For reasons of conciseness, I only outline the general structure and reference the predictor variables in generalized form.

Table 4.4 shows the summary of the posterior coefficients of the analysis with a credible interval of 0.89. The parameters specific to the Student-t family σ and ν are given separately at the foot of the table.

We can infer from the table that there are various co-dependencies between the *Spread* parameter and the other parameters in the accepted runs. For example, both *Obstacle spreading* and the *Innovation* parameter are inversely correlated with *Spread*. This indicates that the agent-based model finds a balance between these three parameters insofar as, if either *Obstacle spreading* or *Innovation* is high, the innovations need to spread more slowly in order to still reach a good fit to the data. This effect is enhanced if both *Obstacle spreading* and *Innovation* increase. The interaction parameter indicates an increased effect of both parameters on *Spread* if both parameters likewise increase.

Positively associated with *Spread* are both innovation timing parameters. The reason for this lies in the fact that if innovations are timed later (i.e. the parameters increase), *Spread* must likewise increase to yield a good fit. Similar to *Obstacle spreading* and *Innovation*, the positive effect of both innovation parameters is increased for higher values of both innovation parameters.

Finally, we can deduce that there are various co-dependencies between parameters on the outcome of the simulation. These co-dependencies are mostly specific to the modelling itself and have no analytical value that could yield insights into the structure of the data. However, they enable the analysis of data distributions and patterns that are artefacts of the method. As the main model contains parameters more reflective of the data, analysing the co-dependencies of agent-specific parameters can yield valuable insights.

As an intermediate summary, we can observe from the parameter estimations that, by analysing the posterior distribution coefficients alone, we cannot show the full picture. Rather, each of those needs to be interpreted under consideration of interactions with other parameters. For example, the innovation parameter being estimated poorly is the result of an interference from the innovations 1 and 2 since ultimately they determine when innovations occur. Thus the innovation parameter itself, while crucial to the mechanic of the simulation, is not informative for a subsequent analysis.

Furthermore, in most cases, informative priors perform better than uniform priors; however; without external information, the innovation timing parameters perform better with weaker priors. In the main simulation, this problem will be side-stepped as we feed external information to the simulation and build the priors such that they are more grounded in the probable parameter regions.

Analysing the runs

As a next step, we can go further and look at the backward inferences we can make using the accepted runs. We can analyse the state of the simulation at each time step to receive estimations about the previous stages of the innovations. To achieve this, we can save the state of every accepted run at a fixed number of ticks (e.g. ticks 0, 20, 40, 60, 80, 100). Afterwards, we can aggregate the runs by stage and thereby overlay the simulations. This returns merged stages across all simulations and indicates the frequency with which each agent has undergone a particular innovation: if in the aggregate one agent has undergone a particular innovation in many runs, we can assume that the support for this agent having undergone this innovation can be considered high. Akin to the clade support in phylogenetics, I call the frequency of an agent showing an innovation *support*. High support thus means that in most of the accepted runs, this agent shows this particular innovation. It needs to be stressed that the runs of this simulation were only evaluated at the last tick. In effect, the simulation emulates the real-world research situation in which only the outcome is known and the previous stages need to be inferred. The outcome state will henceforth always be the rightmost image in a heat map sequence.

To gauge the support of individual agents and the resulting backward inferences, a variety of methods can be used, a few of which will be illustrated in the following.

Firstly, we can display support as heat maps for both innovations by regularizing the support of each agent relative to the maximum support. This means that every agent's support is calculated as $\frac{s_a}{s_{max}}$ where s_a is the individual agent's support in number of runs where this agent exhibits the respective innovation and s_{max} is the maximum number of runs containing this innovation. Doing this fixes the darkest colour relative to the most supported agent irrespective of the strength of support.

Figure 4.41 shows the 'ground truth' states, i.e. the states that the model was built to infer.

The heat maps show that the model was successful in replicating the approximate extent of the original run in the last frame at tick 100. Further, the previous stages were correctly inferred with regard to location and approximate start of the spreading. However, the earlier the snapshot was taken, the smaller the relative support becomes. The reason for this is that the support has to be seen as a distribution which, for some aspects of analysis, is inadequately

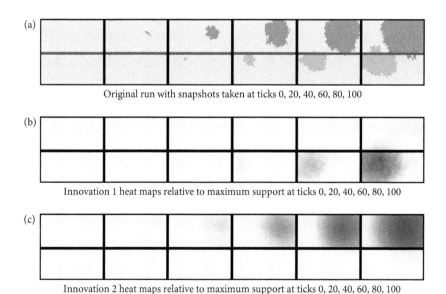

(a)

Original run with snapshots taken at ticks 0, 20, 40, 60, 80, 100

(b)

Innovation 1 heat maps relative to maximum support at ticks 0, 20, 40, 60, 80, 100

(c)

Innovation 2 heat maps relative to maximum support at ticks 0, 20, 40, 60, 80, 100

Figure 4.41 Results from run analysis using maximum support heat maps

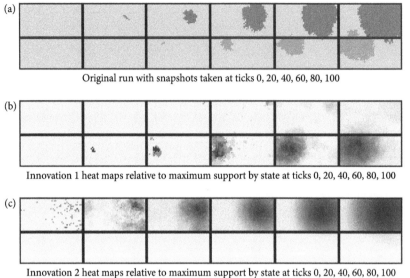

(a)

Original run with snapshots taken at ticks 0, 20, 40, 60, 80, 100

(b)

Innovation 1 heat maps relative to maximum support by state at ticks 0, 20, 40, 60, 80, 100

(c)

Innovation 2 heat maps relative to maximum support by state at ticks 0, 20, 40, 60, 80, 100

Figure 4.42 Results from run analysis using maximum support heat maps

displayed in reference to the peak point of the distribution. Therefore, we need a resolution that highlights the low-support regions of the graph.

This can be realized by normalizing the support by state, i.e. $\frac{S_{a,state}}{S_{max,state}}$. This highlights the high-support agents for every snapshot and lets us investigate earlier states more clearly.

From Figure 4.42 we can infer that most occurrences of Innovation 2 start to arise between tick 20 and 40 and Innovation 1 starts occurring in larger numbers between ticks 40 and 60. Moreover, the origin of Innovation 1 is likely in the centre left of the bottom left quarter whereas the origin of Innovation 2 lies in the upper right corner. When comparing these results to the original runs, we see an accurate inference of the medial stages of the original run. What we can also observe is that the further back the inference is projected, the more inaccurate it becomes. This, however, is mostly due to the fact that only the outcome of the original run is given to the model. In problems where we can estimate an initial state, the uncertainty in the earlier frames is reduced.

It is trivial to state that the number of accepted runs is highly influential on the resolution and accuracy of the analysis. As stated above, the accepted runs were the top 5 per cent out of 3,200 runs used in total. In effect, the number of accepted runs is 160 and resolution and support is therefore low. However, as this is an example to illustrate the mechanics of such an ABM, the resolution was kept low for efficiency reasons.

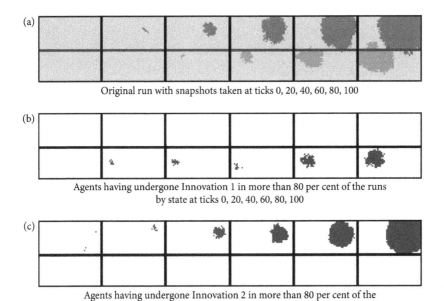

(a) Original run with snapshots taken at ticks 0, 20, 40, 60, 80, 100

(b) Agents having undergone Innovation 1 in more than 80 per cent of the runs by state at ticks 0, 20, 40, 60, 80, 100

(c) Agents having undergone Innovation 2 in more than 80 per cent of the runs at ticks 0, 20, 40, 60, 80, 100

Figure 4.43 Results from run analysis using maximum support heat maps

In the last analysis below (Figure 4.43), only those agents light up that have undergone the respective innovation in more than 80 per cent of the runs present at every state. This returns only the most confident areas at every tick state. This method will display a core area around which the innovations are most likely to be stratified.

The output in Figure 4.43 shows that the model is able to capture the approximate central areas of the innovations at each stage. We have to bear in mind that this 80 per cent confidence map only displays the most likely central area of the runs.

4.9 Model summary

As the individual model parts have been explored in the previous sections, the full model shall be briefly outlined again as a whole in reference to Figure 3.15: Figure 4.44 shows the full model including prior variables.

At the core of the ABM are two data types as observed variables: the geospatial data for every datapoint (D_G), including the approximate locations of the linguistic communities in the final simulated year, as well as the information of the geographical surface, that is, the geographic details of northern and central

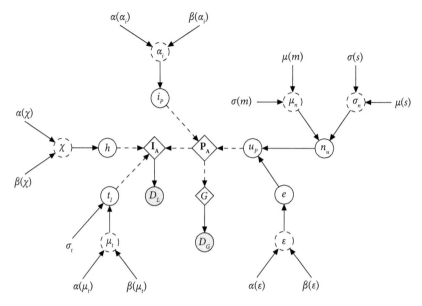

Figure 4.44 Full model graph of the Bayesian agent-based model

Europe. This detail is modelled via an ABM module G which simulates agents on this geographical surface. These agents and their actions in the simulation are governed by parameters which are modelled in the ABM module P_A, meaning a module that handles the parameters of every agent. Secondly, every agent in G is linked to its own linguistic data, namely its own vector of innovations. These linguistic data (D_L) are the second observed variable of the model. They are modelled using the innovation module I_A which handles the occurrence and spread of innovations.

The simulation of the linguistic data is influenced by three factors: each agent's parameters, the innovation timing, and the homoplasy rate. The actions on the basis of agent-specific parameters are provided by P_A and are pertaining to spreading and innovation. The homoplasy rate (h) is a global parameter (i.e. constant during one run of the simulation) which is sampled from the external node χ with constant priors. Futher, each innovation is given an occurrence time which is global. This occurrence time parameter has a fixed standard deviation and a mean sampled from the external node μ_t which has two constant priors.

The second major part of the ABM are the parameters of which each agent has its own set (P_A). These are initialized once at the beginning from the parameter-specific global node i_P. The initialization parameters for each uniform-distributed initialization are drawn from the external nodes α_i and α_i which have constant priors.

Once initialized, the updating process for each parameter during each tick is governed by the node u_P. Here, by how much the parameter changes at a given tick is determined by a normal distribution n_u, the hyperparameters of which (μ_n and σ_n) are themselves external normal distributions. This layering of hyperparameters gives the model freedom in varying the update distribution from tick to tick.

When the update is applied, however, it is mixed with the percentage of local influence by adjacent agents. This percentage is governed by the global node e which is drawn from the external distribution ε with constant priors.

4.10 Prior summary

The following Table 4.5 shows a complete summary of all priors used in the model. The uniform priors were used in those cases where the parameter space is bounded. Recall that the evaluation of this model is not a conventional likelihood function but a distance metric optimized by a Gaussian process regressor. Therefore, using priors with one-sided support is not possible and all priors that have only finite support needed to be uniform. The prior settings in general are rather flat to ensure the parameter space is traversed thoroughly. In future applications, it may further be desirable to test differently informative priors on individual parameters. For now, I used the most agnostic priors possible given the model optimization setup. Note that in preliminary runs it was noticed that the innovation parameter is very sensitive to fluctuations. Therefore, the parameter was initially strongly limited to a small range around 0 which, if necessary, could still be overpowered by the simulation if a higher value of this parameter is beneficial.

4.11 ABM model results

The model was run in 400 optimization instances for 500 simulations each under the setup described above. Hence, the total number of simulations evaluated was 200,000. Of those 200,000 runs, the top 0.2 per cent were selected as the posterior distribution to be analysed further. Recall that this criterion here means that the best-fitting 0.2 per cent of runs were accepted as the posterior runs.

Table 4.5 Summary table of model priors

Type	Coefficient	Parameter	Prior
Hyperparameter agent means	mean	Innovation	normal(0, 3e-05)
		Spread	normal(0, 0.001)
		Spread (sea)	normal(0, 0.001)
		Spread (obstacle)	normal(0, 0.001)
		Align	normal(0, 0.001)
		Spread vulnerability	normal(0, 0.001)
		Migration	normal(0, 0.001)
		Migration (obstacle)	normal(0, 0.001)
		Birth	normal(0, 0.001)
Hyperparameter agent sd.	mean	Innovation	normal(0, 7.5e–07)
		Spread	normal(0, 0.001)
		Spread (sea)	normal(0, 0.001)
		Spread (obstacle)	normal(0, 0.001)
		Align	normal(0, 0.001)
		Spread vulnerability	normal(0, 0.001)
		Migration	normal(0, 0.001)
		Migration (obstacle)	normal(0, 0.001)
		Birth	normal(0, 0.001)
Other		Epsilon	uniform(0, 1)
		Homoplasy rate	uniform(0.0001, 0.1)
		Innovation timing	normal(1-Innovation_ Frequency, 0.2)

4.11.1 The global parameters

Age parameters

The posterior ages for the languages and the origin are displayed as a forest plot in Figure 4.45 and as a summary in Table 4.6.

The figure shows the parameter values on the y-axis, and the x-axis indicates the posterior age of the individual taxa and the family split in 1,000 year steps. The thick and thin black bars indicate the 0.89 and 0.5 credible intervals and the black dot shows the mean of the posterior distribution.

Firstly, the inferred origin time, which in this case means the time of the break-up of the family, is estimated to have occurred between the years 800 BC and 250 BC with the most likely region around 500 BC. The individual languages were estimated relatively uniformly in their given interval (recall that, for all age parameters, the priors were uniform priors). Recall that the taxa

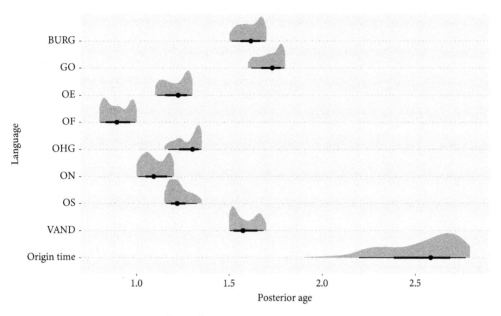

Figure 4.45 Posterior values of age parameters

Table 4.6 Posterior values of age parameters

Taxon	age.mean	age.median	age.lower.89CI	age.higher.89CI
Origin time	2.53	2.59	2.25	2.80
GO	1.72	1.73	1.63	1.80
OF	0.90	0.89	0.81	1.00
OE	1.21	1.22	1.12	1.30
OHG	1.28	1.30	1.19	1.35
OS	1.23	1.22	1.15	1.31
ON	1.10	1.09	1.02	1.20
BURG	1.61	1.62	1.53	1.70
VAND	1.59	1.57	1.50	1.67

ages are not intended to be inferred here. In this posterior summary, we expect the posterior taxa dates to resemble the uniform priors to some degree as the constraints are narrow to facilitate inferring the origin time and to calibrate the model to actual time. They are listed in the summary mainly to contextualize the origin time inference and to check the behaviour of the model.

Some posterior distributions of the individual languages' ages are observed to be bimodal. This is especially true for Vandalic, Old English, Old Norse, and,

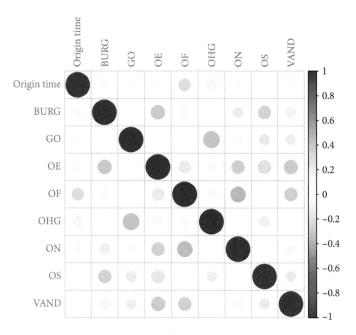

Figure 4.46 Correlation plot of posterior ages

to a lesser degree, Old Frisian. In this simulation, bimodality of age parameters can arise since the parameter estimates are not entirely independent. In other words, it makes a difference for Vandalic at which time Gothic or Burgundian are attested. Bimodality is a biproduct of a function having two high-probability regions conditional on the ages of the other distributions. To investigate this issue further, I devised a correlation plot (Figure 4.46[10]) which shows the pairwise correlations between the age parameters. In this figure, the colour indicates the direction of the correlation whereas the size of the circles indicates the strength of the correlation.

We can observe that the bimodal distributions of Old Norse and Vandalic are negatively correlated with the other bimodal distributions Old English and Old Frisian. This means that these two language pairs are oppositely distributed, in that they are inversely related. In other words, when one parameter shifts to an older age, the other parameter shifts to a younger date. This means that between these language pairs there are specific attestation date combinations that yield a better fit. However, more research is needed for two reasons: on the one hand, the bimodality is often biased towards one peak (e.g. for Vandalic and Old English) which might indicate a weaker pattern for the

---

[10] Plot generated using the R-package *corrplot* (Wei and Simko 2017).

bimodality. On the other hand, the peaks, especially the less dominant one, are not strongly different from what would be expected from a uniform distribution. This raises the question of how strong bimodality is in fact for these distributions.

Homoplasy rate

The inferred homoplasy rate can be seen as a posterior plot in Figure 4.47 below. There, the histogram represents the posterior distribution, whereas the dashed line represents the prior. Moreover, the line segment marks the 0.89 credible interval boundaries and the black dot indicates the mean of the distribution. Note that this plot has two x-axes which indicate two different scales. The axis above (marked 'Rate') shows the raw rate of occurrence of a homoplastic event as inferred by the model, and the lower axis (marked 'p/c') is a re-scale of the raw rate and indicates the number of homoplastic events per century.

As we can see in this graph, the credible intervals are large but the median rate is in the leftmost third of the plot. Moreover, we see a spike between 0 and 1 homoplastic events per century where the point estimate is located. The shape of this plot along with the prior type is indicative of how the parameter influenced the data. Firstly, we have to assume, since there is no clear and narrow credible interval, the parameter had difficulties in overpowering the prior. This can occur when the parameter has some influence on the outcome but the influence is too weak to be easily detectable. Yet we can also infer that

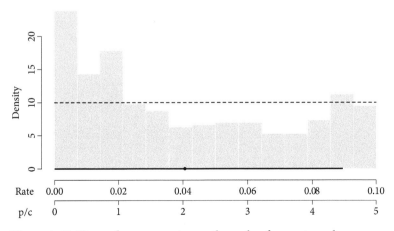

Figure 4.47 Homoplasy parameter on the scale of raw rate and homoplastic events per century (p/c)

the parameter was not negligible since it shows a clear tendency towards lower values.

Recall that the homoplasy parameter governs the rate at which homo-plastic events occur in the simulation, meaning how often innovations can occur more than once. For a dataset with 479 innovations, around 2 per cent of innovations will be innovated in parallel over the course of 1,000 years. In this simulation, the posterior distribution shows that for a dataset of this size, in a setting such as this, the data can be explained best when the parallel innovations do not exceed this level by a significant amount.

Degree of environmental independence

The environmental independence parameter is the percentage of each update consisting of the mean of the parameter values of the neighbouring agents. This means that, if this parameter is high, the agent is more independent and its parameter settings are updated solely based on the random values drawn. If this percentage is low, the random drawn value only influences a fraction of the update and the agent's parameter moves more towards the parameter values present in the environment. We can observe the posterior distribution of the parameter estimate in Figure 4.48.

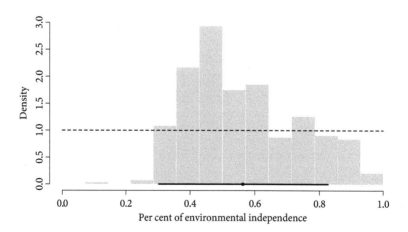

Figure 4.48 Environmental independence of agents from 0 (entirely dependent on the neighbouring agents) to 1 (completely independent from neighbouring agents)

The distribution shows two notable properties: an elongated tail to the right and a steep increase on the left side of the distribution. This indicates that higher values of this parameter are somewhat compatible with the data, yet values lower than 0.3 are very unlikely. In turn, we can interpret this as a sign that, in order to yield the geospatial and linguistic pattern we see, the environmental influence from neighbouring agents is unlikely to be very high. Most runs show mid-range values for this parameter, suggesting that there are adjacency effects between agents, the levels of which, however, do not assume extreme values.

Update parameters

The **hyperparameters** are those parameters that set the updating hyperdistribution for each region. Recall that, for each update, a random value is drawn from a normal distribution with mean μ and standard deviation σ. Depending on the shape of the distribution, the agent's parameters gradually increase, decrease, or remain at the initial level when the value for μ is positive, negative, or close to zero. Moreover, the σ parameter adds random fluctuations, allowing for more extreme outliers. In essence, both hyperparameters decide what trajectory each region assumes over the course of the simulation. For example, one region might start out with a small value for a given parameter which gradually increases over the course of the simulation rather than, for example, showing a high value at the beginning which does not change notably during the simulation. Whether or not a parameter increases or decreases, the trajectory of a region can be seen in the posterior estimates when the lower or higher credible interval boundary is above or below 0. This would mean that, in the most probable 89 per cent of runs, the trajectory of the parameter updates was positive/negative.

An important point to note is that a lack of detectable trajectory does *not* mean that the parameter remains the same for all agents during the simulation. It solely means that there is no *region wide* bias towards an increase or decrease during the simulation. As will become clear in section 4.11.2, the regions are different in certain parameters but these differences arise out of the randomness of the simulation rather than due to some strong bias. Refer to section 4.5.5 (esp. Figure 4.18) for a more detailed explanation of how different trajectories can arise even when an unbiased random normal updating process is underlying.

The global parameters discussed here are hence indicative of strong region-specific patterns whereas the later consensus run analysis reveals the more detailed and fine-grained patterns.

Table 4.7 Posterior estimates of μ-hyperparameters

Parameter	region	mean	median	lower-89CI	higher-89CI
align	OF	−0.0011	−0.0000	−0.0050	0.0027
	OS	−0.0023	−0.0015	−0.0073	0.0011
	OE	−0.0002	−0.0002	−0.0040	0.0037
	ON	−0.0012	−0.0011	−0.0058	0.0018
	OHG	−0.0008	−0.0002	−0.0041	0.0017
	Eastern	0.0009	0.0003	−0.0030	0.0071
birth	OF	0.0001	−0.0006	−0.0064	0.0049
	OS	−0.0005	−0.0010	−0.0022	0.0074
	OE	−0.0003	−0.0004	−0.0034	0.0029
	ON	0.0008	0.0006	−0.0026	0.0053
	OHG	−0.0007	−0.0003	−0.0047	0.0038
	Eastern	−0.0016	−0.0017	−0.0049	0.0020
migration	OF	−0.0014	−0.0015	−0.0083	0.0029
	OS	−0.0007	−0.0006	−0.0035	0.0031
	OE	−0.0008	−0.0009	−0.0047	0.0029
	ON	0.0009	0.0006	−0.0028	0.0061
	OHG	−0.0007	−0.0006	−0.0031	0.0037
	Eastern	−0.0006	−0.0006	−0.0043	0.0045
innovation	OF	−0.0000	−0.0000	−0.0001	0.0001
	OS	−0.0000	−0.0000	−0.0002	0.0001
	OE	0.0000	0.0000	−0.0001	0.0001
	ON	−0.0000	−0.0000	−0.0002	0.0001
	OHG	0.0000	0.0000	−0.0001	0.0001
	Eastern	0.0000	0.0000	−0.0001	0.0001
river crossing	OF	−0.0008	−0.0002	−0.0041	0.0055
	OS	0.0004	−0.0001	−0.0022	0.0056
	OE	−0.0000	0.0001	−0.0029	0.0028
	ON	−0.0000	−0.0001	−0.0040	0.0043
	OHG	−0.0001	−0.0000	−0.0047	0.0035
	Eastern	0.0003	0.0006	−0.0046	0.0059

The posterior estimates of the μ-hyperparameters (Table 4.7) shows only one clear trend we can observe, namely the increased *spread vulnerability* in the eastern area. This indicates that, as we will analyse in more detail in section 4.11.2, this parameter was steadily increased in this region over the course of the simulation. The effects of this are discussed in that section.

Regarding the σ-hyperparameters (Table 4.8), we find large credible intervals meaning that a wide variety of standard deviations were likely to yield

Table 4.7 (cont.) Posterior estimates of μ-hyperparameters

Parameter	region	mean	median	lower-89CI	higher-89CI
river spreading	OF	−0.0002	−0.0001	−0.0040	0.0034
	OS	0.0014	0.0012	−0.0024	0.0074
	OE	0.0012	0.0005	−0.0029	0.0131
	ON	0.0010	0.0008	−0.0027	0.0069
	OHG	−0.0009	−0.0004	−0.0056	0.0028
	Eastern	0.0006	0.0003	−0.0024	0.0046
spread hyperprior	OF	0.0013	0.0005	−0.0015	0.0036
	OS	0.0016	0.0009	−0.0023	0.0053
	OE	0.0009	0.0009	−0.0041	0.0057
	ON	0.0013	0.0008	−0.0012	0.0079
	OHG	0.0014	0.0010	−0.0021	0.0040
	Eastern	0.0009	0.0018	−0.0042	0.0043
spread sea	OF	0.0001	0.0001	−0.0041	0.0046
	OS	−0.0009	−0.0010	−0.0049	0.0035
	OE	0.0000	−0.0000	−0.0024	0.0037
	ON	−0.0014	−0.0012	−0.0055	0.0023
	OHG	0.0004	−0.0001	−0.0038	0.0073
	Eastern	0.0011	0.0013	−0.0036	0.0047
spread vulnerability	OF	0.0020	0.0016	−0.0024	0.0068
	OS	0.0027	0.0026	−0.0006	0.0050
	OE	0.0017	0.0020	−0.0015	0.0048
	ON	0.0015	0.0010	−0.0016	0.0062
	OHG	0.0039	0.0040	−0.0006	0.0061
	Eastern	0.0074	0.0077	0.0036	0.0106

the data we see. Here, too, the distributions are close to the prior settings and therefore the standard deviation of the update distributions do not show a notable impact. A few noteworthy patterns are the smaller standard deviation of innovation spread across the sea in the Old Frisian region or the elevated standard deviation of the migration parameter in the Old High German region and the alignment parameter in the Old Norse region. This means that in those regions, for those parameters, there were stronger or smaller fluctuations.

As demonstrated in section 4.8, agent-based models can date innovations via parameters that are called **innovation timing** parameters in this particular model. The results of these innovation timings show that most parameters can only be dated with great uncertainty. This uncertainty is due to the fact that the innovations are numerous and the parameters are subject to strong randomness in their occurrence times. The full list of posterior innovation

Table 4.8 Posterior estimates of σ-hyperparameters

Parameter	region	mean	median	lower-89CI	higher-89CI
align	OF	0.0041	0.0029	0.0000	0.0089
	OS	0.0047	0.0044	0.0002	0.0094
	OE	0.0042	0.0036	0.0000	0.0088
	ON	0.0058	0.0060	0.0021	0.0100
	OHG	0.0055	0.0058	0.0015	0.0100
	Eastern	0.0064	0.0076	0.0019	0.0100
birth	OF	0.0047	0.0047	0.0003	0.0089
	OS	0.0057	0.0067	0.0009	0.0100
	OE	0.0053	0.0051	0.0014	0.0098
	ON	0.0049	0.0051	0.0007	0.0091
	OHG	0.0045	0.0040	0.0000	0.0092
	Eastern	0.0051	0.0053	0.0000	0.0090
migration	OF	0.0046	0.0044	0.0002	0.0086
	OS	0.0055	0.0055	0.0007	0.0098
	OE	0.0057	0.0062	0.0010	0.0100
	ON	0.0059	0.0067	0.0013	0.0100
	OHG	0.0056	0.0055	0.0021	0.0100
	Eastern	0.0045	0.0039	0.0000	0.0093
innovation	OF	0.0000	0.0000	0.0000	0.0001
	OS	0.0000	0.0000	0.0000	0.0001
	OE	0.0000	0.0000	0.0000	0.0001
	ON	0.0001	0.0001	0.0000	0.0001
	OHG	0.0001	0.0001	0.0000	0.0001
	Eastern	0.0001	0.0001	0.0000	0.0001
river crossing	OF	0.0053	0.0057	0.0000	0.0091
	OS	0.0045	0.0040	0.0000	0.0091
	OE	0.0049	0.0051	0.0006	0.0089
	ON	0.0053	0.0048	0.0015	0.0100
	OHG	0.0053	0.0058	0.0009	0.0100
	Eastern	0.0051	0.0055	0.0000	0.0091

dates is given in the appendix. There, the range of the credible interval is given which is a measure of how certain the innovation could be dated. Some innovations, however, stand out as they could be dated with relative accuracy. For example, the monophthongization of PGmc *ai > ē in Northwest Germanic, Gothic, and Vandalic (in the latter two languages likely to be a parallel innovation) was dated very early at 480 BC with a standard deviation of 280 years. The lower half of the distribution falls exactly in the time of Northwest Germanic. Moreover, the dummy innovation discussed in Chapter 2 was correctly shifted

Table 4.8 (cont.) Posterior estimates of σ-hyperparameters

Parameter	region	mean	median	lower-89CI	higher-89CI
	OF	0.0048	0.0044	0.0012	0.0097
	OS	0.0051	0.0055	0.0007	0.0095
river spreading	OE	0.0050	0.0049	0.0008	0.0092
	ON	0.0054	0.0055	0.0012	0.0100
	OHG	0.0054	0.0056	0.0014	0.0100
	Eastern	0.0042	0.0038	0.0000	0.0086
	OF	0.0046	0.0044	0.0000	0.0088
	OS	0.0045	0.0040	0.0000	0.0092
spread hyperprior	OE	0.0059	0.0063	0.0023	0.0100
	ON	0.0054	0.0054	0.0011	0.0100
	OHG	0.0046	0.0040	0.0000	0.0093
	Eastern	0.0050	0.0049	0.0009	0.0100
	OF	0.0037	0.0032	0.0000	0.0074
	OS	0.0046	0.0046	0.0000	0.0081
spread sea	OE	0.0048	0.0041	0.0000	0.0092
	ON	0.0052	0.0050	0.0009	0.0097
	OHG	0.0049	0.0043	0.0014	0.0100
	Eastern	0.0038	0.0037	0.0000	0.0073
	OF	0.0043	0.0038	0.0000	0.0088
	OS	0.0050	0.0052	0.0004	0.0093
spread vulnerability	OE	0.0057	0.0062	0.0013	0.0099
	ON	0.0049	0.0046	0.0006	0.0100
	OHG	0.0043	0.0036	0.0000	0.0092
	Eastern	0.0055	0.0061	0.0010	0.0100

to the late end of the timeline with a mean of 980 AD and a narrow standard deviation of 300 years. The reason for this is that since this feature does not contribute to any evaluation, as it is a dummy feature, it is estimated to have occurred only at the last possible moment. This shows that the model is able to date the most salient innovations. This property of the model, however, is not very accurate at the current state of the model architecture. More refinements are necessary to improve upon the dating mechanic.

Better than innovation dating, the model can detect innovation ordering. For example, in only 27 per cent of all runs, the West Germanic innovation of $^*K_w > {}^*$Kw was dated earlier than the Northwest Germanic innovation *ā > *ē. However, this is unlikely to be very revealing since most of the issues connected to relative chronology do not have clearly distinct occurrence times. In other words, this test shows that the model can detect and recover the approximate relative chronology and occurrence time of an innovation, which shows that the model is correctly specified but it is likely to yield inconclusive results for occurrence times and chronologies that are temporally too close to be determinable using traditional methods.

4.11.2 The consensus runs

After the analysis of the global parameters, the more insightful step in the investigation is to examine the posterior runs in detail. The global measures can only yield broader and more general trends in the data but are of limited use. Individual runs, however, can show more subtle patterns and were examined for a larger variety of aspects.

To do this, the agents were extracted from each of the posterior runs at a time interval of 100 in-simulation years. To reduce the size of the data, squares of nine adjacent agents were merged using the median value of this patch as the cluster median. As a result, each simulation summary consists of a series of time steps containing larger patches of agents. Since the simulations start and end at different ages, the scale is not discrete in spite of the discrete snapshots taken from each simulation.

The resulting dataset contains 4.5 million agent clusters divided into 400 posterior runs.

Innovation completion times

Firstly, we analyse the innovation completion times of the individual languages by analysing how, in each region, the respective language gradually becomes more similar to the data. To achieve this, a smooth line was fitted to the data for each language indicating the mean of the population over time. Since different languages fit unequally well to the data, I standardized the distance measure MCC to make the languages comparable. Figure 4.49 shows these fitted lines.[11] It is important to note that, for this analysis, the height of the curve (i.e. the x-axis value) is irrelevant. The steepness of the curve alone indicates the development of the relative fit over time.

This figure shows that we have two main groups of languages at the beginning of the simulation: Burgundian, Vandalic, and Gothic show a steep drop in distance, increasing their fit at the beginning. They plateau at age 2.5. Their fit does not improve much after the age of 2.5.

---

[11] Plots were created using the R-package *ggplot2* (Wickham 2016).

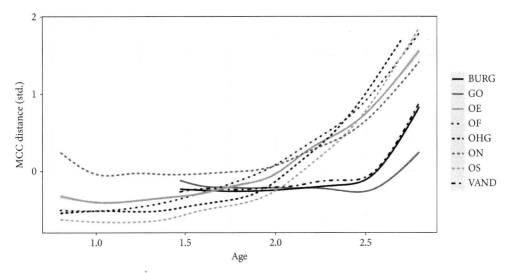

Figure 4.49 Development of the linguistic fit metric MCC (std.) as a function of age (in 1,000 years before present). Shaded areas around the mean curve indicate confidence intervals

The other languages improve their fit for a longer time with Old Norse levelling off at around 2.0 whereas Old Frisian, Old English, Old High German, and Old Saxon further improve their fit slightly until 1.5.

This means that the most important innovations for these languages as simulated in the model are estimated to have occurred by these time points. This is not to be confused with the completion of the *last* innovation undergone in each language recorded in the data; it is solely an abstract time frame by which those innovations have occurred that are most defining for a language in contrast to the other ones in the dataset. In a sense, the plateauing of the fit curve marks the earliest time point at which the most idiosyncratic innovations have been undergone in the model. For Gothic, Burgundian, and Vandalic, this would mean a date at or shortly after 500 BC, for Old Norse a date at, or shortly after, the beginning of the Common Era, for Old Frisian, Old English, Old High German, and Old Saxon this would correspond to a date at or shortly after 500 AD. Regarding Old Frisian, the data even show a slight further decrease in distance from the data until the year 1,000 AD, yet this trend might be too small to be statistically reliable.

Regional diversification

Another important measure that can be scrutinized is how languages in their different regions become more dissimilar from the other languages over time.

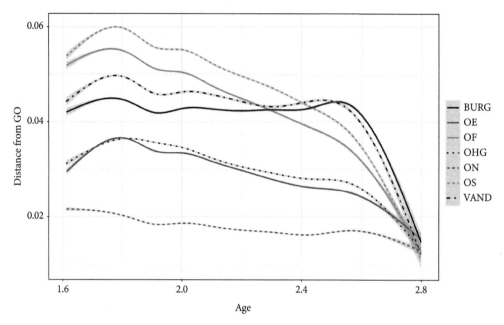

Figure 4.50 Distance from Gothic fit as a function of age

To do this, one can calculate the distance (measured in MCC) of each agent cluster to each of the linguistic datasets and then take the distance from the language fit to the fit to the other languages. For example, in the Old Saxon area, we can calculate each agent cluster's fit to all languages and then calculate the distance of the fit to the Old Saxon dataset to, for example, the fit to the Old Norse dataset. The end result is a function showing how rapidly the agents in that particular region become dissimilar from the fit to the other languages. This shows the agent's behaviour regarding their fit relative to the other languages. Figure 4.50 shows the results of these calculations.

The Gothic fit distance over time shows that in the Eastern region, the distance to the other fits rapidly increases at the beginning with only Old Norse being close to Gothic with a slight upward trend. Moreover, Old High German and Old English maintain a smaller level of distance from Gothic throughout the time. It is important to note that the distances are to be interpreted as *relative* expressions rather than absolute fits which means that Gothic is relatively closer to Old Norse than to the other languages. The effects we see for Old English and Old High German, however, might be indicative of adjacency effects from Old Norse and the eastern area, yet it is unclear how much of this effect might be spurious. One notable result is that we see Burgundian and Vandalic rapidly increasing at the beginning before levelling off, whereas

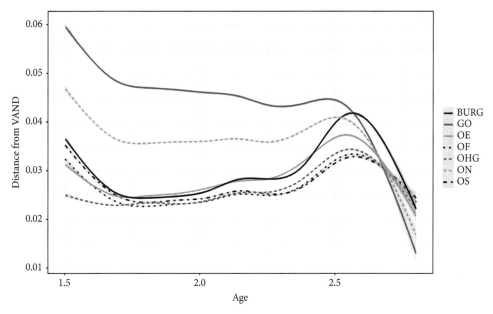

Figure 4.51 Distance from Vandalic fit as a function of age

the distance to other languages increases steadily. This might indicate that the most decisive innovations that differentiate Gothic and Burgundian or Vandalic occur early in the simulation runs.

The fits for Vandalic (Figure 4.51) and Burgundian (Figure 4.52) show a similar picture. In both cases, the distance to other languages rapidly increases, with Old Norse and Burgundian being the most distant.

The later decrease in distance for Old English, Old Saxon, Old High German, and Old Frisian calls for comment: the analysis makes it seem that Burgundian and Vandalic become more similar to these languages over time. This is an interesting finding as, in a straightforward diversification process, we would expect to see a distance increase over time, which might eventually level out but remain stable. That this is not the case for these two languages is indicative of a convergent pattern in the diversification process. Some later innovations in the data seem to be shared between these languages, whereas the early innovations are still distinct. What we see here is congruent with the pattern we would expect to see in convergent processes due to contact and areal spread. The model thus yields a situation where the inferred later innovations draw these languages closer together. For Vandalic, for instance, one of these innovations could be the realization of the outcome of Holtzmann's law which is the same as in West Germanic. Such innovations are interpreted by

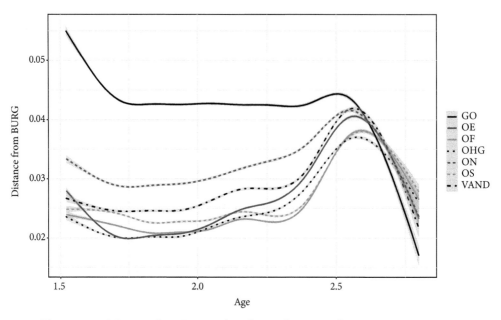

Figure 4.52 Distance from Burgundian fit as a function of age

the model as later convergences. It needs to be stressed that this convergence does not imply that the languages are more likely to be directly related. The model solely finds a pattern in which these languages become closer to one another at later times due to convergent factors after initially diverging.

A peculiarity in all of these figures is the anomalous behaviour of the far left hand side of the curves. It seems as the distance to other languages has changed radically over the last few hundred years. This behaviour is likely due to the fact that the agents become fewer towards the end of their attestation periods: since each of the posterior runs has a unique starting and end point, only a few languages have many datapoints at the very beginning and end of the attestation range given by the model. The reason for this is that, due to the origin time and the taxa ages being sampled from prior distributions, the start and endpoints can differ, which reduces the accuracy at the very ends of every curve. The beginning end of each curve therefore has to be interpreted with greater caution as smaller deviations in the greater trend may cause the line to shift as there are fewer datapoints to counterbalance this trend.

The fit distances for the Old Norse region (Figure 4.53) show a rather homogeneous initial development where only the distance to the immediately adjacent languages Old English and Gothic (and Old High German for reasons explained above) plateaus earlier.

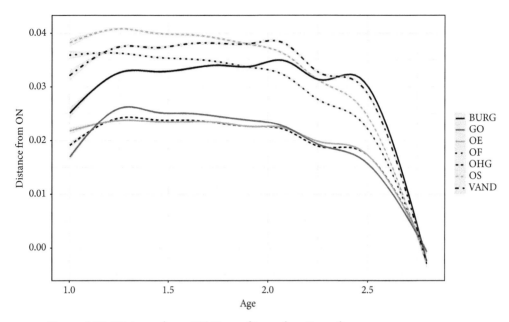

Figure 4.53 Distance from Old Norse fit as a function of age

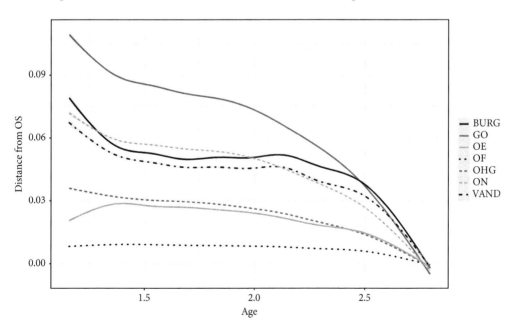

Figure 4.54 Distance from Old Saxon fit as a function of age

The fits of the Old Saxon (Figure 4.54) and Old High German (Figure 4.55) agents are quite similar in their patterns. In all cases Old English, Old Frisian,

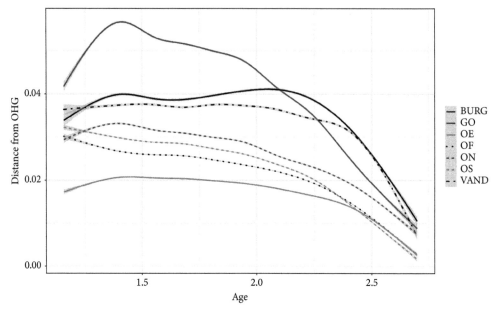

Figure 4.55 Distance from Old High German fit as a function of age

and Old Saxon/Old High German remain similar for the entire course of the simulations. Old High German and Old Saxon, however, differ in what language they are closest to. Old Saxon behaves most similarly to Old Frisian whereas Old High German shows a greater similarity to Old English; the difference between this and the distance to Old Frisian and Old Saxon, however, is smaller than for the Old Saxon area.

The Old English (Figure 4.56) and Old Frisian (Figure 4.57) areas are quite different from one another regarding their fit distance. While both show the same pattern regarding Burgindian, Vandalic, and Gothic, Old Frisian, for instance, shows a greater distance towards Old Norse than Old English. This might be an adjacency effect that Old English seems to be closer in fit to Old Norse in this regard. Further, Old Frisian is closest to Old Saxon whereas Old English is similarly close to the fits of Old Saxon, Old High German, and Old Frisian.

The analysis of these plots highlight certain important points. The model finds that Gothic, Burgundian, and Vandalic are the most distant languages from the rest, with evidence that Burgundian and Vandalic undergo convergent developments with Northwest Germanic languages. Nevertheless, the three languages diverge themselves already at the beginning suggesting that

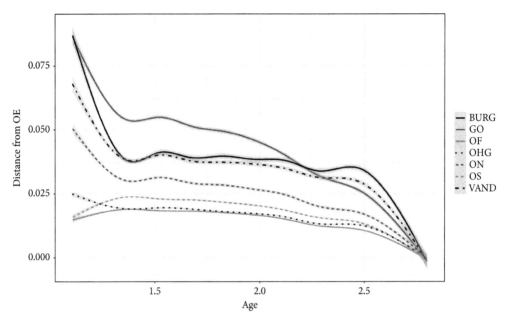

Figure 4.56 Distance from Old English fit as a function of age

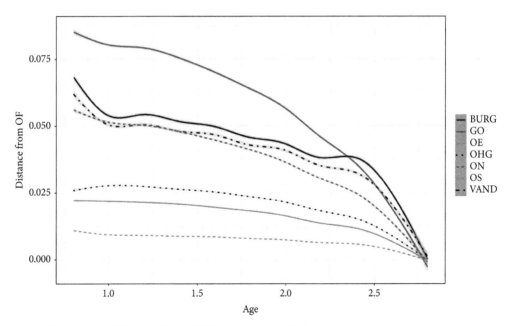

Figure 4.57 Distance from Old Frisian fit as a function of age

although they are more different from other languages, they are not necessarily closer to one another.

The development in the Northwest Germanic area is inconclusive. The model shows clear adjacency effects as Old Norse is closer to Old English and Old Frisian is closer to Old Saxon in the Old Frisian area.

Parameter developments

As a next step, we examine the developments of the parameters in every region as a function of age. The plot type remains the same as before, this time only showing the smooth mean of the parameter values.

The *innovation* parameter (Figure 4.58) shows a rather similar pattern for Old Saxon, Old Norse, and Old Frisian whose trajectories are downwards. The Old High German area and the eastern area show generally higher innovation values than the other regions.

The development of the *align* parameter (see Figure 4.59) is rather diverse across the different regions. Whereas the initial values start at similar parameter values, the eastern area shows a strong increase in this value until the age of 2.25. This means that innovations in this area can be more easily replaced and overridden. On the other hand, the Old Norse and Old Saxon areas show

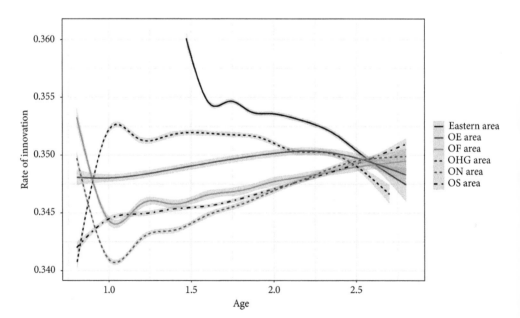

Figure 4.58 Development of the *innovation* parameter in each region over time

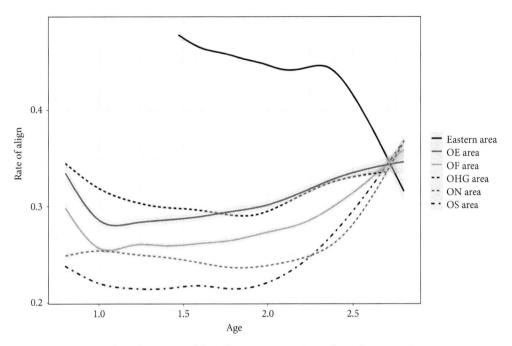

Figure 4.59 Development of the *align* parameter in each region over time

very low values of the parameter especially at earlier ages. This means that, in these areas, innovations are more easily sustained in the region.

Over time, the *spread* parameter (see Figure 4.60) is clearly increasing for all areas, suggesting that we see an acceleration of innovation spread the more the simulation progresses. It is especially interesting to see that this trend seems to hold for all areas. The only diverging pattern is a slim deviation of the eastern area from this trend where the spreading rate remains the same for the first centuries of simulated time.

Closely related is the *spread vulnerability* parameter (see Figure 4.61) which is the percentage of agents in a surrounding area affected by a linguistic spread. A lower rate suggests a more fragmented spread type whereas high parameter values indicate a broader and more uniform spread. Like with the *spread* parameter itself, *spread vulnerability* increases for all regions. The notable exceptions are the eastern region where the parameter increases to a maximum after a short time. This means that while the spreading parameter itself remains low at the beginning, *spread vulnerability* increases. This suggests a more uniform spread of few and regionally confined innovations at the beginning.

The Old Norse area is another anomaly where the *spread vulnerability* parameter caps at around 0.6 after slowing down since the age of 2.0. This

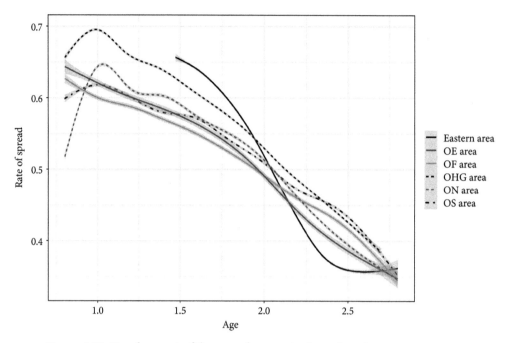

Figure 4.60 Development of the *spread* parameter in each region over time

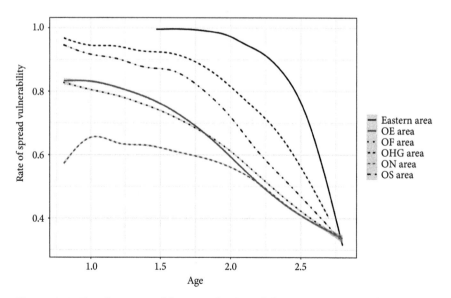

Figure 4.61 Development of the *spread vulnerability* parameter in each region over time

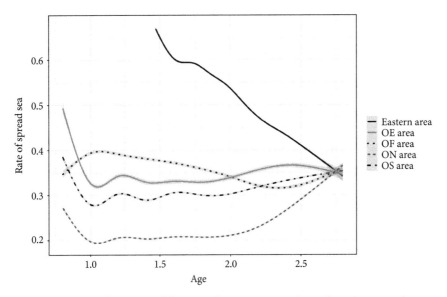

Figure 4.62 Development of the *spread sea* parameter in each region over time

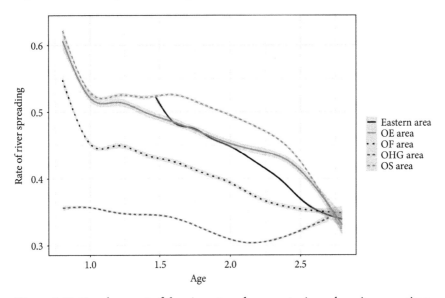

Figure 4.63 Development of the *river spread* parameter in each region over time

suggests that the innovations in this region spread less uniformly, affecting only a few agents at a time.

The obstacle spreading parameters *spread sea* (Figure 4.62) and *river spread* (Figure 4.63) have diverse effects in the individual regions.[12]

---

[12] Note that those areas are not present in the plots for which the parameter is not applicable. For example, the Old High German area does not border a sea region, therefore *spread sea* is not applicable.

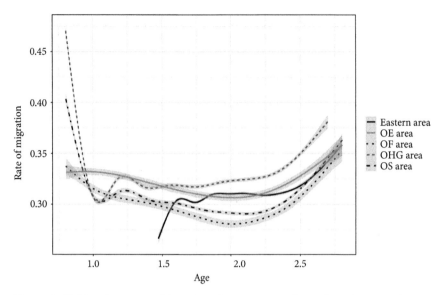

Figure 4.64 Development of the *migration* parameter in each region over time

The parameter *spread sea* is especially high in the eastern area whereas it is especially low in the Old Norse area. This means that in most simulations, innovations crossed the sea more easily from the eastern area outward than from the Old Norse area. The Old Norse area insulates itself insofar from other regions as it does not propagate changes across the sea in the simulation.

River spreading sees high rates for most linguistic groups, yet the Old High German area shows rather low rates. Given that the Old High German area borders a river obstacle to the west and several river obstacles to the east, this indicates that the spread from this area was predominantly northward than to the west or east.

Migration in this model seems to be fairly uniform as most simulations plateau at a value around 0.3 (see Figure 4.64). The only slightly elevated region is Old High German which not only starts out higher but also remains the highest-valued language for the first half of the process.

Regarding the parameter *river crossing* (see Figure 4.65), we find that especially the eastern area acquires a higher value in this parameter, whereas the Old Frisian region displays a below average crossing parameter.

Likewise, the Old Norse area does not have vacant border regions to migrate to, therefore the *migration* parameter is not applicable.

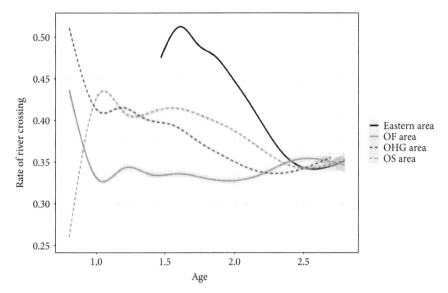

Figure 4.65 Development of the *river crossing* parameter in each region over time

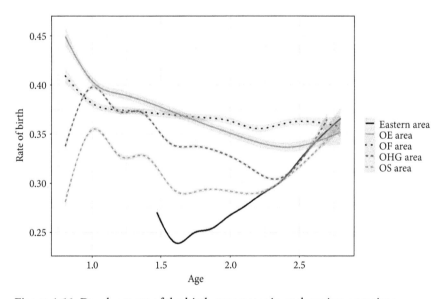

Figure 4.66 Development of the birth parameter in each region over time

The *birth* parameter (Figure 4.66) which governs the occurrence of new agents does not seem to have a strong impact on the course of the simulation as it levels out for most languages at the starting value. Only the eastern area sees a decrease in this value which corresponds to a decreasing potential to expand over time.

Three-dimensional diversification

So far we have examined the model results as two-dimensional graphs which show the relationship of the different languages or regions to one another as different trajectories. However, in many wave model implementations such as historical glottometry or dialect geography, the languages are plotted in two-dimensional graphs where proximity in the plot equals linguistic distance. Such a plot type can be approximated by an agent-based model analysis by using *principal component analyses* (PCAs) to plot the difference between the agent clusters in a two-dimensional space. It further adds time as a third dimension which is usually missing in traditional wave-like depictions of linguistic distance.

To achieve this, the age dimension was discretized by rounding every time step to the nearest first age digit (i.e. an age value of 2.21 was rounded to 2.2). Moreover, the posterior runs were averaged using the mean for every agent cluster at each time step such that the agent clusters represent the consensus for this cluster at this time step across the posterior runs. Afterwards, the linguistic fits in each region were standardized and analysed with a PCA using the R-package *FactoMineR* (Lê, Josse, and Husson 2008) and visualized using *factoextra* (Kassambara and Mundt 2020).

A PCA is in essence an algorithm which takes in multidimensional data and projects the main patterns onto a two dimensional surface (made up of the two most explanatory *principal components*). There, more similar individuals, in this case agent clusters, are projected more closely together. In this case, a PCA was conducted for time steps of 200 years to visually track the linguistic diversification over time. It needs to be kept in mind that the plot is based on the distance between agents and not on languages themselves. Moreover, these plots can only show agents' differences in different regions, therefore the eastern languages have to be grouped together despite being quite heterogeneous themselves.

On these plots, we can see all agent clusters in the consensus plotted in reference to one another based on their mutual distance. The agent clusters are differently shaped and coloured dots where the colour and shape represent the geographical region they belong to. Further, ellipsoids were drawn around a particular region of the plot. These are 95 per cent confidence intervals encompassing the area that most clusters fall into. The percentage given on every axis

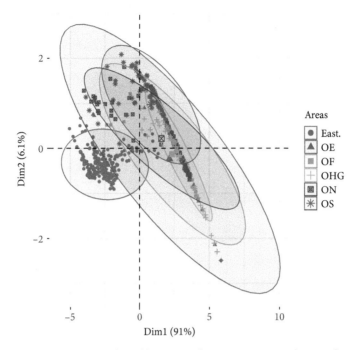

Figure 4.67 PCA plot of linguistic distance at age 2.4 (400 BC)

represents the percentage of variation between the agent clusters attributable to the particular dimension.

Note that every time a PCA is calculated on a different dataset, the principal components and the results differ. This means that to compare different time steps below, we can only interpret the relative positions of the regions to one another. Their absolute position on the surface may vary as an artefact of the PCA algorithm.

Figure 4.67 shows the situation of the simulated diversification process at the year 400 BC. Here, we can see that most ellipses of the different areas overlap, mostly covering the same area. This is different for the eastern area: the agents in this ellipse are outside of most other cluster areas but still overlap to some degree. This suggests an early detachment of the eastern area.

The second plot in Figure 4.68 shows that, now, the centres of the Northwest Germanic languages no longer neatly overlap. Instead, we see shifts from the earlier relative position especially in the Old High German and Old Saxon area. Nevertheless, these clusters overlap significantly, hence we can only speak of a shift in position rather than a detachment. This is somewhat true

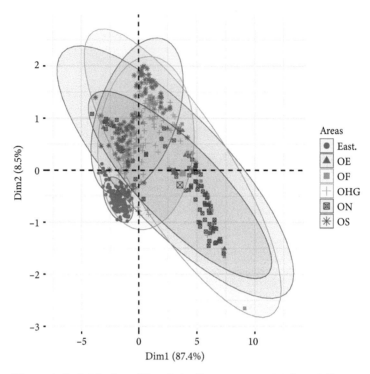

Figure 4.68 PCA plot of linguistic distance at age 2.2 (200 BC)

for the eastern area as well, which maintains its outward rim position only overlapping with a few other clusters.

At the age of 2 (Figure 4.69), we can already see a disturbance in the cohesiveness of the Northwest Germanic areas with a high number of especially Old Norse agents moving to the outer areas of the plot. The fact that the eastern area encompasses a smaller area is indicative of a clear distinctness from the other areas.

Over the course of the next two age steps (Figures 4.70 and 4.71) from 200 AD to 400 AD, we can see that Old Norse moves continuously away from the other areas while still overlapping with Old English and Old Frisian. Still overlapping with Old English and Old Frisian are Old Saxon and Old High German, which follow a joint trajectory.

The following two simulated centuries (see Figures 4.72 and 4.73) see strong outliers for Old High German and Old Saxon which might be due to random fluctuations as the ellipsoid positions remain relatively unchanged. At the year 800, the Old Norse cluster is now mainly outside of any other cluster with the Old English cluster having only little overlap with Old Saxon and Old High

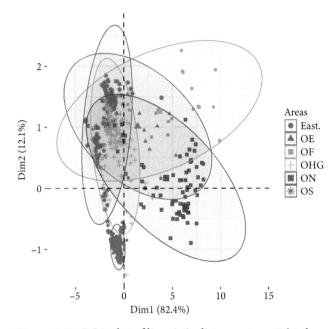

Figure 4.69 PCA plot of linguistic distance at age 2 (at the beginning of the Common Era)

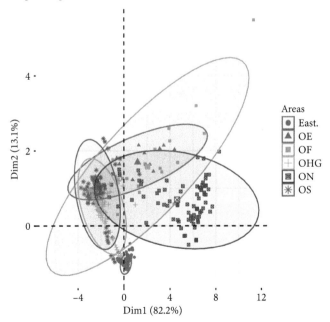

Figure 4.70 PCA plot of linguistic distance at age 1.8 (200 AD)

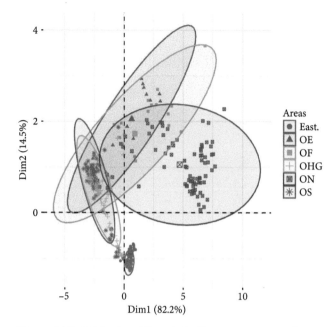

Figure 4.71 PCA plot of linguistic distance at age 1.6 (400 AD)

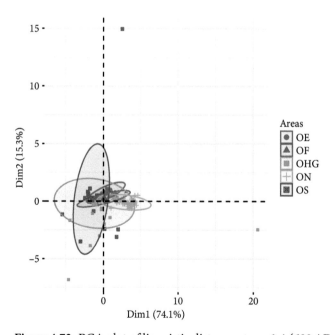

Figure 4.72 PCA plot of linguistic distance at age 1.4 (600 AD)

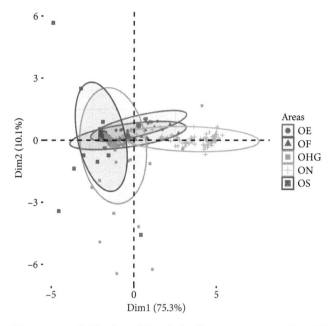

Figure 4.73 PCA plot of linguistic distance at age 1.2 (800 AD)

German, mostly remaining close to Old Frisian, which itself is more integrated in the other two clusters.

To conclude this analysis, we have seen that the simulated data obtained from the models can be displayed as a series of time-progressing clusters which are similar in appearance to previous non-computational two-dimensional depictions. Other than those, the ABM approach further adds the temporal dimension to these displays. For the current purposes, the temporal dimension was discretized to be plotted as consecutive plots, yet for future applications in other contexts, it would be possible to convert the temporal dimension as a third dimension in the form of a cubical plot or a video clip which shows the clusters in continuous progression. For these methods, however, a method other than the particular PCA algorithm used here would need to be employed.

Further, the linguistic developments displayed here suggest an early detachment of the eastern languages followed by internal diversifications in Northwest Germanic of which Old Norse maintains some overlap with Old English and Old Frisian. The latter overlap with Old Saxon and Old High German which themselves remain mostly congruent.

Parameters and geography

Another advantage of agent-based models is that they make use of the geographical component to plot parameter developments in a more fine-grained way on a geographical surface. This is in essence a three-dimensional geospatial variant of what Figures 4.50 to 4.57 outlines using two-dimensional graphs. The two following figures are example plots of the two most interestingly distributed parameters: the *spread sea* and the *spread* parameters. The figures themselves are contour plots devised with the R-package *ggplot2* (Wickham 2016) subdivided into six discrete 200-year time steps from 400 BC to 600 AD. In these plots, the lightness of the colour indicates the parameter value: lighter shades indicate higher values.

The map is essentially a north-oriented map of central and northern Europe with the agents removed in the eastern area from the year 500 AD onwards.

The most salient feature of this distribution (Figure 4.74) is that, from the very beginning, the Old Norse area shows small values for spread across the sea, whereas the rest of the Northwest Germanic area exhibits average values with the exception of Old Saxon. The high values of the eastern area first appear in the east of the region before spreading westward. As discussed above,

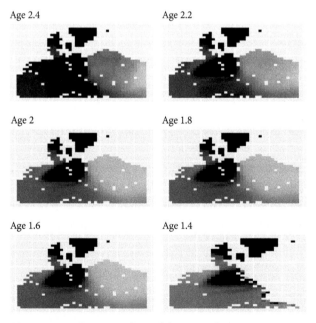

Figure 4.74 Contour plots of the *spread sea* parameter at different ages

Age 2.4   Age 2.2

Age 2   Age 1.8

Age 1.6   Age 1.4

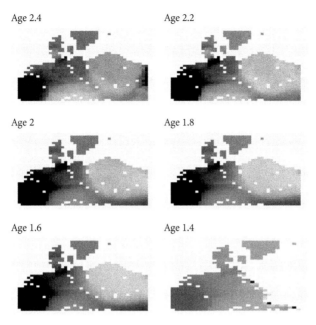

Figure 4.75 Contour plots of the *spread* parameter at different ages

it is unclear whether this high value is actually indicative of a higher spread rate for this region across the sea.

The other interesting parameter to examine geographically is the *spread* parameter which, as shown in Figure 4.75, seems to have three epicentres. Over time, the Old English and Old High German areas show high values, with the south of the Old High German area being especially prominent. Yet, over time, by the age of 1.8 (200 AD) these parameters are overshadowed by higher values in the eastern regions. There, the spread values appear first in the border regions to the west which are best visible in the subplots for the ages 2.4–2. This suggests that in the eastern area, innovations spread more easily within the area, and from and to the outside, whereas the west shows generally higher values but there seem to be epicentres in the simulation driving this development.

5

Genealogical implications and Germanic phylogeny

5.1 Prelude: society and identity in pre-Roman and migration-age central Europe

Before we can investigate the cladistic history of the Germanic languages, we need to address the social and political structures of this time. Regularly, we encounter issues that can only be addressed when bearing in mind these particular circumstances.

The fact of the matter is that we know little about pre-Roman and migration-age Germania[1] regarding precise historical events, interactions between groups, and chronology. We know, however, that the modern conceptions of group identity as political, ethnic, or religious does not apply in the time in question. The Germanic-speaking population of northern and central Europe was organized in small units of political commonalities such as allegiance to a leading figure (cf. Heather 2009: 6; and Wolfram 1997). These units were rather small and agriculturally less developed than in neighbouring regions (Heather 2009: 5) but could organize regionally and even suprare-gionally in loose confederations or alliances with other groups, break away, or merge with other communities (cf. Todd 2009: 29–31). The identities of these groups or allegiances were not formed along linguistic or ethnic lines. We rather see group coherence that transcends the modern understanding of identity (cf. Heather 1996: 3–7). As a result, any political group in this time, be it during the time of the first encounters between the Roman republic and Germanic groups, or in later centuries during the 'migration age', groups that Roman and Greek sources identify as coherent communities could in fact be

---

[1] The term *Germania* is in the historical and archaeological field predominantly a term for the approximate geographical area east of the Rhine and north of the Danube which, in most definitions, does not include Scandinavia. In the following, this term is used in an unorthodox way to mean the entire Germanic-speaking area in northern and central Europe for the sake of convenience. However, note that in other fields, the distinction between Scandinavia, mainland Germania, and eastern Germania is often much sharper.

Germanic Phylogeny. Frederik Hartmann, Oxford University Press. © Frederik Hartmann (2023).
DOI: 10.1093/oso/9780198872733.003.0005

multilingual political units whose members were from different origins and backgrounds (Frey and Salmons 2012: 6).

This view of the societal structures and group identities has changed considerably. When earlier literature on linguistic matters referenced the identity between group and language, they relied mostly on the notion of Germanic 'tribes' as proto-nations with a congruence of ethnicity, language, religion, and political allegiance (so, for example Von Der Leyen 1908; Wrede 1886). The realization that groups identified by Roman sources and linguistic units are very different is a necessary condition for the further investigation of early Germanic linguistic relationships. Not only can Roman sources not be taken at face value, the linguistic situation in this region during classical and late antiquity is much more intricate than group-language assignments on a map could show (Steinacher 2020).

In reality, the region of Germania was a highly opaque and intricate network of groups and political units with regional differences regarding material and perhaps societal development.

5.2 Origin and disintegration of Proto-Germanic

5.2.1 Brief remarks on the stages of Proto-Germanic

The most common nomenclature to refer to the development of the Germanic family up until the point of disintegration is usually divided into pre-Proto-Germanic (or sometimes pre-Germanic) and Proto-Germanic. The former denotes the time period between the separation of the Germanic clade from its most recent ancestor it shares with another linguistic family and said Proto-Germanic. The latter refers to the state of the language shortly before its breakup which is in part determined by the methods of reconstruction (see discussion in section 5.2.2). Following this definition, pre-Proto-Germanic encompasses a long timespan containing all defining developments of pre-Proto-Germanic history ending in a relatively short but ultimately indeterminable Proto-Germanic period where the language had undergone all (or at least most) common Germanic innovations but not yet broken up into smaller units. This is the definition of these terms that are used in this study. Among the most notable of these aforementioned innovations that occurred before the break-up of Proto-Germanic are, for example, Grimm's law (Ringe 2017: 113–140), accent shift (Van Coetsem and Bammesberger 1994: 82–93), and the development of a weak and a strong verb class (Fulk 2018: 254–255).

Some researchers, however, have previously attempted to partition the Proto-Germanic period into discernable and datable stages (Early and Late Proto-Germanic are the most common divisions, e.g. in Antonsen 1965; and Voyles 1992).

In the definition used in this study, I refrain from assuming and dating individual stages prior to the Proto-Germanic level. This is not to say that there is no determinable linguistic relative chronology (see, for example, the detailed relative chronology of sound-changes that is summarized in Ringe (2017: 176) in the form of a flow chart). Rather, I assume that these developments have all taken place in the period of pre-Proto-Germanic leading up to the completion of these innovations which is how these terms are defined. The decision to not divide the period further is predominantly based on the inability to make precise statements about the temporal relationships between the individual changes. It seems likely that, in the prehistory of Germanic, developments came in clustered bursts rather than being evenly distributed over the entire pre-Proto-Germanic period (cf. Koch 2020: 38–39). To make reasonable statements about sub-pre-Proto-Germanic divisions, we lack knowledge about the temporal chronology of the changes. Alternatively dividing only relatively datable developments into two distinct periods would further be an arbitrary choice with little value to the particular study at hand.

5.2.2   The origins of the Germanic clade

Any investigation of Germanic phylogeny and Proto-Germanic inevitably needs to present, even if briefly, the research into the relationship between Germanic and other branches of Indo-European. The importance of this discussion is that in order to understand the break-up of the family into daughter lineages, we need a firm understanding of the conditions of this family shortly before the dissolution of its linguistic unity. This requires an outline of where Proto-Germanic came from historically and cladistically, and what the state of the language was, at, and shortly before, the break-up (see e.g. section 5.2.3). Note, however, that since this investigation primarily rests on linguistic evidence from Germanic daughter languages, the methodological possibilities at this point are limited vis-a-vis higher-order clades and subgroupings beyond Proto-Germanic. It is therefore not possible to investigate the cladistic prehistory of Proto-Germanic in the scope of the study at hand. Instead, I will focus on previous investigations to briefly outline pre-Germanic cladistic history which then leads to insights into the state of the family at the time from where this study starts.

First of all, the research question this investigation starts is, as repeatedly mentioned, the time of the break-up of the Germanic family. This point is set both by methodological and theoretical considerations. The latest reconstructible layer of Germanic, Proto-Germanic, is the point on the eve of Germanic disintegration. That is, without further internal reconstruction and comparison with other IE sister languages, the comparative method can only take us back as far as the latest point where Germanic was still a (somewhat) coherent group. Moreover, the Bayesian phylogenetic and agent-based models estimate or simulate the break-up point as the start point of the analysis. Thus, neither computational nor qualitative methods address questions of the origin of Germanic.

Unsurprisingly, this definition is an artificial point which does not necessarily map onto the actual proceedings of disintegration of Germanic. Rather, it marks the point in time where the last common Germanic innovation has taken place and right before the first Germanic daughter diverges. We have to be aware of the fact that this split-terminology, especially in the Germanic context, might not be adequate. The more likely scenario is a gradual diversification process under which the Eastern Rim becomes diversified more quickly than the rest of the core area. This means that a 'day before the split' did not exist, not even allegorically. The start of the disintegration therefore has to be interpreted as a gradual process spanning a certain amount of time—at the longest until the individual subgroups had undergone enough divergent innovation to be detectable as independent.

As described above, the methods used in this study, both traditional and computational, set the earliest investigated time point to the time of the family break-up. However, to be able to analyze the Proto-Germanic origins of the family, we need to at least briefly discuss the pre-Proto-Germanic history.

A plethora of studies and discussions have researched the placement of the Germanic branch in the wider Indo-European family tree.

Many contemporary studies and overviews place Germanic in the *Central Indo-European* branch in which there are other families placed such as Balto-Slavic and Indo-Iranian.[2] In this view, Germanic is more closely related to, for instance, Balto-Slavic than to Italo-Celtic. Subclades below Central-IE are very much still a matter of debate. Phylogenetic studies, however, find differing subgroupings. Gray and Atkinson (2003) and Chang et al. (2015) find Germanic more closely related to Italo-Celtic than to Balto-Slavic. Yet, in both mentioned

---

[2] See Ringe (2017: 5–8) and references for a summary of the current state of research.

studies, the branch lengths are small, meaning that the actual clade differences are clear but not large.

Earlier computational studies place Italic, Celtic, Balto-Slavic, and Germanic closer together (e.g. Holm 2000) as does Euler (2009). Moreover Ringe, Warnow, and Taylor (2002) have found specifically the position of Germanic, modelled using conventional tree structures, to be difficult as the family does not seem to possess features that let it be easily placed in a tree with determinable splits. The view that the placement of Germanic is difficult to assess is often acknowledged in overview works of the topic (e.g. Clackson 2007: 13–14). It is clear that the languages of central Europe in pre-Proto-Germanic times were very much in contact through trade and geographic proximity.[3] Moreover, we can assume that the central and northern European IE languages formed, at least in the beginning, a larger dialectal area with mutual influence (Fulk 2018: 6).

The linguistic split of pre-Proto-Germanic from its most recent ancestor is often placed in southern Scandinavia (Fortson 2010: 338) and perhaps northern Germany (E. König and van der Auwera 1994: 1) at around 2000 BC (cf. Chang et al. 2015: 199 and Polomé 1992: 55–56), with estimates from archaeology suggesting that this date is perhaps the latest possible time of divergence (cf. Koch 2020: 37–38). At around this time, the Germanic branch started to develop distinct features that can clearly be identified as uniquely Germanic.

5.2.3 Proto-Germanic—a dialect continuum?

Since the first reconstructions of the most recent common ancestor of the Germanic languages, researchers have discussed the question of the internal coherence of the Proto-Germanic language before its break-up.[4] Early research viewed Proto-Germanic as the language of unitary Germanic proto-nations as described by Roman and Greek sources such as Tacitus (e.g. Streitberg 1896: 15). Since this time, as our understanding of the societal structures and conditions of early Germanic have improved, the issue has been raised whether or not to regard Germanic as a dialect continuum. Researchers have

---

[3] An extensive analysis of Celto-Germanic contact is provided by Koch (2020).

[4] I am using the term Proto-Germanic language for a dialect continuum here and below which is strictly speaking an oxymoron in some sense, as protolanguages are by definition linguistic constructs, however they are rooted in reality. In this view, a protolanguage cannot be a dialect continuum; rather, a dialect continuum can produce daughter languages which can in turn be used to reconstruct an approximation to the common properties of this dialect continuum. However, for convenience, I use Proto-Germanic to denote the reconstructed language which is representative of the dialect continuum underlying the reconstruction.

noted that reconstructed Proto-Germanic is both lexically and grammatically homogenous (e.g. Euler 2009: 41–43). On the other hand, little to no detectable variation in the Proto-Germanic language is not so much a feature of the language itself but rather an artefact of the method and an inherent property of most protolanguages (cf. Fulk 2018: 11). As linguistic reconstruction entails the systematic comparison of a particular family's daughter languages, it produces a rather artificial language representing the 'common ground' of features in the varieties of the Germanic language that existed at the time we reconstruct Proto-Germanic. In the same way, we can reconstruct a single Proto-Romance language while knowing for a fact that the Romance varieties in late antiquity were more heterogeneous and varied than the reconstruction suggests (see Alkire and Rosen 2010: 40). This is not to say that Proto-Germanic did not exist as a linguistic area but that our picture of this are obtained by the comparative method is more unitary and smooth than it most likely was. The current standpoint therefore is that early Germanic already was a dialect continuum when it began to disintegrate (cf. Euler 2009: 41–43; Seebold 2013: 58–59). It was a geographical space of individual groups speaking Proto-Germanic varieties which were all mutually intelligible (cf. Frey and Salmons 2012: 21).

5.2.4 Time estimations of Germanic diversification

The time of the end of the Germanic dialect continuum and the start of the diversification process is dated ambiguously in previous literature. The methodologically sound definition of Proto-Germanic is the point in time just before the first languages split from the common dialect continuum (see also section 5.2.2). However, as it is likely that the linguistic unity persisted for some time before disintegrating, there was a possibly several hundred year-long period around the time of the diversification where Germanic had slowly started to disintegrate. We therefore have to bear in mind that this transitional phase from relative unity as a language (or a group of closely related varieties) can span decades or centuries.

Previous researchers have suggested a break-up period of around 500 BC (for a more extensive list of references and suggested dates see 3.2.1). Other researchers such as Mallory (1989: 87) cite 500 BC as the most likely point in time when Proto-Germanic has completed all major innovations, thus shifting the time to a later date.

Phylogenetic and computational evidence by Chang et al. (2015: 226) dates the break-up of Germanic at ~ 2,000 years before present. As established in section 5.3.4, the break-up of Germanic unity was completed with the fragmentation of the Eastern Rim languages.

The most probable Bayesian phylogenetic tree discussed in section 3.2.5 shows for the origin parameters a highest density 89 per cent credible interval between 2.12 and 2.69, which translates to a time span between 690 and 120 BC. The mean sampled origin is 2.42 or 420 BC. This suggests a most likely disintegration of Proto-Germanic around, but mostly shortly after, 500 BC. Among the chief reasons for such large credible intervals is the uncertainty connected with the attestation dates of the individual taxa.

The ABM evidence lies on the earlier side of the time estimates with a mean age of 2.53 (590 BC). Yet the credible intervals suggest a large range of values between 250 BC and 800 BC that mostly overlap with the phylogenetic evidence but shifted to a later date by about 100 years.

In conclusion, we can summarize that both computational methods estimate the diversification date in a time interval around 500 BC with mean values enclosing the time interval between 420 BC and 530 BC, which is in line with traditional assumptions.

5.3 The Eastern Rim languages

The languages of eastern Germania, including Gothic, Burgundian, Vandalic, and more, are commonly referred to as the 'East Germanic' languages. This term, however, comes with difficulties with regard to definition. Still to this day, this term is often used to refer to these languages as a coherent subgroup descended from an East Germanic protolanguage. At least in this reading, the term is highly problematic, as I will argue in the following section. Drawing on previous literature and the computational models applied in this study, I will aim to draw a coherent picture of the emergence and the development of the languages in eastern Germania.

5.3.1 The provenance of Gothic—a linguistic perspective

To shed light on the origins of the languages in the east of the Germanic-speaking area, we have to start assessing the area in which the linguistic emergence occurred, (i.e. the linguistic *Urheimat*). The discussions surrounding the provenance of Gothic are paralleled for other alleged East Germanic languages such as Vandalic and Burgundian. For this reason, I will use Gothic as an example to outline the issue, but the notions that hold for Gothic are likewise comparable for Vandalic and Burgundian as well. We have to keep in mind that historical and archaological *ethnogenesis* and *Urheimat* are closely linked, albeit not identical. That is, as political and societal groupings do not necessarily map onto one another, evidence from historical and archaeological sources need to be treated differently and, for linguistic purposes, may serve solely as additional external evidence. In other words, the question of the linguistic *Urheimat* of Gothic takes precedence over Gothic ethnogenesis in this study.

Scandinavia and the *Gotho-nordic* hypothesis

Early literature on the Gothic language relied mostly on Roman sources for the accounts of the Gothic *Urheimat*. Especially Jordanes was taken as the predominant source on this issue. Jordanes' most important work regarding the Goths is the sixth-century *Getica* which presents itself as a historiographic account of the prehistory of the Goths. In this work, he claims the Goths originated in Scandinavia ('Scandza') and migrated to the Vistula area in modern-day Poland before migrating again to the area surrounding the Black Sea in later centuries.[5]

The Roman historiographical sources are mirrored and argumentatively intertwined with the Gotho-Nordic hypothesis up to a point where some researchers have criticized the confusion of historiographic and linguistic arguments in earlier research (e.g. Nielsen 1995). After the then-common consensus of the tripartite division of the Germanic languages was established, researchers were investigating further subgrouping of two of the three assumed clades North Germanic, West Germanic, and East Germanic. Until the debate was settled starting with Kuhn (1955) in favour of a Northwest Germanic group, some scholars adhered to the notion of a Gotho-Nordic subgroup (cf. Schwarz 1951: 184–187). This debate was by no means unaffected by the early stance of many historians who took Jordanes' account at face value. Although researchers favouring Gotho-Nordic present linguistic evidence, a vital part in many of these discussions, especially in the early debate, is reliant on the axiomatic assumption that there is a close genealogical link between the Germanic-speaking populations of Scandinavia and the Vistula region (see e.g. Maurer 1952; and Hutterer 1975: 133).

One of the issues with Gotho-Nordic as a subgroup is that the proposed evidence in many cases involves retentions rather than shared innovations.

---

[5] Heather (1996: 11–30) discusses the topic from the perspective of the historic sciences.

Moreover, many of the proposed changes are themselves questionable.[6] For example, the similarity in the second person singular preterite ending in strong verbs, as proposed in Lehmann (1966: 17) and masculine a-stem noun nominative singular endings, are both shared retentions (examples drawn from Antonsen 1965: 18–20; and Fulk 2018: 14).

The mainly cited noteworthy common feature of Gothic and North Germanic is the reflex of Holtzmann's law (*Verschärfung*) in both languages: the PGmc glide sequences *-ww- and *-jj- have stop outcomes in Gothic and Old Norse. Previous research, however, has cast doubt on the earlier assumption that the *Verschärfung* had arisen through a common innovation (for discussion see Fulk 2018: 17–20). Whether it might be a parallel innovation is unclear and the research is deemed inconclusive so far (cf. Ringe and Taylor 2014: 65).

It is worth noting that the stop outcome of Holtzmann's law is not shared by Vandalic which makes this phenomenon exclusive to Gothic and Old Norse (cf. Hartmann 2020).[7] In the phylogenetic models applied in previous sections, the Gotho-Nordic split shows a vanishingly small clade credibility which is a computational result of a low probability that the linguistic innovations in favour of this split suffice to establish a subgroup.

Moreover, in the agent-based models, Old Norse and Gothic remain separate from the early beginnings of the simulations. It is true, however, that Old Norse and Gothic according to some measures are modelled as closer to one another in absolute terms than to the West Germanic languages; this, though, only indicates that there is some overlap in shared retentions. In the developmental trajectory, Old Norse sides with the West Germanic languages in all cases.

It becomes clear that the evidence in favour of a Gotho-Nordic grouping is meagre and no clearly demonstrable common innovations can be identified. Moreover, judging from the greater cohesion of Northwest Germanic due to the greater number of innovations clearly attributable to a Northwest Germanic stage (see section 5.4), a Gotho-Nordic subgroup most likely did not exist.

Indigenous Gothic hypotheses

Other views, to which I collectively refer here as 'indigenous Gothic' theories, assume that the Gothic language originated in central Europe in the eastern

---

[6] For an overview of the proposed Gotho-Nordic changes see Antonsen (1965: 18–20).
[7] It is difficult to assess this situation for Burgundian as no reflexes of this change survive in the data (Hartmann and Riegger 2022).

parts of Germania. The key aspect that these views have in common is that they do not presuppose an early migration from Scandinavia. In most cases where an *indigenous Gothic* hypothesis is voiced, it is often the result of a refutation of Gotho-Nordic. Archaeological evidence does not show patterns in the archaeological record that require a need for the population to have descended from Scandinavian emigrants (cf. Heather 1996: 11–30). Thus, a large part of the indigenous Gothic notion assumes Gothic to have arisen where the Goths are located by current historians and archaeology—in the Vistula region.

There is, however, dissent among the proponents of this notion. Manczak (1987), for example, argues for an *Urheimat* of Gothic in the very south of Germania, to the southeast of what would later become the West Germanic linguistic area. Accordingly, he suggests redefining West Germanic as 'Mittelgermanisch' ('central Germanic') and Gothic as 'Südgermanisch' ('South Germanic') (Manczak 1982: 137).

Similarly, Kortlandt (2001) agrees with this theory, arguing, along the same lines as Manczak's proposals, that Gothic was linguistically closer to languages of southern West Germanic (chiefly Old High German) than to any other Germanic variety.

This view has roots in earlier research (e.g. Wrede 1924) proposing a closer relationship of Gothic to Old High German. A considerable proportion of the arguments in favour of this theory stem from the identification of purported Gothic loanwords in Old High German. Yet critical reviews of later researchers have identified flaws in the identification of loanwords (e.g. Kufner 1972).

More generally, we can assert that the linguistic evidence for a Gothic homeland located on the southern border of Germania is problematic when resting predominantly on loanwords. Since there are to date no clearly demonstrable contact phenomena between Gothic and either northern West Germanic or southern West Germanic, abandoning the Vistula region origin as a hypothesis of Gothic *Urheimat* is not well-founded.

Evaluating the evidence
Pertaining to the Gothic *Urheimat*, an out-of-Scandinavia theory could only possibly arise in one of two scenarios:

(1) The migration from Scandinavia occurred in early times during the time of the Proto-Germanic dialect continuum. As a result, we cannot expect to find linguistic evidence linking North Germanic and Gothic, at least not to the exclusion of West Germanic languages.

(2) The migration from Scandinavia occurred in post-PGmc times where the Gothic language was either completely descended from or strongly influenced by Scandinavian varieties.

From a linguistic perspective, scenario (1) is irrelevant for two reasons: the hypothesis lies beyond the reach of linguistics as it would entail that a linguistically (un-reconstructably) similar group had migrated to the southern shores of the Baltic sea. Secondly, by the definition of the linguistic *Urheimat*, the important factor here is whether or not Gothic must have necessarily developed in Scandinavia or the Vistula area. Moreover, the computational results of this approach do not indicate a large Scandinavian influence to the mainland.[8] If anything, the linguistic influence is on a below-average level suggesting that a large Scandinavian to mainland influence is unlikely to account for the data we see.

The possible argument that Gothic emerged as a language in Scandinavia but at a date early enough for modern-day research to be unable to uncover the earliest shared innovations between Gothic and North Germanic is problematic since the most defining Gothic innovations even predate uniquely North Germanic features. In other words, if indeed a historical tie between Scandinavia and the speech community of the language that would later develop into Gothic existed, we would find Gothic innovations in Northwest Germanic or at least chronologically predating any independent North Germanic innovations.

And with the evidence from Vandalic and Burgundian which inhabited the same region, it becomes unlikely that Gothic emerged as an independent variety in Scandinavia, then relocated to the Vistula region to undergo areal and contact changes with Vandalic and Burgundian all in a matter of a short timespan relative to the number of features that have evolved in Gothic in the earlier periods.

The main issue with the Scandinavian provenance of the Goths is that by the time the Goths become a political actor in contact with the Roman empire in Dacia and the Black sea coast, historical continuity is not necessarily given. In other words, the group called the Goths in the third and fourth century cannot be deemed identical with an emigrating group that may have left Scandinavia several hundred years earlier. To modern-day researchers, a group only claiming Scandinavian ancestry but having formed as a political actor in the Vistula region or even later at the Roman border in the Balkans and the Black Sea would be indistinguishable from a group that indeed collectively remembers Scandinavian origins.[9] The fact that the origin myth was formed after the Goths had become an important political factor is reminiscent of a

---

[8] For the corresponding results, see section 4.11.2 and the discussion of Figure 4.62.

[9] On the mutual independence of factual and fictional notions of *Urheimat* in the context of Germanic origin myths see e.g. Plassmann (2009: 13–27).

post hoc self-attribution of a glorious mythical past. Given the societal and political structures in late Iron-age Scandinavia and Central Europe (as discussed in section 5.1), it is more likely that the Goths in the third and fourth century were of diverse linguistic origin consisting of a number of closely related varieties that had formed a political group but originated from various groups previously seated in the Vistula region.

It is, moreover, not uncommon for groups in European antiquity to trace their ancestry back to a mythological past—especially those that come to considerable political and military power. One prominent example of this is the Roman Republic and Empire which, according to their founding mythology, were descended from Aeneas who was originally from Troy. Founding mythologies are commonplace rather than the exception and fulfil predominantly mythological needs of explaining. This means that a heroic origin story is more desirable for a political group or a Roman historiographer than a true account of the likely origins and is often constructed (cf. Hachmann 1970: 451). Moreover, the purported ancestry lies hundreds of years back—likely beyond the reach of orally passed on stories. In the Germanic context, these myths have a special importance as many Germanic-speaking groups in the late Antiquity had their own origin myths. These origin myths even constitute a type of literature in that time period named *origo gentis*. The stories included in the origines gentium predominantly feature narrative motifs of migration, exploration, and colonization of a new territory (Wolfram 1990). The most important examples is the arrival of the Saxons in Britain under the leaders Hengist and Horsa (cf. Plassmann 2009: 65–66).

In conclusion, there is little linguistic evidence for the hypothesis of the Gothic language, or any Eastern Rim language for that matter, originating in Scandinavia. Moreover, we can conclude, in accordance with the historical sciences (cf. Heather 1996), that the most likely linguistic *Urheimat* of the Gothic language lies in the area south of the Baltic sea in the eastern part of Germania. At the very least we can assert that the *linguistic* origins of Gothic are perfectly compatible with an indigenous emergence of the language in modern-day Poland.

5.3.2 Widening the view: Vandalic and Burgundian

Besides Gothic, we know of several scarcely attested Germanic languages (sometimes called *Trümmersprachen* 'fragmentary languages'), almost exclusively associated with eastern Germania. One exception is Lombardic which is deemed a West Germanic language in the current consensus view (cf. Nedoma 2017: 883). These scarcely attested languages share a common record tradition insofar as the circumstances under which the linguistic record was formed are similar.

They are all attested in the second quarter of the first millennium AD when the speech communities first come into contact with the Roman empire. Around the third century, the records grow of scattered linguistic material in Roman historiography and ethnogeography. The vast majority of these records contain names of political figures associated with the political units of the regions in the eastern Germania. It needs to be noted that Germanic onomastics is an important source for linguistic enquiry in cases where the source material is scarce. This is facilitated by the fact that early Germanic names usually consist of one or more name elements derived from common words. Thus we find names such as the name of the ruler *Theodoric* which is a Latinized version of a name derived from the Gothic name elements *þiuda* 'people' and *reiks* 'ruler'.

The contact of these groups intensifies during the fifth century when some of these speech communities relocated to parts of the Roman empire. The Vandals, for example, cross the Rhine in the early fifth century and move southwards through Gaul and the Hispanic peninsula to establish a permanent political presence in northern Africa in the mid-fifth century. Similarly, the Burgundians arrive at the western slopes of the Alps during the early and mid fifth century and form a kingdom. Both the rule of the Vandal and the Burgundian kingdoms were short-lived and their power and influence diminished by being absorbed by larger political units in respective regions—the Frankish kingdom in France and the Byzantine empire in northern Africa during the sixth century. Despite the brief duration of the Vandalic and Burgundian political presence in these areas, we see the attestations grow notably as the increased contact with the Roman empire caused native Germanic names to be written in legal documents, on coins, on buildings, and on gravestones. Further, we find native writing, albeit rare, in Roman records such as Burgundian legal terms (e.g. the word *morginegiba* in Latin legal texts; Bleiker 1963: 39) or the Vandalic *Vandal epigram* and Kyrie eleison (both discussed in Hartmann 2020: 85–87). After the demise of the Vandal and Burgundian kingdoms, the attestations continuously fade before vanishing from Latin and early Romance sources by the end of the seventh century.

Their attestation history is in many ways similar to the history of the Gothic language. Gothic, too, was a language prevalent in a Germanic political group in intense contact with the Roman empire. Unlike the Goths, they never had a literary tradition dominant enough to produce the texts Gothic is attested in. However, just like the speakers of Gothic, they were absorbed into the dominant linguistic community, Latin or early Romance in this case.

These groups, the Goths included, cannot be seen as uniform ethnic entities. Rather, they were loose coalitions of people from various linguistic and ethnic backgrounds. What united them in the eyes of the Roman historiographers was their joint political actions (see discussion in Hartmann 2020: 10–13). As a result of this situation, the languages we deem Vandalic, Burgundian, and even Gothic are select attestations of heterogeneous groups which we can describe in much less breadth than their later Germanic sister languages of large corpora containing textual records across a wide time and date range.

Vandalic

The Vandalic language is one of these scarcely attested languages. It is mostly recorded in names and a few common words in northern Africa during the fifth and sixth century. Vandalic shares many archaic features with Gothic and was therefore often regarded as closely related to Gothic and sometimes even identical with Gothic (e.g. Reichert 2009). However, in recent studies, this view has been challenged, outlining the salient differences between the two languages (Francovich Onesti 2002; Hartmann 2020). Most notably, divergent developments between Gothic and Vandalic point to a more distant relationship. For example, we find that Vandalic lacks the Gothic generalized raising of PGmc $*/e/$ to Goth $/i/$ and shows a different outcome for the reflexes of Holtzmann's law (Hartmann 2020: 114–115). The minor changes attributable to a common development—such as monophthongization in stressed syllables—are either easily repeatable changes or likely to arise through areal or contact changes. Moreover, the evidence for the different developments suggests an early divergence between the two languages (Hartmann 2020: 115–121). The main issue with evaluating the Gotho-Vandalic relationship is the relatively archaic form of these languages which is likely, but possibly not solely, a result of their early attestation date. As a consequence, it is difficult to find common developments that are not either repeatable changes or shared retentions. Therefore, it cannot be determined that Vandalic is related to Gothic via a common protolanguage.

Burgundian

The relationship between Vandalic and Gothic is mirrored in the relation between the latter and Burgundian. Although we find fewer clearly divergent innovations, the picture is not as clear-cut as a common development would

demand. Although Burgundian shows the Gothic generalized raising of PGmc
*/e/ > Goth /i/, it retains PGmc *-Vnh- sequences (cf. Francovich Onesti
2008: 278), diphthongs, and inflectional suffixes (cf. Hartmann and Riegger
2022) in contrast to Gothic. Although considered as 'East Germanic' by previous research (e.g. Haubrichs and Pfister 2008; Tischler and Moosbrugger-Leu
1982), the textual evidence does not warrant an indisputable proposal of a
Gotho-Burgundian subgroup.

Other languages
Several other languages with small corpora are commonly associated with the
eastern Germania: Gepidic, Bastarnic, Rugian, and Crimean Gothic (cf. Fulk
2018: 19).

  Gepidic, Bastarnic, and Rugian are so scarcely attested that the corpora
are even smaller than those of Vandalic and Burgundian (cf. Schwartz 1968:
123). Bastarnic, for instance, is only attested in a few names and Romance
loanwords, according to some researchers (cf. Schulte 2011). Crimean Gothic
on the other hand is attested with a reasonably well attested corpus compared with other small Germanic languages. Crimean Gothic is a language
that was prominently first recorded by Ogier de Busbecq, a Flemish-speaking
ambassador in Constantinople in the latter half of the sixteenth century.
He recorded a Germanic idiom from an acquaintance from the Crimean
peninsula.[10]

  Despite some counterarguments, most prominently voiced by Grønvik
(1983), the current state of research has adopted the view that Crimean Gothic
is actually descended from, or closely related to, biblical Gothic (see e.g.
Nielsen 2017; Nedoma 2017: 880: Miller 2019: 4–6; Stearns 1989).

5.3.3 A dialect continuum on the Eastern Rim

The subgrouping of the languages discussed in this section has always been
a matter of debate. In the following, I attempt an evaluation of the evidence
obtained from previous research and the phylogenetic and agent-based models used in this study to approximate an answer to the question of the coherence
of these languages and ultimately a common 'East Germanic' subgroup.

  In all Bayesian inference models, East Germanic was supported with low
clade credibility, meaning that the evidence obtained from this phylogenetic

[10] For a detailed discussion see Nielsen (2017).

model suggests that there is no coherent picture from a phylogenetic viewpoint regarding further subgroupings among the languages Gothic, Burgundian, and Vandalic.

The ABM approach differentiates this view even more: we see that the Eastern Rim behaves similarly in comparison with the rest of the Germanic-speaking area, yet the languages themselves that make up this area are much more distinct. This diversification, moreover, occurs very early on in the simulations, suggesting that these languages diverged early and more rapidly from one another, thus being a region that falls apart into different varieties while still remaining a high-contact area. The spreading of innovations there was high very early, suggesting that the earliest post-Proto-Germanic innovations occurred in this region. The high *alignment* values of this region further suggest that we find these innovations to be unstable and regionally fractured (i.e. having no continuous uniform spread).

Moreover, as outlined in section 5.3.2, Vandalic, Burgundian, and Gothic do not share discernible common innovations that may point towards a common development of these languages. For this reason, we can assert with relative certainty that an East Germanic protolanguage never existed. Moreover, the notion of East Germanic is flawed as it is used in many cases.

At the same time, there is little evidence to suggest that any of the three languages is more closely related to Northwest Germanic. Both Vandalic and Burgundian share no clearly identifiable common innovations with Northwest Germanic beyond features that can be deemed repeatable, coincidental, or chronologically inconsistent (see Hartmann 2020: 121–125; Hartmann and Riegger 2022: 62–67). In the computational models, none of the three languages are inferred to be more closely related to Northwest Germanic (see sections 3.2.5 and 4.11.2).

In a purely cladistical sense, 'East Germanic' implies a subgroup akin to Northwest Germanic or West Germanic with the same properties. As we have seen above, there is little evidence to support genuine East Germanic innovations. However, in previous research, scholars differ strongly in their usage of the term 'East Germanic' and the subsequent assumptions that are stated explicitly or implicitly.[11]

---

[11] It has to be noted that the implicit claims in previous literature are difficult to evaluate as, when not stated directly, the actual scholarly claims can only be inferred from how the term 'East Germanic' is discussed in the surrounding context. Therefore, in the following discussion, the presentation of the interpretations of this term is mostly based on how the individual scholars treat the concept in their discussions.

East Germanic as a protolanguage

The strongest claim about East Germanic as a protolanguage is found predominantly in earlier literature (e.g. Prokosch 1939; Streitberg 1896: 17; Krause 1953: 42–44; Krahe 1948: 21–23; Wrede 1886). Yet also more recent studies invoke the notion of an East Germanic protolanguage in linguistic analysis (e.g. Reichert 2009; Francovich Onesti 2002; Haubrichs 2014). The foundation of this claim is that the earliest split that occurred in Germanic was between Northwest Germanic and East Germanic with both lineages exhibiting common features due to common development. However, as discussed above, the vast majority of those common features can be considered shared retentions (cf. Hartmann 2020; Hartmann and Riegger 2022) which do not suggest a common development as a subgroup. Nevertheless, adherents of this notion view East Germanic as a proper subgroup with discernible linguistic features.

East Germanic as a dustbin-category

One of the more common modern perspectives is the—almost exclusively implicitly stated—notion of East Germanic as a group containing languages which do not belong in the Northwest Germanic clade. Research subscribing to this notion often acknowledges the existence of 'East Germanic' as a valid grouping entity but characterizes Gothic or other minor languages on the Eastern Rim of Germania predominantly in contrast to Northwest Germanic (e.g. Fulk 2018: 12–13; Miller 2019: 6–7). This is not to say that this research assumes East Germanic to be a protolanguage but rather that the treatment of alleged East Germanic features is done by contrasting those with Northwest Germanic innovations.

East Germanic as Gothic

The third scholarly stance is the most agnostic towards the existence of East Germanic of the three positions. This research foregoes the question of the existence of an East Germanic protolanguage by focusing predominantly on Gothic (e.g. Ringe 2017: 241; Voyles 1992: 88; Fortson 2010: 350–353). Here, East Germanic is not so much used as a term itself but as a stand-in for Gothic.

The root of the discussions surrounding East Germanic most likely lie in the fact that still to this day, Gothic remains the 'East Germanic' language most rigorously and frequently scrutinized regarding its phylogeny and position in the Germanic family with modern methods. As it undoubtedly is distinct from Northwest Germanic, it was rightly placed outside of the North and West

Germanic lineages. With the inclusion of Vandalic and Burgundian evidence, however, the coherence of an East Germanic group is called into question.

Instead, it is appropriate to abandon the notion of East Germanic as a subgroup and posit the adoption of a different grouping paradigm for these languages. The term I used before for these varieties is *Eastern Rim languages* which is a naming proposal opting for removing the protolanguage concept the term 'East Germanic' often presupposes. In this view, the Eastern Rim languages were a number of Germanic varieties that simultaneously and independently diverged from common Proto-Germanic in a gradual way, detached from Northwest Germanic. Speakers of these languages lived on the eastern edge of the Germanic-speaking areas in central Europe. Their close proximity and relative linguistic isolation from Northwest Germanic yielded high-contact situations and areal changes which are reflected in the languages at the time of their attestations.

The term *Eastern Rim languages* therefore illustrates the notion that these languages can only be grouped together when contrasting them with Northwest Germanic and via a geographical rather than a linguistic term. Also, this grouping term is not the name of a tree node in a linguistic phylum but joins languages according to horizontal criteria (as e.g. the term 'Balkan sprachbund' does). The term itself is thus rather defined geographically than linguistically. What further unites the languages in this area is that they are the first languages that become detached from Northwest Germanic innovations and develop separately. They do so however not jointly as a group, but rather they develop in different directions.

5.3.4 The development of the Eastern Rim

The roots of the Eastern Rim languages doubtlessly lie in the linguistic situation of late Proto-Germanic. As established in section 5.2.3, the Proto-Germanic area was a patchwork of different dialectal variants of the language and speakers of the eastern part of the linguistic area became gradually dissimilar from the rest of the Germanic region. They did not become jointly detached from the rest of core Proto-Germanic as a subgroup but were geographically at the far end of the dialectal area where innovations and edge effects take place. Potential candidates for these changes are repeatable and chronologically late innovations common in at least two of the languages Gothic, Vandalic, and Burgundian. This includes monophthongizations and word-final devoicing (cf. Hartmann 2020: 112–113) or raising of earlier *e (cf.

Hartmann and Riegger 2022). We cannot say for certain whether the Eastern Rim languages underwent innovations that distanced them from the rest of the area or whether Northwest Germanic underwent innovations that left out the Eastern Rim. Both notions are problematic as they require fundamental changes to have made these languages strongly differ from one another and blocking horizontal transmission in the form of a dialect continuum. On the contrary, it is more plausible that while the Northwest Germanic languages were more strongly connected, the languages on the Eastern Rim had, due to their geographical locations less exposure to Northwest Germanic while still forming a dialect continuum with the west. However, we cannot demonstrably show that there have been observable contact changes between Northwest Germanic and the Eastern Rim languages (see for discussion Hartmann 2020: 121–123). This is because we either cannot clearly attribute changes to contact situations or because the contact in the western border region of the post-PGmc Eastern Rim dialect continuum was too short-lived to spark any lasting, detectable contact-induced changes. In other words, it was, in the early stages, likely a slow divergence process between Northwest Germanic and the Eastern Rim languages that, probably geographically conditioned, became more and more different without fully breaking the connections. This is also what the computational model results suggest (section 4.11.2). Therefore it is a superfluous question to ask which linguistic area underwent innovations that detached it from the rest of the linguistic area. It is rather a simultaneous dissimilation process with one of the main variables being geographical distance and edge effects.

Moreover, the Eastern Rim being a dialect continuum meant that the different varieties developed independently, undergoing innovations of their own and retaining features that spread fully in Northwest Germanic. The reason for this detachment from the western areas is likely extralinguistic as some sociocultural factors may have contributed to the different developments of the northwest and the east. Archaeologically, for instance, we find that the eastern regions of Germania are notably different regarding agriculture and material culture (cf. Heather 2009: 8).

It has sometimes been discussed whether there was in fact an asynchronous development regarding linguistic innovations in the east and the northwest. Grønvik (1998: 148), for example, suggests that the earliest disruption of Germanic linguistic unity occurred when a more innovative Northwest Germanic branch became detached from a more conservative East Germanic branch. The question of synchronicity of development is likely not applicable to this scenario. The divergence of Eastern Rim languages from one another and

Northwest Germanic is to be placed in the same period. Therefore it is unlikely that the eastern languages remained conservative (or even unchanged) for a considerable time while Northwest Germanic underwent several innovations. Moreover, if a rapidly changing Northwest Germanic would have left behind a conservative East Germanic area, we would not observe a fragmentation of these languages from the very beginning. It is undoubtedly the case that while this dissociation in the east was ongoing, the remaining area continued to undergo innovations, but the early divide of the Eastern Rim languages was unlikely to have been a necessary after-effect of Northwest Germanic innovations. More likely, these processes were synchronous and the fragmentation in the east not caused by a faster developing Northwest Germanic.

The roots of the fragmentation of the Eastern Rim and the common innovation of Northwest Germanic lie in the same phenomenon. While in earlier periods, when the Proto-Germanic dialect continuum was intact, changes could spread easily among the Proto-Germanic variants, after the Eastern Rim languages had become increasingly detached, the subsequent innovations only spread in the north and the west. In that view, we cannot speak of one 'innovative' and one 'conservative' variant. The disruption of the Germanic continuum and the independent development of the individual Eastern Rim languages and Northwest Germanic occurred synchronously. It is more the case that Northwest Germanic continued the Germanic dialect continuum whereas we find fragmentation in the east.

While Burgundian was probably closer to Gothic for a longer period of time (perhaps due to geographical proximity)—in these early stages, Vandalic, for instance, was likely not more different from Gothic than from Northwest Germanic when considering that a similar number of innovations sets apart Vandalic from both Gothic and Northwest Germanic (see Hartmann 2020: 99–106). Only over time did the different trajectories of change become accelerated. This was aided by the upcoming movement of populations and smaller groups into eastern Europe which cemented the Gothic, Vandalic, and Burgundian split beginning in the second century AD (cf. Todd 2009: 149). There, in fact, we can assume a splitting event which drew apart a dialect continuum of languages that up until that point had already been diversifying for some time. The view that the (south-)eastward migrations were responsible for the cementing of the divide between Gothic and other languages is shared by, for example, Nedoma (2017: 879), but others such as Penzl (1985: 161) view the departure as the most important step in the diversification of the Eastern Rim. According to this, the Eastern Rim continuum cannot have lasted longer than the second century AD.

The runic inscriptions that are sometimes taken to be 'East Germanic', for example the Kowel spearhead and the ring of Pietrossa, would then be definitively Gothic (for detailed discussion of the current state of research on runic inscriptions suggested to be Gothic see e.g. Fulk 2018: 22–24; and Miller 2019: 6–7). The ring of Pietrossa is a metal ring with a fourth-century inscription found in modern-day Romania and the spearhead inscription found in Kowel, Ukraine dates to the third century (Miller 2019: 6–7). Their time of attestation points towards a language stage that followed the stages of Gothic when it was part of the Eastern Rim dialect continuum.

We cannot determine with certainty which innovations took place before and after this split of the Eastern Rim languages from this dialect continuum but there are enough identifiable areal changes that might have occurred during the time of the dialect continuum. Therefore we can assume that by the time Gothic, Vandalic, and Burgundian are attested between the fourth and fifth centuries, the languages had experienced centuries of independent development.

What needs to be stressed at this point is that this analysis does not assume the groups of the Vandals, Goths, and Burgundians to have existed as coherent groups on the Eastern Rim at the time of the fragmentation. Rather, these three languages, speakers of whose ancestors we know originated in the Eastern Rim area, are momentary snapshots taken at a later time that indicate a great linguistic diversity in the Eastern Rim. Moreover, the properties we would expect to see had there been a common protolanguage are missing. Insofar they can be seen as linguistic samples from an area that exhibits linguistic common traits only as a result of mutual contact and the relatively isochronous diversification away from a larger ancestral entity.

5.4 Core-Germanic

5.4.1 The beginning: Core-Germanic vs. Northwest Germanic

Core-Germanic came into existence by the fragmentation of the Germanic east which had been brought forth by a disconnect between the two areas (see section 5.3.4). The East–Northwest dichotomy is therefore a product of the linguistic method of the tree model that creates a language node after a furcation event. We do see this furcation event in the east, yet this leaves the remaining Germanic area in a position where one geographic region becomes detached from the other and results in the area being cleft into two geographically defined regions. The larger part of both regions continues Germanic unity more or less unchanged for a short amount of time whereas in the east we cannot determine the existence of a protolanguage at all.[12]

This view was not shared especially by the earlier literature until the idea of Northwest Germanic as a subgroup was prominently supported by several researchers in the 1950s (Grønvik 1998: 70–71). Chief among those is Kuhn (1955) who suggests a split of East Germanic away from the rest of the continuum, proposing Northwest Germanic–East Germanic as the earliest Germanic split.

Voyles (1968: 734–736) further made the case that Gothic was the language to split first from Proto-Germanic thus leaving the remaining linguistic group as a clade of its own using exclusively phonological data. The early proponents of Northwest Germanic were met with some criticism which proposed reformulations of the theory. Further, Nielsen (1989: 11) defined Northwest Germanic as only consisting of Ingvaeonic and North Germanic under the exclusion of Old High German. He argued in favour of this grouping with reference to changes that are not found in Old High German.[13] Today, Northwest Germanic as a clade is uncontroversial in most research on Germanic linguistics; an extensive review of research history on Northwest Germanic is provided by Grønvik (1998).

The resulting picture is that of languages in the east independently drifting away from a common core relatively synchronously (see especially section 4.11.2). In the technical sense, according to the tree model, we would then need to assign both parts as individual nodes. While this is methodologically rigorous, it might not be the ideal framework to describe the linguistic situation at this time. It is, in fact, not a bifurcating event where the developmental pathways of two communities part, but a phenomenon where a smaller part of the entire area disintegrates, leaving most of the earlier network intact. This issue is captured in the ABM results where the east shows parameter values that indicate early innovation spread with simultaneous non-uniformity of innovation spread. The earliest innovations therefore likely occurred in the east as a result of the simultaneous disintegration of the varieties in this region.

Therefore, I adopt the term 'Core-Germanic' to be used as a less loaded nomenclature describing the remaining linguistic entity after the genetic departure of the Eastern Rim languages. This term is by no means intended to

---

[12] Among others, Seebold (2013: 59–60) has previously voiced this view; however, he assumes an East Germanic that departed from the core continuum by migration. See also Kuhn (1955: 45) for an early statement of this idea and Penzl (1985: 163) for additional discussion.
[13] For further discussion see Stiles (2013) and below.

replace the previous term 'Northwest Germanic' but to introduce a term that captures a different aspect of this stage of the diversification process. In this study, I use both terms to describe different angles of the same phenomenon: 'Northwest Germanic' is hence used to refer to the *linguistic* grouping of the languages Old Frisian, Old Norse, Old High German, Old English, and Old Saxon. It refers to the phenomenon that, after the linguistic ties to the Eastern Rim languages are severed, a new node in the family tree model is created under the exclusion of Gothic, Vandalic, and Burgundian. This term fails to capture the fact that it is not an equidistant split comparable to that between North and West Germanic where two areas develop into different directions but rather a shattering of unity and linguistic exchange in one smaller part of the entire area as detected in the computational simulations (section 4.11.2). Therefore we are presented with a situation where one part continues the previous unity and the other part disintegrates. The term 'Core-Germanic' therefore describes the situation better as it directly outlines the continuity between the Proto-Germanic and the Northwest Germanic language continuum.

Concretely, Core-Germanic is intended to denote the Germanic variety that continued to develop as a language *in situ* after the diversifications on the eastern rim of the former Proto-Germanic area. I introduce this term specifically to discourage the interpretation of Core-Germanic and the Eastern Rim as a symmetric east–west split. Indo-European cladistics knows this 'asymmetric' or 'continuation-type' split from the breakup of Proto-Indo-European where Anatolian first diverged from the ancestor language, leaving behind a still intact continuum which would continue to exist for some time after that (cf. Mallory 1989: 26–28). In that way, an analogy can be drawn from Core-Germanic to Core-IE which is often used to depict a similar situation in the history Indo-European (see Ringe 2017: 7).

5.4.2 The decline of Core-Germanic

As we have established above, Core-Germanic was a continuation of Proto-Germanic in a smaller area. Naturally, it continued to undergo innovations for some time before its demise.

There is no doubt that the innovations we take as common Northwest Germanic are indicative of this continuation as they suggest a common language lived on in western and northern Germania (Ringe and Taylor 2014: 14). The nature of this common language was, very likely, unchanged from the Proto-Germanic starting position—namely a dialect continuum (cf. Haugen 1984: 140–141). Yet other than in the east where we see no common developments but only horizontal spread and contact-induced changes, Core-Germanic in fact was a dialect continuum whose varieties were linguistically close and connected enough for discernible changes to spread along this network of varieties. The question is therefore not whether Core-Germanic was a continuum but to what degree and we can state with relative certainty that the region remained fairly interconnected from the northern shores of the Baltic sea to the central parts of modern Germany.

Equally salient, however, is the fact that we can only make out few changes that can be attributed to the post-PGmc stage in the west and north.

For example, one of the most salient changes is the lowering of PGmc $*\bar{e}$ to PNWGmc $*\bar{a}$ (cf. Ringe and Taylor 2014: 10–13). The changes are so few that the computational analyses conducted in section 3.15 do not yield reliable results for this clade. Tree support is low and credible intervals are large for this subgroup. In those samples where it does surface as a clade, the branch length shows a mean between 0.14 and 0.15, that is, an existence of 140 to 150 years in total. As a reference, West Germanic is estimated to have a mean existence time of 0.45 (i.e. 450 years in the Hardbounded-VarRates model) (in both cases see Table 3.11).

The diversification time of this area is equally problematic to pinpoint. The earliest diverging trajectories of the northern region and the area to the south can be approximately dated between 400 and 200 BC with Old Norse gradually drifting away especially from the more southern languages.

This supports the argument that while we can speak of a Core-Germanic group, it is rather the direct successor of Proto-Germanic (i.e. a Proto-Germanic without the Eastern Rim) where the last innovations of Germanic unity in these regions were carried out. The small number of clear detectable changes indicates that these innovations percolated through a still tightly connected but already dissolving Core-Germanic continuum (for extensive discussion of these changes see Ringe and Taylor 2014: 10–40).

The end of the Core-Germanic continuum had likely started only a few centuries after the common Proto-Germanic period ended. The tentative dating of this time on the basis of computational evidence can be set at around 300 to 200 BC given that the final days of common Proto-Germanic are dated between 500 and 400 BC.

Other dates set for the existence of Northwest Germanic are 500–200 BC (Grønvik 1998: 145). Some researchers posit an even later date of the

Northwest Germanic break-up dating it to the fourth or fifth century AD (e.g. Markey 1976).

There is not much evidence to shed light on the proceedings of this division between north and south, yet it had the effect that the ties between the two linguistic areas were gradually severed and exchange networks between both areas were weakened and the ties to the respective core areas strengthened. Whether this reshaping of the linguistic landscape had intralinguistic reasons or was rooted in sociopolitical shifts needs to remain unanswered at this point (see also discussion in section 5.4.3).

The result of this split is, however, not a neat cut which detached both communities from one another. The evidence rather points towards a situation in which North Germanic influence still persisted well into the time after the two communities had separated (cf. Stiles 2013: 26–28; Ringe and Taylor 2014: 10). For example, both Old English and Old Norse retain a reflex of the PGmc ending *-urz (see Stiles 2013: 30). Although we can assert that both areas gradually gain distance from one another, it evidently took time for both communities to be separated and not exchange innovations.

The computational ABM results further show that it is especially the Northern area that is insulated as we see the parameters, such as linguistic spread across the sea, diminish. This isolation ruptures the further development of the agent communities in the simulation. There is, however, evidence for continued influence as especially the Old English area (and the Old Frisian to a lesser degree) remains close to the North Germanic area.

In this line of reasoning, the date of 300–200 BC marks only the point of the *beginning* of disintegration of both communities—not the end. We might reasonably assume a looser network of exchange between southern North Germanic and northern West Germanic continuing for several centuries without actually shifting the main orientation of the West Germanic group to a closer cladistic alignment with the north.

The definitive end of North and West Germanic as reference systems of their own, embedded in a larger but looser Northwest Germanic exchange area is marked by the emergence of individual languages in the early first millennium AD. At the latest, the emerging migration age disruptions saw the demise of this entity with the development of individual languages in the north and the south. The development of Proto-Norse around 500 AD (Grønvik 1998: 139) would be such an event.

The much-debated status of the earliest runic language (between 200 and 500 AD) would then fall in the time of the earliest Proto-Nordic period (on this notion see also Grønvik 1998: 119; Nielsen 2000: 290–293) where Core-Germanic influence and north–south exchange was still highly prevalent. The Northwest Germanic features noted in previous research (e.g. Nielsen 1995: 121; Penzl 1989) therefore do not contradict this view. It is rather the case that, with linguistic methods, we can establish a date of 200 BC as the start of North and West Germanic diversification; due to mutual influence and a prolonged time as part of a common linguistic area, the clearly discernible features of Proto-Norse show up at a time late enough that earliest Runic still exhibits mostly Northwest Germanic properties. Thus Antonsen (1965: 36) concludes that as the Runic inscriptions in the common era lack clearly Gothic features, they have to be considered Northwest Germanic. This, of course, demonstrates mainly that Runic was not equal to Gothic; the argument presented in the aforementioned research assumes a binary system in which lack of Gothic features makes a closer relationship with Northwest Germanic more likely.

5.4.3 Linguistic and social orders in transition

I close the discussion of Core-Germanic with a tentative outlook on the sociocultural factors that may have contributed to the rapidly succeeding diversification events of the Eastern Rim and Core-Germanic. With this out-look, I attempt to reopen the question of whether there are archaeologically identifiable social phenomena that coincide with, and are perhaps causally linked to, the linguistic diversifications in these areas.

For the reasons given above, it might be important to view Northwest Germanic not as a lineage created by splitting from a larger body, but rather as a continuation of the core Proto-Germanic continuum after the Eastern Rim languages had broken off. Instead of seeing the post-Proto-Germanic period as dominated by a Northwest Germanic clade and multiple languages in the east, the Eastern Rim languages depart from the continuum while in the remaining 'Core-Germanic' regions, now reduced to the north and the west, the original continuum lingers on. Before Core-Germanic itself breaks up into two sub-continua, a small number of innovations take place in this area.

This means, however, that although the Core-Germanic continuum lived on for some time, the linguistic separation of the Eastern Rim languages marked the beginning of the end of this continuum. It is unclear how long Core-Germanic continued to exist; it might have been a relatively short time of only a few hundred years (perhaps not even more than 200 years in total). In any case, what we see is a period of 200 years at the beginning of the second half of the first millennium BC in which the Germanic family is severely ruptured by a disintegration process in the east and, shortly thereafter, in the southwest and the north. We may observe the fractioning of Germanic unity as two events (Eastern Rim disintegration and north–west split) but they are perhaps not exclusively independent events. It is possible that the two events are discrete snapshots of a longer trend in early Germanic, where a cataclysmic period in Germanic linguistic history yielded the fracture of the existing order. This period coincides with the transition between Bronze and Iron age in northern Europe (Van Coetsem and Bammesberger 1994: 145–147), yet it is difficult to align this period with concrete observations.[14] Nevertheless, it is beyond the scope of this study to identify sociohistorical or political factors that may have converged in this period, triggering this linguistic upheaval. A task for future research therefore lies in the investigation of this period of linguistic disruption in central and northern Europe, for which certain starting points for such inquiry can be identified.

Indeed, the Iron Age in northern Europe coincides with archaeologically identifiable changes, yet these changes coincide with different time periods than outlined by Van Coetsem and Bammesberger (1994). It is not the introduction of imported iron material culture that saw changes to societal structures in the Germanic-speaking area, it is rather the development and improvement of the population's own iron technology that occurred in this timeframe in the transition between the early and the late Pre-Roman Iron Age (see e.g. Brumlich 2020: 150–152). This leads to an archaeologically discernible discontinuity in northern and central eastern Europe (see Martens 2017). At the same time, we find a difference in societal organization between the southern and the northern part of the Core-Germanic area, leading to a north–south contrast especially in Jutland (see Brandt 2014; Martens 2014). Taken together, the societal restructurings identified by archaeological research fall exactly into the timeframe of repeated linguistic diversification events. It would therefore be a forward-looking endeavour to scrutinize the linguistic and archaeological finds in more detail.

---

[14] Van Coetsem and Bammesberger (1994: 187–188) suggest that the similarities between sociopolitical factors and linguistic breaking points may be spurious.

5.5 West Germanic and its daughters

5.5.1 West Germanic origins

The West Germanic period followed the unified linguistic stage of Northwest Germanic. Yet as discussed before in section 5.4.3, the emergence of West Germanic did not represent a clear disconnect with North Germanic. We need to interpret the NWGmc diversification as a slow process of opposing orientation of linguistic contact networks that commenced in the south of this area with the earliest distinct properties. These, despite starting the process of diversification, were in the beginning not numerous enough to cause a sudden disconnect between the northern and southern area.

How to view this linguistic group has been debated ever since Kuhn's endorsement of Northwest Germanic. In the beginning, scholars suggested that West Germanic was not in fact a Germanic subclade but rather a geographically defined group of related languages (see discussion of these viewpoints in Nielsen 1989: 92–93). Yet subsequent research clearly demonstrated several common innovations in West Germanic, thereby excluding the possibility that West Germanic was a mere geographical region containing already differentiated languages. Among the earliest proponents of this string of research is Voyles (1971) who shows that West Germanic is not a loose conglomerate of languages but a linguistic phylum with a reconstructible protolanguage. Other researchers have since followed this line of reasoning (e.g. Ringe and Taylor 2014; Stiles 2013) such that a West Germanic protolanguage is uncontroversial.

The common features identified as the most compelling are, for example, gemination of consonants, most notably preceding earlier $*j$ (cf. Ringe and Taylor 2014: 48–54).[15]

This view is paralleled in the phylogenetic findings which show strong support for a West Germanic clade. Likewise, the ABM simulations result in coherent trajectories of the languages Old English, Old Frisian, Old Saxon, and Old High German at the beginning while, early on, the North Germanic region follows a distinct development. This is also found in individual parameter developments where West Germanic in most cases is a more coherent set of languages during the simulated times between 200 BC and 200 AD.

---

[15] For an extensive review of the common West Germanic developments see Grønvik (1998: 96–117) and Stiles (2013).

It is important to stress that a notion of a West Germanic protolanguage does not exclude a gradual diversification process. The existence of Proto-West Germanic can be attributed to a strong West Germanic exchange network along which several exclusive innovations occurred. Yet nevertheless, North Germanic influence especially in the border regions is likewise observed as innovations (Stiles 2013: 30–32).

The early and middle stages of West Germanic therefore were a clear sub-clade of Germanic, sharing many features and being strongly interconnected. As discussed earlier, this does not exclude the fact that there are several innovations that only parts of this subgroup share with North Germanic exclusively.

It is thus reasonable to view West Germanic as a strongly connected network of speech communities of varieties of West Germanic, so as to make it possible to reconstruct a protolanguage. The linguistic distance of West Germanic varieties from one another was smaller than to the north which gave a common point of reference. However, the distance was not so strong as to exclude outside influence. This is especially true for the northernmost varieties of West Germanic.

5.5.2   West Germanic disintegration

The further development of the West Germanic continuum from this point onward is a process of gradual dissimilation of linguistic communities especially in the later periods of West Germanic unity. In this period, we expect to see the early signs of further diversification in the form of emerging subgroups and independent languages. The issues often discussed in this regard are the Ingvaeonic question, and, nested therein, the question of North Germanic influence, the status of Old High German, and the Old High German–Old Saxon relationship.

Research into this matter, however, is intricate as we see various parallel innovations that may distort the analysis (cf. Grønvik 1998: 95).

Ingvaeonic and the status of Old High German

Ingvaeonic is a long-standing discussion point in Germanic cladistics. The term was first used in linguistic contexts in earlier research focusing on socio-cultural aspects of the speakers of late West Germanic (e.g. by Wrede 1924) and is predominantly used for a hypothetical grouping of the languages Old Frisian, Old English, and Old Saxon. The term Ingvaeonic itself goes back to the concept of a grouping unit back to Pliny's subgrouping of Germanic tribes (Ludwig et al. 2017: 986).

As it is often the case with such subgroups, there is no unified definition of what Ingvaeonic is assumed to be. Whereas this term can be used to refer to the three languages in the northern part of the West Germanic linguistic area, a grouping also implies the existence of a determinable subgroup. While current research by no means assumes an Ingvaeonic protolanguage, the issue is worth addressing as it has implications both on how we view late West Germanic developments and the relative position of Old High German within West Germanic.

It is clear that Ingvaeonic can be easily defined by what it is not. Old High German does not share several features that were prevalent in the Ingvaeonic area. Moreover, Ingvaeonic languages exhibit areal innovations found in North Germanic (see, for discussion, Stiles 2013). Yet both observations are predominantly geographical properties of Ingvaeonic. The Old High German varieties are, due to their position on the southern edge of the Germanic-speaking area and extensive contact with non-Germanic languages to the south and west, geographically detached from the northern, and apparently more densely interconnected, languages in the coastal regions of the North Sea (cf. Stiles 2013: 24). In this environment, both contact and non-contact related innovations spread more easily along the societal networks in this area yielding a gradual detachment of Old High German varieties. In many regards, Old High German is seen as more conservative (e.g. Stiles 2013: 18).

Old Saxon is, in many ways, in a medial position, both geographically and linguistically as we find influences both typical of Ingvaeonic and Old High German. For example, in weak verb inflection (2nd class), it shows both the Ingvaeonic form and the form that Old High German exhibits (see Stiles 2013: 20). Because of these idiosyncrasies, some previous researchers have suggested that Old Saxon was a mixture language between the Old High German varieties and Ingvaeonic (e.g. Nielsen 1989: 79; and Grønvik 1998: 139).[16]

The phylogenetic analysis shows a peculiar situation: Ingvaeonic has full clade support in the models where only innovations are counted but no clade support in all other models. The reasons for this oddity lie in the conceptual architecture of substitution models. When we see such a stark contrast in clade support depending on the weighting of the base innovation rate, it

---

[16] For detailed discussion and outline of the Old Saxon material and its relation to other Germanic varieties see Krogh (1996, 2013).

means that the Ingvaeonic innovations we see are numerous enough to be informative of a subgroup but can be explained better by other tree topologies. In the case of Ingvaeonic, it is likely a confluence of two factors: Old Saxon takes a medial position between Old Frisian and Old English on the one hand and Old High German on the other. It shares, as discussed above, areal innovations with both sides, which shifts the weighing away from Ingvaeonic and, additionally, the remaining Ingvaeonic innovations are regarded by the model as easily influenced by randomness and are, in turn, weighted less since the non-Ingvaeonic innovations of Old Saxon are exclusively shared with Old High German. In this way, the computational phylogenetic topology is both an artefact of the method and indicative of an important pattern: while many of the Old Saxon innovations identified certainly align more with Ingvaeonic than with Old High German, we need to regard those as less reliable. This is to say that Ingvaeonic as a grouping has merit insofar as it describes a linguistically more aligned network of mutual influence and contact. However, it is difficult to demarcate it to the south—if not impossible. The pattern we see in the linguistic record is indicative of a gradual transition of Ingvaeonic and Old High German with Old Saxon in a medial position, exhibiting contact features both with the north and the south, despite being slightly more northwards-oriented.

In the ABM context, West Germanic is modelled much more as a gradually diversifying area where especially geographical proximity is a predictor for similarity in the development. The spread in this area is propelled forward from two epicentres in the north and the south. Elevated spreading parameters in the Old High German area along with lesser probabilities of spread across natural barriers to the west and east suggest that a part of West Germanic family disintegration can be explained by southern linguistic innovations radiating northward and northern innovations being shared in the northern regions of the West Germanic area.

This is a crucial point in the treatment of late West Germanic: the issue is not so much to identify genetic subgroups that withstand any level of scrutiny but to take the sub-relationships of West Germanic as a question of *degree* rather than discrete categories. Thus, we can identify an Ingvaeonic point of reference for the northern West Germanic varieties which entailed influence from North Germanic and a tighter exchange network but the southern parts of this area are more southward-oriented, giving Old Saxon its characteristic medial position between the linguistic communities of the south and the northwest.

The Anglo-Frisian controversy

The Anglo-Frisian controversy—the proposal (e.g. by Karstien 1939: 12–13; Nielsen 1981: 253–259) to group together Old English and Old Frisian in a coherent subgroup has been challenged by an increasing number of researchers (see overview in Stiles 1995). It needs to be noted that the problems underlying the scholarly debate of Anglo-Frisian as a subgroup are the same that underlie Ingvaeonic. At least, they stem from the same cause—the late West Germanic continuum. We know that Old Frisian and Old English were in close contact, mainly because speakers of this group lived in close proximity to one another at least until the departure of the linguistic ancestors to Old English to the British isles. We have seen above in the case of Ingvaeonic how much mutual influence there was, especially between the northern West Germanic languages. This mirrors the Anglo-Frisian situation where we expect strong horizontal transmission of innovations and extensive contact. It is therefore a given that, through the lens of diversification in a closely connected dialect continuum, the lines between genetic (clearly vertical) relatedness via a common protolanguage and similarities transmitted via a dialect continuum are far from clear-cut.

Nevertheless, scholars like Fulk (2018: 26) and Colleran (2017: 135–136) suggest that the Anglo-Frisian ancestor hypothesis is valid. In the latter study, linguistic changes and extralinguistic evidence are employed to propose an ancestor-linked relationship between Old English and Frisian.

The phylogenetic evidence (i.e. non-significant clade support) points towards a situation that cannot be captured with a vertical transmission model. Rather, it supports the thesis of Anglo-Frisian as a phenomenon of a dialect continuum.

Old English and Old Saxon are closely adjoined in the ABM simulations, but cross-cut different linguistic areas. Moreover, their modelled developments are distinct to a degree that suggests primarily geographical reasons for their similarity. This is in line with Stiles (1995) who concludes that there is little support for an Anglo-Frisian protolanguage and that the similarities we observe are most likely a by-product of two gradually differentiating languages submitted to a high-contact continuum with other closely related languages.

It is without doubt that individual pairings of discrete snapshots of a dialect continuum as we have in the form of Old Saxon, Old English, and Old Frisian exhibit exclusive features that raise the question of a shared ancestor. Yet the context of these changes is such that no coherent common development can be established for these languages. The shared features that have been adduced in previous research are not numerous and exclusive enough to securely infer a shared subgroup between any pair of the three aforementioned languages. This is supported by both the phylogenetic and agent-based model results (sections 3.2.3 and 4.11) where the topological certainty is not strong enough to assume further subgrouping.

The role of subgroups in West Germanic

Following the conclusions regarding possible further subgroupings in West Germanic, it needs to be stressed that neither computational nor traditional approaches yielded conclusive results for clear subgroups. This is not necessarily indicative of our lack of abilities to find a coherent subgroup or due to data scarcity. Instead—and this seems the more likely conclusion—there might not be any discernible subgroups in West Germanic. Two viewpoints can be taken here: either we do not find subgroups because we lack the data and methods or we cannot find subgroups as there are none. Both views result in the same lack of establishable pairings but are fundamentally distinct in their theoretical assumptions. The models and traditional examinations alike suggest West Germanic to be a highly fluid and geographically determined region where innovations are spread due to proximity rather than group cohesiveness, a fact which is currently recognized by the majority of researchers (e.g. Kortlandt 2017; Stiles 2013). This results in multiple unclear or crosscutting innovations that are not a result of common genetic relationships. In this view, there *cannot* be subgroups in West Germanic in the classical sense that there is a West and North Germanic. The differences arise due to geographical proximity and contact rather than due to common developments during a protolanguage period. This means that while we can establish that Old English and Old Frisian show similar developmental features when contrasted with Old High German, these similarities are the result of geographical distribution rather than a shared common ancestor.

Dissolution of the continuum

The point in time when West Germanic dissolved is hard to determine in a situation where a continuum of languages dismembers. Arguably, it is impossible. While its beginnings can be tentatively defined as a gradual shift away from a joint Core Germanic ancestor with continued contact with North Germanic neighbours, West Germanic, in some sense, does not have such an endpoint. There are two main angles one can take on the end of West Germanic: the early end and the late end. Both viewpoints are equally valid as they depend on one's definition of the West Germanic continuum.

The early end of West Germanic

In one interpretation, akin to the situation in Northwest Germanic, West Germanic starts to dissolve when the first languages started to diverge. This was likely the case when the outermost languages at the edges of the West Germanic area underwent their own innovations. When the earliest ancestor of Old High German or Old Saxon acquired innovative features, some of them left some areas of West Germanic untouched. Following this definition, many scholars such as Grønvik (1998: 139, 145) date the end of West Germanic some time in the second or third century AD.

The phylogenetic estimates support this dating as they estimate a break-up of West Germanic between 170 BC and 370 AD. The ABM results see a diversification of this area at 200 AD at the latest (see e.g. Figure 4.70).

What we have to keep in mind, however, is that despite these dating attempts, the contact and horizontal transmission of innovations remained extensive, as the analyses of the Anglo-Frisian and Ingvaeonic hypotheses show. Moreover, we need to be aware of the fact that, especially for the West Germanic area, a 'diversification date' is unlikely to exist. As it is a continuous process, we can only pinpoint the approximate dates where the languages start to become distinct to a noticeable degree. But the diversification process had likely started long before this point.

The late end of West Germanic

In the interpretation of West Germanic as a more or less homogeneous dialect continuum, the period ends with the definitive disruption of this contact network by the dissociation of Old English (or its ancestor language) from continental West Germanic. Although Old English developed most of its core innovations before the break-off (cf. Grønvik 1998: 82), its departure cemented the rupture of the unity among the West Germanic languages.

In some sense—in the literal sense—the West Germanic continuum has never ended. After Old English had left the continental network, the existing structures, contacts, and innovations continued to evolve: continental West Germanic is still a dialect continuum (cf. Seebold 2013: 58). The languages today are not nearly as mutually intelligible as they were two thousand years ago, yet the linguistic borderlines are still continuous and oftentimes mutually intelligible on both sides. As long as there are gradients of linguistic distances between Flemish, Dutch, Frisian, Low German varieties, and High German varieties, where linguistic difference increases with spatial distance, the West Germanic continuum lives on between the modern languages and their varieties.

5.6 The development of the Germanic family—final considerations

5.6.1 The central aspects of Germanic phylogeny

The history of Germanic can be tentatively sketched with the following outline:

(1) Around 2000 BC (± ~ 300 years), the Indo-European variety that would later become Germanic broke off from a Central Indo-European ancestor. In the time that follows, Germanic developed as an independent branch of Indo-European whose speakers inhabited the rough geographical area of southern Scandinavia and the southern shores of the Baltic sea in central Europe. This Germanic was a language made up of a network of closely related varieties that were linguistically similar and remained in close contact for several centuries.

(2) It is then at 500 BC (± 100 years) that the original continuum was disrupted by a diversification event in the eastern part of the Germanic-speaking area. Likely due to their geographically edge position and the resulting prolonged detachment from the more interconnected northern and western parts of the continuum, several languages underwent independent innovations that set them apart both from one another and from the core area. Due to their geographical proximity, a small number of areal features arose and were shared, but in general, these languages underwent independent developments. At a later stage, speakers from this area would relocate to the east and south, thus consolidating the disintegration of the Eastern Rim. In contact with the Roman empire three of these groups would then be called 'Goths', 'Vandals', and 'Burgundians'. Their group-specific origins are unknown but are likely to have formed at a later stage during the time of migration. What we can observe, however, is that the three groups linguistically originate in the earliest diversified area of Germania.

In this context, it is important to note that what we observe is not an east–northwest split, but a fragmentation of the Eastern Rim languages with the northwestern regions of Germania merely maintaining the original stability.

(3) After the Eastern Rim languages had diversified, the original Germanic unity continued for some time in the west and north. What continued was specifically the unity of the earlier contact and dialect continuum. For approximately another 200 to 300 years, this Core-Germanic network remained intact and went on developing new innovations. These were few in number, however, as a diversifying element of that period prompted further diversification.

Around the year 300–200 BC, we see newer linguistic regions emerging in the south and the north that gradually drifted away from one another. This may have started with several late Core-Germanic innovations not being shared by the entire linguistic area, and a potential sociopolitical reorientation of speech communities toward their closest reference points in the north and south, producing a growing north–south divide in this region.

(4) From then on, the ties between the north and the south became looser; both regions continue contact and exchange, areal changes, however, only spread to the nearest adjacent regions instead of penetrating the area as a whole. By this time, common innovations in the north and the south respectively had become numerous enough and the group-coherence sufficiently distinguished that we can speak of supraregional protolanguages emerging in the north and the south: North Germanic and West Germanic.

(5) In the first centuries of the common era, the West Germanic language that had itself arisen only ~ 400 years earlier started to come apart. The once relatively homogeneous protolanguage gave rise to gradually more independent lower-order groupings. This effect is most salient when comparing the northwest of the area (i.e. the north sea coastal region) and its south (i.e. the southern varieties that would later become the Old High German varieties). Yet still, this area remained a continuum where adjacent areas are closer to one another than to the respective ends of the geographical distribution of West Germanic.

The definitive end of West Germanic as a coherent and at least somewhat interconnected group is marked by the split of Old English through migration to the British Isles. The now reduced continental West Germanic varieties continued to diverge gradually until the rise of the individual regional varieties that are attested in textual records.

The history of the Germanic languages can therefore be framed in terms of the dichotomy of disruption and maintenance of continua and exchange networks. We see repeated events of gradual disintegration in an evolving speech community from the Proto-Germanic continuum until the end of antiquity. In this time, Germanic unity fractured and shrunk, divided up and persisted in different stages of linguistic history. In this way, Germanic does not lend itself to clear genealogical characterizations—it is rather best captured by frameworks that take into account the specific processes present in dialect continua.

This viewpoint is not new—researchers have, in the past, repeatedly called for a reframing of certain aspects of Germanic cladistics to be understood in terms of dialect continua (e.g. Stiles 2013; Grønvik 1998: 136; and Roberge 2020: 414).

The processes in these continua follow sociopolitical lines in addition to lines of linguistic networks of contact and exchange that are maintained and severed. Thus, we do not observe clear splits between languages, and where linguistic communities are spatially separated, such as the Gothic and the Old English communities, they had begun to diverge from the Germanic/West Germanic core some considerable time before their separation. A clear split is only visible post hoc after several centuries and with a wide enough scope of view. The actual processes themselves were long under way by the time the data show overt splits between linguistic varieties.

Hence, Germanic phylogeny is an intricate mesh of varieties that show relationships to one another which arose through an almost 1,000-year process of gradual and incremental dismantling of the core unity.

5.6.2 Attempt to construct a stemma

Having established that the early Germanic relationships cannot be captured in a conventional stemma, this section aims to alter the existing family tree to arrive at the stemma below. There, dashed lines between languages indicate a dialect continuum.

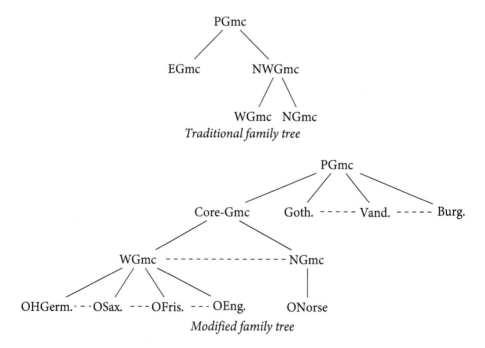

Traditional family tree

Modified family tree

The issue with this stemma is that each node suggests a coherent or at least in part reconstructible protolanguage which is not the case for Core-Germanic and the subsequent Northwest Germanic continuum. What Proto-Northwest Germanic represents is the late stage of the continuum before disintegrating into North and West Germanic sub-units. Early Core-Germanic is therefore identical with Proto-Germanic and only slowly transforms into a Northwest Germanic continuum. Moreover, it cannot capture the relative proximity of the languages in the continua. For example, it does not capture the medial position of Old Saxon which is influenced by Old High German from the south and the ancestors Old Frisian and Old English from the northwest. This situation is therefore ill-represented by a tree diagram where node proximity can only be represented by drawing two nodes next to one another. However, the depiction of a genetically close language cluster is more difficult.

The following circle plots (Figures 5.1 to 5.4) are an attempt to show different horizontal relationships of the early Germanic languages in consecutive stages. In these plots, solid circles indicate individual (proto)languages with

Figure 5.1 Germanic unity until ~ 500 BC (± 100 years)

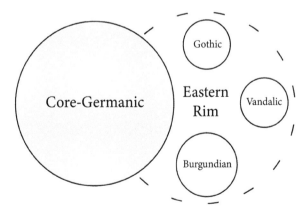

Figure 5.2 The fragmentation of the eastern part of the area and the formation of a geographically defined contact zone *Eastern Rim*

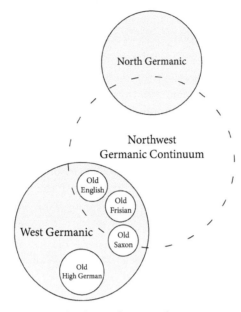

Figure 5.3 The diversification of Core-Germanic

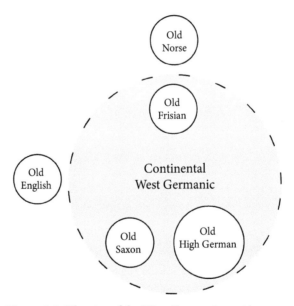

Figure 5.4 The rise of the West Germanic continuum

empty circles representing coherent dialect continua. Dashed empty circles denote dialect continua where mutual influence is less strong or solely based on contact.

Following this is a gradual transition of a unitary Core-Germanic into a well-connected but already differentiating Northwest Germanic continuum until ~ 200 BC (± 100 years). In the eastern parts of Germania, the Eastern Rim begins to dissolve, with the loose continuum finding an end at the start of the Gothic, Vandalic, and Burgundian movements.

In the time that follows, North and West Germanic begin to differentiate further with some languages being more affected by the fading Northwest Germanic continuum especially on the contact points between the speech communities. This situation gradually progresses until ~ 200 AD (± 100 years).

In the late period, we find the disintegration of the West Germanic languages very much completed with the continental West Germanic languages maintaining a loose continuum. The diversification of common West Germanic is completed at the latest with the detachment of the Old English speech community during the fifth century AD.

6

Computational tree and wave models—final remarks

This study has shown that a computational wave-theory approach using ABM simulations can yield valuable insights for real-world applications. Applied to the Germanic diversification case, it was shown how tree-based phylogenetics and wave-based simulations detect different parts of a diversification process, each model with its own advantages and disadvantages.

For the languages Gothic, Burgundian, and Vandalic, for example, the phylogenetic model did not yield reliable results. Further, the specific inter-relations between the West Germanic languages remain uncertain under this model. The wave-model ABM could step in where the phylogenetic model yielded inconclusive results, showing that East Germanic was a gradual diver-sification process with strong cross-linguistic contact on the eastern rim of the Germania region rather than a true subclade of Germanic with its own protolanguage. Equally, it showed subclades below West Germanic cannot be established as the diversification process in this region likely did not run along the lines of tree-like splits. It, too, was a dialect continuum influenced by con-tact lines between languages and geographical proximity. ABM wave models are, however, computationally more resource-intensive and custom-built for the specific task at hand.

This chapter will be a retrospective, a reassessment of computational wave-based and tree-based models for genealogical diversification which out-lines their strengths and weaknesses. This meta-level perspective is intended to map out a path forward to refining and improving the computational methods in the future. The discussion about advantages and disadvantages of wave-like ABM implementations over Bayesian phylogenetic models in section 6.1 will be purely from a computational standpoint. The following section 6.2 discusses tree and wave implementations from a theoretical and interpretive perspective.

Germanic Phylogeny. Frederik Hartmann, Oxford University Press. © Frederik Hartmann (2023).
DOI: 10.1093/oso/9780198872733.003.0006

6.1 Rethinking wave models under a computational paradigm?

Firstly, the advantages of tree-based phylogenetics and the wave-based ABM presented in this study, as is the case with most quantitative and computational approaches, is that they follow a stringent and repeatable process in which every decision can be criticized and improved. In this respect, they complement more traditional methods in historical linguistics by making certain aspects of linguistic problems quantifiable and more transparent. While it is not possible in a Bayesian ABM framework to replicate a study exactly because of the inherent randomness in the task, nevertheless the individual parts of the models can be replicated, changed, and extended according to the researcher's modelling preferences.

The main advantage of an ABM approach is that, beside modelling linguistic diversification as a gradual process, it takes extralinguistic parameters into account. Especially factors that contribute to the geographical position of a speech community with regard to its neighbours, and the adjacent landscape can be fed into the analysis. Introducing this geographical variable complements the purely linguistic analysis by making it sensitive to the factors at play in a geography-dependent diversification process such as the emergence or breakup of a dialect continuum. Agent-based models can also model a variety of different pathways of linguistic spread which can be adjusted based on the current linguistic theory. Issues such as founder effects due to population growth and migration can also be taken into account.

Due to this parametric versatility and the gradual nature of the underlying process, it can show diversification nonlinearly. In other words, convergences and divergences between languages or speech communities that are confined to certain periods of a diversification process can be detected. This makes it easier to model temporally limited contact and horizontal convergence events between speech communities.

The disadvantages of the agent-based models are mainly related to their complexity. For Bayesian phylogenetic inference, there are currently many different off-the-shelf methods that follow a building blocks system where a researcher can choose each model part based on the theoretical underpinnings of the problem at hand. Agent-based models are, mainly by virtue of their flexible nature, inherently more complex to set up as the basic model architecture needs to be implemented from the bottom up. Moreover, because of this complexity, the interpretation of the results is more intricate and needs a variety of different complementary methods such as clustering algorithms or regression models to extract valuable insights.

Further, they are very much resource intensive. Even extensively using parallel computation on large-scale computing clusters it can take fifteen to twenty days for 200,000 simulations to finish. In comparison, Bayesian phylogenetic algorithms take from minutes to a few hours to finish their calculations. Running multiple agent-based models or repeatedly improving certain model aspects proves difficult when the time delay between model programming and model results is a matter of weeks. Of course, there are ways to improve the efficiency and smaller models can run faster in less time, but, for the time being, simulating several thousand agents in one simulation over the course of more than 1,000 simulated years is resource intensive nevertheless.

It is clear that the agent-based model proposed in this study is only one of the possible set-ups of a computational wave-theory implementation. That is, there are numerous possibilities to set up such a model. What this study has demonstrated, however, is that the results obtained from ABM implementations can complement tree-based methods such as Bayesian phylogenetics.

As described above, the main advantage of ABMs is simultaneously their biggest weakness: whereas Bayesian phylogenetics is based on more or less straightforward algorithms that make use of the dimensions of a tree (branch lengths and rates, tip dates, branching order, and branching times), agent-based models are much more flexible in how they can be implemented. The upside of this feature is that the researcher can incorporate many problem-specific factors into the model. The downside is that, due to this property, each model is unique to a problem and knowledge cannot be effectively shared between a specific ABM implementation for one language family and an implementation for another. The main lines of discussion will pertain to the model parameters that are similar between both models. Unlike ABMs, Bayesian phylogenetic model architectures can more easily be applied to other problems by switching out the data and the priors.

It is also clear that the model in this study is merely the beginning of hopefully subsequent research into the best modelling techniques, limits, and benefits of Agent based models used for wave-like language diversification. Many of the aspects of the model presented here need to be refined in the future—Germanic thus served as a test case for an early computational wave model.

Some of the aspects in particular that will need to be investigated further are:

Data types: Can ABM wave models model the innovation and spread of features other than raw innovations? Research is needed into how a model needs to be designed to simulate the spread of competing variants (e.g. lexical).

Weighting of innovations: Is there a benefit of using only a specific subset of innovations to be modelled (only phonological innovations or only regular sound changes)? Do the different types of change need to be differently weighted?

Missing data estimation: Does an ABM implementation benefit from approximating missing data? When datapoints are missing, is there an alternative to leaving them out of the evaluation? Techniques exist in other fields of quantitative research that compensate for missing data. For example, multiple imputation is widely used to recover approximate values of a missing variable based on the other variables in the dataset. It is to be investigated whether missing datapoints can effectively be modelled themselves in the simulation to reduce their impact.

Improvement of optimization: The optimization process used in this study is very resource-intensive and inefficient. How can the posterior estimation of the ABM be improved to save time and computational resources?

Model comparison and model choice: In this study, I only presented one model as an early example of an implementation using ABMs. Yet unlike with Bayesian phylogenetic models which have a variety of goodness-of-fit estimations for model comparison, there is no consensus in how the fit of agent-based models can be compared. Although there are possible starting points such as the sum of the posterior model fit, measures for model comparison need to be found to make it possible to generate multiple competing models for one problem particularly for the linguistic datasets.

Partitioning of the model: As it stands, the ABM proposed here contains a large number of variables and factors that each contribute to the result in some form. Yet it is to be investigated whether certain modules of the model can function on their own or if a smaller model will yield more precise answers to more narrow-scope questions. For example, it might be possible to devise a small model just to investigate the relative chronology of a few innovations. The geographical spread of innovations and the resulting isoglosses could potentially be modelled very precisely in a limited geographical area.

Finally, it is important to compare the results obtained in this study with the findings in Agee (2018) since this allows comparisons to be drawn between three methods in quantitative cladistics: Bayesian phylogenetics, agent-based models, and historical glottometry.[1]

The results of the study show five subgroupings with high subgroupiness values, namely West Germanic, Ingvaeonic, Northwest Germanic, Teuto-Saxon, and Anglo-Frisian in descending order of subgroupiness (Agee 2018: 49). These findings are partially supported by the investigation at hand where West Germanic and Northwest Germanic were meaningful subgroups identified by the agent-based and phylogenetic models. However, in the phylogenetic approach, Northwest Germanic was found to be only weakly supported as a subgroup (see e.g. section 3.2.5) which was taken as a sign that it was relatively short-lived (see section 5.4). Yet in the study by Agee (2018), we see that Northwest Germanic is calculated to be the third-best supported subgroup. This difference might be due to the fact that exclusively shared innovations are very important in historical glottometry (Agee 2018: 12–13) which can enhance subgroups that share few but mostly exclusive innovations.

Further, the subgroups Anglo-Frisian and Ingvaeonic found by Agee (2018) are not supported by the findings in this study. The reason for this might be that, as mentioned above, historical glottometry weights exclusively shared innovations more strongly. On the other hand, ABM and Bayesian phylogenetic approaches account for randomness and parallel innovations which results in less weight being put on individual innovations.

It is worth noting that, interestingly, the Teuto-Saxon subgroup that Agee finds is reflected as a meaningful subgroup in the phylogenetic model (section 3.2.3). This indicates a parallel in results between the tree-based phylogenetic algorithm and the glottometric wave-model implementation while the ABM approach finds Old High German and Old Saxon to be not more closely aligned (see Figures 4.54 and 4.55). One interpretation of this is that both the phylogenetic and glottometric approaches weight aspects of the data higher, which the agent-based approach does not. Since the ABM takes temporal and geographical factors into account, this could mean that the closeness between the languages in the data becomes insignificant when adding a geographical variable and an innovation spreading mechanism. It cannot be decided at this point which interpretation comes closer to the actual diversification process, yet this observation itself is an important starting point for future investigations. More research is needed to examine in which situations this discrepancy between ABM approaches and phylogenetics/glottometry arises and what the underlying causes are.

---

[1] For a comparison between the modelling strategies themselves see section 6.2.

6.2 Of hammers and nails

The prize of solving these issues in the future is the promise of computational wave models that can investigate linguistic families with a wide range of geographical and horizontal factors underlying their diversification by using a complementary method to Bayesian phylogenetics, which can yield novel insights into the processes of change. Concretely, aspects of the history of, for instance, the Romance family could be better understood. This links back to the discussion of the usefulness of tree and wave model in linguistic research, as with a reliable and empirical wave model method that captures temporal and spatial diversification, wave-like spreads might gain explanatory power which they did not have before.

The question is therefore not *whether* tree models can and should be used in computational cladistics but rather *in which cases.* In the present study, the tree model, despite yielding valuable insights into the support of certain relationships, does not fully capture the geospatial and dialectal disintegration processes in Germania. The wave model implementation was more useful in outlining the general trajectories of Germanic diversification. Yet this does not devalue the tree model per se but the agent-based approach presents a novel method to complement the robust tree models.

There is, however, an epistemological issue raised in the applications of either method. A famous quote by the twentieth-century psychologist Abraham Maslow states, paraphrased, that if the only tool available is a hammer, every problem will be treated like a nail. This hammer and nail problem is a widely referenced metaphor for scientific bias towards known methods. In its most simple interpretation, the questions we have about real-world issues might be answered using the tools we have available—from the perspective of the tools themselves. In the worst case, our methods to approach a topic shape our understanding of the process not by leading us to new insights but by suggesting that the obtained results are the real process.

This viewpoint is intended as a caveat for any discussions regarding computational tree or wave models. Although we can analyze the linguistic data both with tree-based and wave-based methods, we have to be aware that the results of each method will mostly fit within the framework of the method itself. It is therefore crucial to be aware of the limits of every method. Not in the sense of where the model is inaccurately making assumptions about model-internal issues but where the model entirely fails to capture a vital aspect of the real-world process. In other words, we must be aware that both wave and tree models in computational contexts are blind to certain aspects regarding which they are not merely inaccurate but which they a priori disregard as an artefact of the method itself. It is the researcher who is responsible for contextualizing the results of each method to gain a more complete understanding of certain aspects of the real-world process.

This discussion above and of what follows, therefore, is a call to assume a meta-level viewpoint in which the issue of tree and wave models is not a question of *either/or* but what each method, in its limited scope, can contribute to a broader understanding of the subject matter.

It is therefore clear that the tree model as a tool for genealogical analysis cannot—and should not—be abolished. If anything, the analysis has shown that only a confluence of both methods can yield results that take a broad scope of linguistic diversification into account. This means that we cannot discard one or the other method when computationally analysing linguistic relatedness.

In general, we have to distinguish between *modelling* language diversification and how we assume the *actual* diversification process of a particular language has developed. As pointed out numerous times (Drinka 2013; François 2015), the pure tree model has numerous issues when assumed to be the only form of linguistic diversification. However, as a modelling technique, computational tree model implementations capture certain scenarios better than wave implementations. For example, tree and subgroup dating in computational Bayesian phylogenetics runs along a rigorous site-dependent tree that approximates intermediate stages and can take into account and even reflect uncertainty in the diversification process. Moreover, linguistic diversification resulting from migration processes (such as, perhaps, early Indo-European) is best captured in a tree model. In many cases, a highly horizontally influenced diversification process may even result in poor subgrouping results with regard to clade support, making the model indicate that the process is more intricate than can possibly be captured in a tree. In non-computational contexts, the advantages of a tree are even more pronounced as the standard comparative method operates in a way where it assumes relatively homogeneous protolanguages (Fox 1995: 128–133). At the end of a comparative reconstruction stands a tree-like confluence of linguistic features into a single protolanguage.

There is no doubt that a computational wave-theory implementation can yield more insights than a Bayesian phylogenetics could on its own but it is exactly this: a complement. In the Germanic case, the tree model as a phylogenetic *analysis* tool is of vital importance and by no means subordinate to the agent-based wave model implementation. However, the *results* have shown that Germanic in particular is less well captured in a pure tree-like display which would entail more abrupt splits between groups with a following relative isolation. Rather, Germanic is a highly connected web of mutual influence and the diversification processes take place in gradually disintegrating communities in a dialect continuum. Whereas for Germanic, this question can be answered quite clearly in favour of a wave-like diversification process, this does not translate to other language families. The finding that for Germanic a gradual process is preferred neither invalidates the tree model being applied to other language families nor does it show that tree-model-based analysis practices are to be abolished. In a sense, we need both approaches to be applied to a problem in order to arrive at the conclusion that one might be preferred over the other. Whether or not a tree-like scenario can be subsumed under the wave-theory as François (2015: 171–172) attempts, would be a different question not related to the issue of modelling.

As the ABM approach is a computational implementation of the wave theory, it is important to examine its relationship to historical glottometry, the most prominent quantitative wave-model implementation to date as outlined in François (2015), tested and fleshed out in Daniels, D. Barth, and W. Barth (2019) and applied to the Germanic family in Agee (2018).

The most salient difference between the agent-based approach proposed in this study and historical glottometry is that, while the former is a computational simulation model, the latter is a calculation method based on a series of equations operating on the number of shared or cross-cutting innovations in various possible subgroups. In other words, while the ABM simulates pathways of diversification across time, historical glottometry calculates the credibility ('subgroupiness') of a certain subgroup within an innovation-based dataset as a numerical value (François 2015: 181–184). Therefore, both methods are, despite being quantitative in nature, substantially different in their complexity and assumptions. Historical glottometry outputs a single value based on weightings of shared innovations governed by a predetermined set of equations whereas the ABM approach seeks to give the model freedom to infer parameter values from the data during the process, outputting a variety of different parameters, linguistic distances, and geographical properties.

Due to this difference, both methods are differently complex in their output interpretation. Yet the simulation-based, and therefore more complex, agent-based model has advantages concerning the ability to directly account for fluctuations and uncertainty in the data as well as to report the uncertainty regarding specific parameters and model results. Historical glottometry has, in its current form, no metric which can report the 'significance level' of subgroupings to be accepted as valid. Some studies consider subgroups to be valid above a certain number of exclusively shared innovations, yet depending on different cutoff points, the accepted subgroups may include false positive due to many parallel innovations (cf. Daniels, D. Barth, and W. Barth 2019: 106). This is moreover the case when the subgroupiness values of two groupings are very close to one another as small errors or uncertainties regarding individual innovations can distort the values.

Further, this can lead to shared innovations being weighted higher than in other methods. The results in the study by Agee (2018), for example, show both Ingvaeonic and Anglo-Frisian as valid subgroups (Agee 2018: 49). However, the agent-based approach and the phylogenetic algorithm found these two subgroups to be spurious and likely to be an artefact of the linguistic discretization of languages in a diversifying dialect continuum.

Lastly, the factors considered for the computation of the results are, crucially, different since historical glottometry is a purely linguistic computation method that attempts to determine subgroups based on the association strengths between individual languages as part of subgroups with shared and cross-cutting innovations. On the other hand, the agent-based approach models the diachronic development of a linguistic family by taking into account geographical and linguistic factors.

As a complementary method for modelling linguistic diversification, the agent-based approach has therefore proven effective in modelling aspects of linguistic history that trees are not able to fully capture. Moreover, the model is the first computational and non-descriptive wave-theory implementation that takes diachrony and temporal progression into account, which previous methods such as historical glottometry do not. It is therefore an improvement on previous methods which have frequently been criticized for not modelling the temporal aspect of wave-like diversification processes (e.g. Jacques and List 2019).

Appendix

Table A.1 Innovation dataset

Innovation	GO	ON	OE	OF	OS	OHG	VAND	BURG
*ē > *ā/ [+stress]	0	1	1	1	1	1	0	0
*-ī > *-i / _#	0	1	1	1	1	1	?	?
*-ō > *-u/ [-stress] _#	0	1	1	1	1	1	0	0
*-wū > *-u	0	1	1	1	1	1	0	0
*a > *u/ _*m	1	1	1	1	1	1	?	?
*a > *i / [-stress] _ n	1	1	1	1	1	1	?	?
*ai > *ē	1	1	1	1	1	1	1	0
*u > *[o]/]σ [-high]	0	1	1	1	1	1	0	0
*ō > *ū / _ [σ	0	1	0	1	1	1	1	0
*V12 > *V̄ 3	0	1	1	1	1	1	0	0
*kʷ > *kw	0	1	1	1	1	1	?	?
*kw > *kkw	0	1	1	1	1	1	?	?
dual > Ø	0	1	1	1	1	1	?	?
3 imp. > Ø	0	1	1	1	1	1	?	?
pres. pass. > Ø	0	1	1	1	1	1	?	?
*-miz, *-maz > *-maz	0	1	1	1	1	1	?	?
*-aiz- > *-ez-	0	1	1	1	1	1	?	?
*-ded-, *-d- > *-d-	1	1	1	1	1	1	?	?
voc. > Ø	0	1	1	1	1	1	?	?
*-um(m)ē > *-um	0	1	1	1	1	1	?	?
*-ēm > *-um	0	1	1	1	1	1	?	?
*-ū-	1	1	1	1	1	1	0	?
-u(-) (appearance)	0	1	1	1	1	1	?	?

Table A.2 Innovation dataset (cont.)

Innovation	GO	ON	OE	OF	OS	OHG	VAND	BURG
-u(-) (spread)	0	1	1	1	1	1	?	?
*þrij- > *þrijō, * þrijǭ	0	1	1	1	1	1	?	?
*tigiwiz	0	1	1	1	1	1	?	?
*hwī	0	1	1	1	1	1	?	?
*hir > *hēr (lengthening)	1	1	1	1	1	1	?	?
*hir > *hēr (lowering)	1	1	0	0	1	1	?	?
*jūz, *jūt > *jīz, *jīt	0	1	1	1	1	1	?	?
*uban-	0	1	1	1	1	1	?	?
Null subject	0	1	1	1	1	1	?	?
*hwaþeraz	0	1	1	1	1	1	?	?
*-(i)ji- > *-ī-	1	1	0	0	0	0	?	?
*d (/ð/) > /d/ / r _	1	1	1	1	1	1	?	?
-a	1	1	0	0	0	0	?	?
*-ā-	1	1	0	0	0	0	?	?
*-z- ~ *-s-; *-d- ~ *-þ-	1	1	0	0	0	0	?	?
*u > *u, *o	0	0	1	1	1	1	0	1
*a, *ą > Ø / _ (*-z)#	0	0	1	1	1	1	1	0
*-u > Ø / CC _#	0	0	1	1	1	1	0	0
*zw, *dw > *ww	0	0	1	1	1	1	?	?
*V[ð]V > *V[d]V	0	0	1	1	1	1	0	0
*Vwu- > *Vu	0	0	1	1	1	1	0	0
*-z > Ø	0	0	1	1	1	1	0	0
*Cj > *ʋjʋj	0	0	1	1	1	1	0	0

Table A.3 Innovation dataset (cont.)

Innovation	GO	ON	OE	OF	OS	OHG	VAND	BURG
*C(l/r) > *CC(l/r)	0	0	1	1	1	1	?	?
*Ṽ# > *V	0	0	1	1	1	1	?	?
*-i, *-u > Ø	0	0	1	1	1	1	?	?
*-ō(r) > *-ā(r)#	0	0	1	1	1	1	?	?
*-Ṽ r# > *-Vr	0	0	1	1	1	1	?	?
*ō > *ū / _n#	0	0	1	1	1	1	?	?
*C(C)V > *C(C)V	0	1	1	1	1	1	?	?
*-jj-, *-ww- > *-ij-, *-uw-	0	0	1	1	1	1	1	?
*-ī- ~ *-ija- > *-i- ~ *-ija-	0	0	1	1	1	1	?	?
*-i- > Ø / -t/d- _ -d-	0	0	1	1	1	1	?	?
*walid- > *waldē	0	0	1	1	1	1	?	?
*/x/ > *[h] / #_	0	0	1	1	1	1	1	0
*z, *r > *r	0	1	1	1	1	1	0	0
*-izd- > *-īd-	0	0	1	1	1	1	?	?
*-īn > *-ī	0	0	1	1	1	1	?	?
dat., inst. > dat.	0	0	1	1	1	1	?	?
*-ī	0	0	1	1	1	1	?	?
*ijōz > *sijā	0	0	1	1	1	1	?	?
*unsiz > *uns, etc.	0	0	1	1	1	1	?	?
*-nVssī	0	0	1	1	1	1	?	?
1g., 3sg. subj. > 3sg. subj.	0	0	1	1	1	1	?	?
*-an	0	0	1	1	1	1	?	?
*-nd-ija- > *-nd-ijō-	0	0	1	1	1	1	?	?

Table A.4 Innovation dataset (cont.)

Innovation	GO	ON	OE	OF	OS	OHG	VAND	BURG
inf. + *-ja-	0	0	1	1	1	1	?	?
*namô (neut.) > *namō (masc.)	0	0	1	1	1	1	?	?
2sg. *-s	0	0	1	1	1	1	?	?
2sg. past indic. > subj.	0	0	1	1	1	1	?	?
*-Ø > *-u/[+heavy] _	0	0	1	1	1	1	?	?
*i (cl. I) > *e (cl. IV/V)	0	1	1	1	1	1	?	?
*mati > *matja- : *sagją-	0	0	1	1	1	1	?	?
*hehaww > *heuw	0	0	1	1	1	1	?	?
*hehēt > *heht	0	0	1	1	1	1	?	?
*-i- > Ø	0	0	1	1	1	1	?	?
*-dēs	0	0	1	1	1	1	?	?
*-st	0	0	1	1	1	1	?	?
*-ik	0	0	1	1	1	1	?	?
*-CijV- > *-CjV-	0	0	1	1	1	1	?	?
[-voice] > [+voice]	0	0	1	1	1	1	?	?
*sī > *si(j)u	0	0	1	1	1	1	?	?
*ijē, *iją̄	0	0	1	1	1	1	?	?
*wilī	0	0	1	1	1	1	?	?
*þits/*þitt(i)	0	0	1	1	1	1	?	?
*sa > *siz	0	0	1	1	1	1	?	?
*þrīz	0	0	1	1	1	1	?	?
*twō + *n	0	0	1	1	1	1	?	?
*dēdē > *dādī	0	0	1	1	1	1	?	?

Table A.5 Innovation dataset (cont.)

Innovation	GO	ON	OE	OF	OS	OHG	VAND	BURG
*þar > *þār; *hʷar > *hʷār	0	0	1	1	1	1	?	?
*þē	0	0	1	1	1	1	?	?
*baum	0	0	1	1	1	1	?	?
*obat	0	0	1	1	1	1	?	?
*rindā	0	0	1	1	1	1	?	?
*waskan	0	0	1	1	1	1	?	?
*wolkn	0	0	1	1	1	1	?	?
*gagang(?) > *gang	0	0	1	1	1	1	?	?
*waht	0	0	1	1	1	1	?	?
[+nasal] > Ø	0	0	1	1	1	0	?	?
*e > *i / _m	0	0	1	1	1	0	?	?
*a, *o > [+front]	0	0	1	1	1	0	?	?
*-lþ- > *-ld-	0	0	1	1	1	0	?	?
*sl > *ls	0	1	1	1	1	0	?	?
*ā, *ē > *ē	0	0	1	1	1	0	?	?
*h > Ø / _CC	0	0	1	1	1	0	?	?
*-z > Ø	0	0	1	1	1	1	?	?
*VfV, *VbV > *VbV	0	0	1	1	1	0	?	?
*-iw- > *-aw-	0	0	1	1	1	0	?	?
*-ō	0	0	1	1	1	0	?	?
*-i- ~ *-ija- > class II	0	0	1	1	1	0	?	?
hund-	0	0	1	1	1	0	?	?
3pl.	0	0	1	1	1	0	?	?

Table A.6 Innovation dataset (cont.)

Innovation	GO	ON	OE	OF	OS	OHG	VAND	BURG
*-ōs	0	0	1	1	1	0	?	?
*-ô > *-a	0	1	1	1	1	0	?	?
-ianne	0	0	1	1	1	0	?	?
*-nō- ~ *-na- > class III	0	1	1	1	1	0	?	?
*a, *o > [+nasal] / _ [+nasal]	0	0	1	1	1	0	?	?
*a > [+round]	0	0	1	1	1	0	?	?
*lagdun : *satte	0	1	1	1	1	0	?	?
*sindi	0	0	1	1	1	0	?	?
*sīn > Ø	0	0	1	1	1	0	?	?
*siz > Ø	0	0	1	1	1	1	?	?
*sek > Ø	0	0	1	1	1	0	?	?
*Þ- + *-s	0	0	1	1	1	0	?	?
*hi- ~ *he-	0	0	1	1	1	0	?	?
*stā-	0	0	1	1	1	0	?	?
*lais- ~ *laiz-	0	0	1	1	1	0	?	?
*i- ~ *e- > *hi- ~ *he-	0	0	1	1	1	0	?	?
*nigun	0	0	1	1	1	0	?	?
*hwat	0	1	1	1	1	0	?	?
*hwaþeraz	0	1	1	1	1	0	?	?
*a > [+front]	0	0	1	1	0	0	?	?
*ō > *ā / [-stress]	0	0	1	1	1	0	?	?
*-w-	0	0	1	1	0	0	?	?
*-ē	0	0	1	1	0	0	?	?

Table A.7 Innovation dataset (cont.)

Innovation	GO	ON	OE	OF	OS	OHG	VAND	BURG
*-s, -þ, -aþ	0	0	1	1	0	0	?	?
*þaizō, *þaimi	0	0	1	1	0	0	?	?
*hwa-	0	0	1	1	0	0	?	?
*hū	0	0	1	1	0	0	?	?
V > Ø / _(C)#	0	1	1	1	1	1	?	?
i-umlaut	0	1	1	1	1	1	0	0
V2	0	1	0	0	1	1	?	?
sé	1	1	0	0	0	0	?	?
*-hw-, *-h- > -h-	0	0	1	1	1	1	?	?
*-dē > *-dō	0	0	1	1	1	1	?	?
*au > ō	0	0	0	0	1	1	?	?
ao > ō	0	0	0	0	1	1	?	?
CR# > CVR#	0	0	0	0	1	1	?	?
*-anu	0	0	0	0	1	1	?	?
-īs	0	0	0	0	1	1	?	?
*-u > Ø / [+light] _	0	0	0	0	1	1	?	?
Ø > -u / [+heavy] _	0	0	0	0	1	1	?	?
1g., 3sg. indic. > 3sg.	0	0	0	0	1	1	?	?
-ōno	0	0	0	0	1	1	?	?
*þi- ~ *þe-	0	0	0	0	1	1	?	?
*hwi- ~ *hwe-	0	0	0	0	1	1	?	?
imu	0	0	0	0	1	1	?	?
-ta	0	0	0	0	1	1	?	?

Table A.8 Innovation dataset (cont.)

Innovation	GO	ON	OE	OF	OS	OHG	VAND	BURG
*a > *æ	0	0	1	1	0	0	?	?
* Ṽ # > V̄ ; *Ṽ # > V; *V# > Ø	1	0	0	0	0	0	?	?
*e, *i > i	1	0	0	0	0	0	0	1
*ē1 *ē2 > *ē1	1	0	0	0	0	0	?	?
*i, *u > [ɛ, ɔ] / _ /r, h, hʷ/	1	0	0	0	0	0	0	1
*h (/x/) > /h/	1	0	0	0	0	0	1	0
-ggw-, -ngw- > -/ngw/-	0	0	0	0	0	0	?	?
*ē > a / [+stress] _	1	0	0	0	0	0	?	?
h > Cα / _ #Cα	1	0	0	0	0	0	?	?
*ai > /ɛ/	1	0	0	0	0	0	1	0
*au > /ɔ/	1	0	0	0	0	0	1	0
*z > s	1	0	0	0	0	0	0	?
*i > Ø / _ *jV	1	0	0	0	0	0	?	?
*a > Ø / _z#	1	0	0	0	0	0	?	?
*-(i)ji- > *-ī-	1	1	0	0	0	0	?	?
*-mz > -m	1	0	0	0	0	0	?	?
r/n > l	1	0	0	0	0	0	?	?
Thurneysen's Law	1	0	0	0	0	0	?	?
ē, ō > /ɛ̄, ɔ̄ / / _ V	1	0	0	0	0	0	?	?
*-jj-, *-ww- > -ddj-/-ggj-, -ggw-	1	1	0	0	0	0	0	?
*-z > Ø / V r/s _	1	0	0	0	0	0	?	0
*fl- > þl-	1	0	0	0	0	0	?	?
*þ > t / _ s	1	0	0	0	0	0	?	?

Table A.9 Innovation dataset (cont.)

Innovation	GO	ON	OE	OF	OS	OHG	VAND	BURG
-aiwa, -aima, -aina	1	0	0	0	0	0	?	?
Ø > j / _ i	1	0	0	0	0	0	?	?
*-n-	1	0	0	0	0	0	?	?
sijai-	1	0	0	0	0	0	?	?
siju-	1	0	0	0	0	0	?	?
-uh > -h	1	0	0	0	0	0	?	?
V > Ø / _-uh/-ei	1	0	0	0	0	0	?	?
*-aiz- > -ai	1	0	0	0	0	0	?	?
*-r-iz > -r-jus	1	0	0	0	0	0	?	?
-a, -o, -o	1	1	0	0	0	0	1	0
-o : -e	1	0	0	0	0	0	?	?
þata	1	0	0	0	0	0	?	?
*-īn- > Ø	0	0	0	0	0	0	?	?
*-at	1	1	0	0	0	1	?	?
*-assu-	1	0	0	0	0	0	?	?
*-ā-	1	1	0	0	0	0	?	?
*-es-	1	0	0	0	0	1	?	?
-and-s	1	1	0	0	0	0	?	?
1g., 3sg. > 1g.	1	0	0	0	0	0	?	?
hʷa	1	0	0	0	0	0	?	?
*hwō	1	0	0	0	0	0	?	?
iusiza	1	0	0	0	0	0	?	?
godai	1	0	0	0	0	0	?	?

Table A.10 Innovation dataset (cont.)

Innovation	GO	ON	OE	OF	OS	OHG	VAND	BURG
alþeis	1	0	0	0	0	0	?	?
*hir > her	1	0	0	0	0	0	?	?
sauil	1	0	0	0	0	0	?	?
*fõr ~ *fun- > fon ~ funin-	1	0	0	0	0	0	?	?
tunþus, fotus	1	0	0	0	0	0	?	?
sehʷun	1	0	0	0	0	0	?	?
wato, watins, etc.	1	0	0	0	0	0	?	?
iddj- ~ iddjed-	1	0	0	0	0	0	?	?
sitan, ligan	1	0	0	0	0	0	?	?
*anguz > aggwus	1	0	0	0	0	0	?	?
nahtam	1	0	0	0	0	0	?	?
*taujan	1	0	0	0	0	0	?	?
stōþ	1	0	0	0	0	0	?	?
wesun	1	0	0	0	0	0	?	?
ufar	1	0	0	0	0	0	?	?
hausjan	1	0	0	0	0	0	?	?
gadaúrsun	1	0	0	0	0	0	?	?
taihuntehund	1	0	0	0	0	0	?	?
*-ô, *-ō > -ō	0	1	0	0	0	0	?	?
*ār > er > ir / [-stress]	0	1	0	0	0	0	?	?
*eu, *iu > i > e	0	1	0	0	0	0	?	?
*ai > ei	0	1	0	0	0	0	1	0
ǫ > u; a > e	0	1	0	0	0	0	?	?

Table A.11 Innovation dataset (cont.)

Innovation	GO	ON	OE	OF	OS	OHG	VAND	BURG
*ai > á/ _ r/h	0	1	0	0	0	0	?	?
e > i	0	1	0	0	0	0	?	?
*eu, *iu > iu	0	1	0	0	0	0	1	0
V > Ø / _(C)#	0	1	0	0	0	0	?	?
Ṽ > V / [-stress]	0	1	0	0	0	0	?	?
R-umlaut	0	1	0	0	0	0	?	?
u-umlaut	0	1	0	0	0	0	0	0
*e > *ea > ja; *e > *eu > jo	0	1	0	0	0	0	?	?
*au > ó	0	1	0	0	0	0	?	?
iu > jú / f, g, k, p	0	1	0	0	0	0	?	?
V > Ṽ	0	1	0	0	0	0	?	?
V > Ṽ / _ CC	0	1	0	0	0	0	?	?
Ṽ > V / _CC	0	1	0	0	0	0	?	?
*ht > tt	0	1	0	0	0	0	?	?
*j > Ø / # _	0	1	0	0	0	0	?	?
w > Ø / # _	0	1	0	0	0	0	?	?
þ > Ø / _ l	0	1	0	0	0	0	?	?
*z, *r > *r	0	1	0	0	0	0	0	0
*kj, *gj > kkj, ggj	0	1	0	0	0	0	?	?
bera	0	1	0	0	0	0	?	?
*i > *e	0	1	0	0	0	0	0	0
á, ǫ > ǫ	0	1	0	0	0	0	?	?
*d > ð / *r _	0	1	0	0	0	0	?	?

Table A.12 Innovation dataset (cont.)

Innovation	GO	ON	OE	OF	OS	OHG	VAND	BURG
*zd, *zn > dd, nn	0	1	0	0	0	0	?	?
mn > fn	0	1	0	0	0	0	?	?
sá	0	0	0	0	0	0	?	?
-r > C / [+alveolar] _	0	1	0	0	0	0	?	?
*w > v	0	1	0	0	0	0	?	?
ðt > tt	0	1	0	0	0	0	?	?
Ø > t	0	1	0	0	0	0	?	?
berið	0	1	0	0	0	0	?	?
*ī	1	1	0	0	0	0	?	?
*hnut > hnot	0	1	0	0	0	0	?	?
*sezō, etc.	0	1	0	0	0	0	?	?
*-nnz > -ðr	0	1	0	0	0	0	?	?
3sg., 2sg. > 2sg.	0	1	0	0	0	0	?	?
-usi/-isi > -r	0	1	0	0	0	0	?	?
góðir	0	1	0	0	0	0	?	?
koma	0	1	0	0	0	0	?	?
cl. IV weak verbs > cl. II	0	1	0	0	0	0	?	?
-u(-)	0	1	0	0	0	0	?	?
-ar	0	1	0	0	0	0	?	?
-inn	0	1	0	0	0	0	?	?
-sk	0	1	0	0	0	0	?	?
a-stems	0	1	0	0	0	0	?	?
i-stems	0	1	0	0	0	0	?	?

Table A.13 Innovation dataset (cont.)

Innovation	GO	ON	OE	OF	OS	OHG	VAND	BURG
Cons. stems	0	1	0	0	0	0	?	?
an-stems	0	1	0	0	0	0	?	?
muga	0	1	0	0	0	0	?	?
nafn, vatn	0	1	0	0	0	0	?	?
lifa	0	1	0	0	0	0	?	?
þrettán	0	1	1	0	0	1	?	?
þér	0	1	0	0	0	0	?	?
vega	0	1	0	0	0	0	?	?
sé	0	1	1	0	0	1	?	?
hann	0	1	0	0	0	0	?	?
nǫkkurr	0	1	0	0	0	0	?	?
gøra	0	1	0	0	0	0	?	?
ugga	0	1	0	0	0	0	?	?
gamall	0	1	0	0	0	0	?	?
karl	0	1	0	0	0	0	?	?
eigi	0	1	0	0	0	0	?	?
kjǫt	0	1	0	0	0	0	?	?
eldr	0	1	0	0	0	0	?	?
margr	0	1	0	0	0	0	?	?
p, *t, *k > pf, ʒ, hh	0	0	0	0	0	3	0	0
*w > Ø / _ r, l	0	0	0	0	0	1	?	?
joh	0	0	0	0	0	1	0	?
*e > i / _ u	0	0	0	0	0	1	1	?

Table A.14 Innovation dataset (cont.)

Innovation	GO	ON	OE	OF	OS	OHG	VAND	BURG
*CC > C	0	0	0	0	0	1	?	?
*h- > Ø / # _ C	0	0	0	0	0	1	?	0
*-hw-, *-h- > -h-	1	0	0	0	0	1	?	?
*-i- > Ø	0	0	0	0	0	1	?	?
Ø > -h-	0	0	0	0	0	1	?	?
i-umlaut	0	0	0	0	0	1	0	0
*ē > ie	0	0	0	0	0	1	0	0
-e > -ea, -ia > -a	0	0	0	0	0	1	?	?
*au > ou; *ai > ei; *eu > iu	0	0	0	0	0	1	0	0
*ō > uo	0	0	0	0	0	1	0	0
*au > ō	1	1	0	0	1	1	0	0
V > Ø / _(C)#	0	0	0	0	0	1	?	?
-w > -o	0	0	0	0	0	1	?	?
ao > ō	0	0	0	0	1	1	?	?
CR# > CVR#	0	0	0	0	1	1	?	?
Ø > V / l/r _ h/w	0	0	0	0	0	1	?	?
ga- > gi-	0	0	0	0	0	1	?	?
*i > *e / _ [+lab./+vel.] [+voc., -hi]	0	0	0	0	0	1	?	?
V1> V2 / _ CV2(C)	0	0	0	0	0	1	?	?
*i > e / [-high] C0	0	0	0	0	0	1	?	?
*-ō > -u	0	0	0	0	0	1	?	?
eo > io	0	0	0	0	0	1	?	?
-m > -n	0	0	0	0	0	1	?	?

Table A.15 Innovation dataset (cont.)

Innovation	GO	ON	OE	OF	OS	OHG	VAND	BURG
iu > [ȳ]	0	0	0	0	0	1	?	?
sk	0	0	0	0	0	1	0	0
-V > -e	0	0	0	0	0	1	?	?
*þ > [t]	0	0	0	0	0	1	?	?
*-dē > *-dō	0	0	0	0	0	1	?	?
*-dum > *-dōm, etc.	0	0	0	0	0	1	?	?
*-anu	0	0	1	1	1	1	?	?
-īs	0	0	0	0	1	1	?	?
1g. -m	0	0	0	0	0	1	?	?
*-zz- > -zt-	0	0	0	0	0	1	?	?
-amu ~ -emu	0	0	0	0	0	1	?	?
*-u > Ø / [+light] _	0	0	0	0	1	1	?	?
Ø > -u / [+heavy] _	0	0	0	0	1	1	?	?
zi ērist	0	0	0	0	0	1	?	?
Abstracts in -ī	0	0	0	0	0	1	?	?
habēta	0	0	0	0	0	1	?	?
u-stem > i-stem	0	0	0	0	0	1	?	?
-ēs	0	0	0	0	0	1	?	?
*þrīz > drī	0	0	0	0	0	1	?	?
-ōnne, -ēnne	0	0	0	0	0	1	?	?
*-ai-	0	0	0	0	0	1	?	?
nom. pl., acc. pl. > acc. pl.	0	0	0	0	0	1	?	?
-er-	0	0	0	0	0	1	?	?

Table A.16 Innovation dataset (cont.)

Innovation	GO	ON	OE	OF	OS	OHG	VAND	BURG
-o	0	0	0	0	0	1	?	?
1g., 3sg. indic. > 3sg.	0	0	0	0	1	1	?	?
2sg. -s > -st	0	0	0	0	0	1	?	?
-ōno	0	0	0	0	1	1	?	?
dual > ∅	0	0	0	0	0	1	?	?
-u > -o	0	0	0	0	0	1	?	?
-in > -en	0	0	0	0	0	1	?	?
fem. jō-stems ~ ī-stems	0	0	0	0	0	1	?	?
ō-stems	0	0	0	0	0	1	?	?
n-stems	0	0	0	0	0	1	?	?
*CReC- > class IV	0	0	0	0	0	1	?	?
-ta	0	0	0	0	1	1	?	?
*þi- ~ *þe-	0	0	0	0	1	1	?	?
*hwi- ~ *hwe-	0	0	0	0	1	1	?	?
sīn	0	0	0	0	0	1	?	?
wellen	0	0	0	0	0	1	?	?
imu	0	0	0	0	1	1	?	?
sāhun	0	0	0	0	0	1	?	?
fateres, fatere, etc.	0	0	0	0	0	1	?	?
*drī + o	0	0	0	0	0	1	?	?
zi	0	0	0	0	0	1	?	?
ir(-)	0	0	0	0	0	1	?	?
doret	0	0	0	0	0	1	?	?

Table A.17 Innovation dataset (cont.)

Innovation	GO	ON	OE	OF	OS	OHG	VAND	BURG
inan > in	0	0	0	0	0	1	?	?
drīzehan	0	0	0	0	0	1	?	?
(h)we-	0	0	0	0	0	1	?	?
sī	0	0	0	0	0	1	?	?
gitar	0	0	0	0	0	1	?	?
bim	0	0	0	0	0	1	?	?
habēt	0	0	0	0	1	1	?	?
gisehan	0	0	0	0	0	1	?	?
sluog	0	0	0	0	0	1	?	?
stuont, stuontun, gistantan	0	0	0	0	0	1	?	?
werdan, wesan	0	0	0	0	0	1	?	?
blint man	0	0	0	0	0	1	?	?
V2	0	1	0	0	1	1	?	?
*[awjwj] > *[auj]	0	0	1	0	0	0	?	?
*w > Ø / _ i	0	0	1	0	0	0	?	?
*a > *æ	0	0	1	0	0	0	?	?
*ai > ā	0	0	1	0	0	0	?	?
ā > o / [-stress]	0	0	1	0	0	0	?	?
*au > ēa	0	0	1	0	0	0	0	0
[+front] > V12	0	0	1	0	0	0	?	?
*hs > x	0	0	1	0	0	0	?	?
*k, *g > [+palatal]	0	0	1	0	0	0	0	0
*-kw- > -k-	0	0	1	0	0	0	?	?

Table A.18 Innovation dataset (cont.)

Innovation	GO	ON	OE	OF	OS	OHG	VAND	BURG
i-umlaut	0	0	1	0	0	0	0	0
/f, þ, s/ > [v, ð, z] / [+stress]σ _	0	0	1	0	0	0	0	0
Ø / C_C	0	0	1	0	0	0	?	?
*i, *u > Ø / _ #	0	0	1	0	0	0	?	?
*þs > *ss	0	0	1	0	0	0	?	?
*b > f / _ #	0	0	1	0	0	0	?	?
*h > Ø	0	0	1	0	0	0	?	?
*æ > a / _ C1[+back]	0	0	1	0	0	0	?	?
i > io	0	0	1	0	0	0	?	?
CR# > CVR#	0	0	1	0	0	0	?	?
æ, i > e	0	0	1	0	0	0	?	?
*-azd- > *-ezd-	0	0	1	0	0	0	?	?
*C(l/r) > *CC(l/r)	0	0	1	0	0	0	?	?
*i > Ø / CV.C _ l	0	0	1	0	0	0	?	?
V̄ > V / _CC(C)	0	0	1	0	0	0	?	?
a = u	0	0	1	0	0	0	?	?
-sr- > -ss-	0	0	1	0	0	0	?	?
io, īo > eo, ēo	0	0	1	0	0	0	?	?
*-ēja- > *-ejV	0	0	1	0	0	0	?	?
*-iz	0	0	1	0	0	0	?	?
hettend	0	0	1	0	0	0	?	?
wæter, wæteres	0	0	1	0	0	0	?	?
-CC-, -rġ-	0	0	1	0	0	0	?	?

Table A.19 Innovation dataset (cont.)

Innovation	GO	ON	OE	OF	OS	OHG	VAND	BURG
*haubud, etc.	0	0	1	0	0	0	?	?
þā	0	0	1	0	0	0	?	?
Abstracts in *-u	0	0	1	0	0	0	?	?
-i	0	0	1	0	0	0	?	?
-æs, -æ, -um	0	0	3	0	0	0	?	?
*-æ-	0	0	1	0	0	0	?	?
heardra	0	0	0	0	0	0	?	?
*-z- ~ *-s-; *-d- ~ *-þ-	0	0	3	0	0	0	?	?
-e	0	0	1	0	0	0	?	?
1g. subj.	0	0	1	0	0	0	?	?
acc. pl., nom. pl > nom. pl	0	0	1	0	0	0	?	?
-u	0	0	1	0	0	0	?	?
*-st	0	0	1	0	0	0	?	?
hæbbe wē	0	0	1	0	0	0	?	?
-tl > -ld	0	0	1	0	0	0	?	?
hrēaw(-), fēawe	0	0	1	0	0	0	?	?
dohtur	0	0	1	0	0	0	?	?
u-stems	0	0	1	0	0	0	?	?
gen. prons.	0	0	1	0	0	0	?	?
-tiġ	0	0	1	0	0	0	?	?
þȳ	0	0	1	0	0	0	?	?
þrīora	0	0	1	0	0	0	?	?
*ni wi- > ny-	0	0	1	0	0	0	?	?

Table A.20 Innovation dataset (cont.)

Innovation	GO	ON	OE	OF	OS	OHG	VAND	BURG
ēode	0	0	1	0	0	0	?	?
þreotīene	0	0	1	0	0	0	?	?
hwæs	0	0	1	0	0	0	?	?
wilt	0	0	1	0	0	0	?	?
*ar-	0	0	1	0	0	0	?	?
eam	0	0	1	0	0	0	?	?
guma	0	0	1	0	0	0	?	?
cwom > com	0	0	1	0	0	0	?	?
*hes > his	0	0	1	0	0	0	?	?
*her- > hir-	0	0	1	0	0	0	?	?
ēow	0	0	0	0	0	0	?	?
*gā-	0	0	1	0	0	0	?	?
ūre	0	0	1	0	0	0	?	?
miklæ	0	0	0	0	0	0	?	?
sīe	0	0	1	0	0	0	?	?
dearr	0	0	1	0	0	0	?	?
hæbbe	0	0	1	0	0	0	?	?
tū	0	0	1	0	0	0	?	?
dæġ	0	0	1	0	0	0	?	?
dōm, dōð, etc.	0	0	1	0	0	0	?	?
dyde	0	0	1	0	0	0	?	?
*ai,*au,*eu > ā, ē, iā	0	0	0	1	0	0	?	?
WGmc *a > PFris *æ	0	0	0	1	0	0	?	?

Table A.21 Innovation dataset (cont.)

Innovation	GO	ON	OE	OF	OS	OHG	VAND	BURG
*g > j	0	0	0	1	0	0	0	0
k > kj > tj > ts	0	0	0	1	0	0	0	0
i-mutation	0	0	0	1	0	0	?	?
*i > iu	0	0	0	1	0	0	0	0
*e > *eu > iu	0	0	0	1	0	0	0	0
loss of u/w after iu	0	0	0	1	0	0	?	?
loss of intervocalic -h-, aha > a	0	0	0	1	0	0	?	?
loss of *ga-/*gi-	0	0	0	1	0	0	?	?
metathesis of r	0	0	0	1	0	0	?	?
loss of -n	0	0	0	1	0	0	?	?
-e- instead of -i-	0	0	0	1	0	0	?	?
1/2. Ps. Sg./Pl Dat. = 1/2. Ps. Sg./Pl Acc.	0	0	1	1	0	0	?	?
fem. -jon/-in-stems adopt strong fem. declension	0	0	0	1	0	0	?	?
v drop after l/r	0	0	0	1	0	0	?	?
endings -ene/-ende	0	0	0	1	0	0	?	?
loss of distinct. feat. in u-/wo-adj.	0	0	0	1	0	0	?	?
stem vowel shortening	0	0	0	1	0	0	?	?
*ō > *ū/ [+stress]	0	0	0	0	0	0	1	0
-anh- > -ah-	1	1	1	1	1	1	?	0

Table A.22 Posterior estimates of feature occurrence times

Feature	Mean	SD	Lower-89CI	Higher-89CI	HDI range
*ē > *ā/ [+stress]	1.9	0.56	0.87	2.57	1.7
*-ī > *-i / _#	1.9	0.59	0.8	2.62	1.82
*-ō > *-u/ [-stress] _#	1.86	0.56	0.93	2.62	1.69
*-wū > *-u	1.82	0.66	0.96	2.79	1.83
*a > *u/ _*m	2.08	0.57	1.25	2.8	1.55
*a > *i / [-stress] _ n	2.22	0.4	1.79	2.78	0.99
*ai > *ē	2.48	0.28	2.2	2.8	0.6
*u > *[o]/]σ [-high]	1.99	0.55	1.16	2.78	1.62
*ō > *ū / _ [σ	1.87	0.67	0.8	2.69	1.89
*V1V2 > *V̄ 3	1.92	0.61	0.9	2.66	1.76
*kʷ > *kw	2.01	0.56	0.97	2.69	1.72
*kw > *kkw	2.05	0.56	1.1	2.8	1.7
dual > Ø	2.09	0.58	1.08	2.8	1.72
3 imp. > Ø	2.02	0.49	1.32	2.8	1.48
pres. pass. > Ø	2.04	0.59	1.1	2.8	1.7
*-miz, *-maz > *-maz	1.96	0.63	0.93	2.74	1.81
*-aiz- > *-ez-	1.87	0.55	0.96	2.72	1.76
*-ded-, *-d- > *-d-	2.28	0.49	1.72	2.8	1.08
voc. > Ø	2.23	0.46	1.48	2.8	1.32
*-um(m)ē > *-um	2.05	0.57	0.81	2.69	1.88
*-ēm > *-um	1.82	0.69	0.93	2.75	1.82
*-ū-	2.33	0.46	1.62	2.8	1.18
-u(-) (appearance)	1.85	0.5	1.21	2.8	1.59

Table A.23 Posterior estimates of feature occurrence times (cont.)

Feature	Mean	SD	Lower-89CI	Higher-89CI	HDI range
-u(-) (spread)	1.96	0.63	0.96	2.72	1.76
*þrij- > *þrijō, *þrijǭ	1.96	0.6	0.8	2.61	1.81
*tigiwiz	1.78	0.58	0.8	2.46	1.66
*hwī	2.04	0.48	1.38	2.79	1.41
*hir > *hēr (lengthening)	2.43	0.31	2.04	2.8	0.76
*hir > *hēr (lowering)	1.96	0.6	0.91	2.78	1.87
*jūz, *jūt > *jīz, *jīt	2.17	0.42	1.72	2.8	1.08
*uban-	2.1	0.61	1.14	2.8	1.66
Null subject	2.2	0.47	1.47	2.8	1.33
*hwaþeraz	1.98	0.65	0.8	2.67	1.87
*-(i)ji- > *-ī-	1.64	0.64	0.8	2.53	1.73
*d (/ð/) > /d/ / r _	2.41	0.35	2	2.8	0.8
-a	1.65	0.66	0.8	2.5	1.7
*-ā-	1.64	0.6	0.8	2.6	1.8
*-z- ~ *-s-; *-d- ~ *-þ-	1.55	0.59	0.8	2.52	1.72
*u > *u, *o	2.17	0.64	0.88	2.8	1.92
*a, *ą > Ø / _ (*-z)#	2.13	0.55	1.18	2.8	1.62
*-u > Ø / CC _#	1.71	0.51	0.8	2.36	1.56
*zw, *dw > *ww	1.87	0.55	1.16	2.75	1.59
*V[ð]V > *V[d]V	1.65	0.64	0.8	2.57	1.77
*Vwu- > *Vu	1.78	0.51	0.82	2.41	1.59

Table A.24 Posterior estimates of feature occurrence times (cont.)

Feature	Mean	SD	Lower-89CI	Higher-89CI	HDI range
*-z > Ø	1.88	0.55	1.1	2.74	1.64
*Cj > *υʲυʲ	1.83	0.6	0.95	2.67	1.72
*C(l/r) > *CC(l/r)	1.83	0.49	0.83	2.46	1.63
*Ṽ# > *V	2.04	0.58	1.18	2.8	1.62
*-i, *-u > Ø	1.65	0.64	0.8	2.55	1.75
*-ō(r) > *-ā(r)#	2.07	0.56	1.16	2.8	1.64
*-Ṽ r# > *-Vr	1.78	0.66	0.8	2.62	1.82
*ō > *ū / _n#	1.77	0.61	0.96	2.78	1.82
*C(C)V > *C(C)V	2	0.54	1.19	2.79	1.6
*-jj-, *-ww- > *-ij-, *-uw-	1.84	0.6	0.81	2.62	1.81
*-ī- ~ *-ija- > *-i- ~ *-ija-	1.91	0.56	1.22	2.78	1.56
*-i- > Ø / -t/d- _ -d-	1.73	0.6	0.8	2.55	1.75
*walid- > *waldē	1.86	0.64	0.96	2.78	1.82
*/x/ > *[h] / #_	1.76	0.68	0.8	2.67	1.87
*z, *r > *r	2.09	0.58	1.05	2.8	1.75
*-izd- > *-īd-	1.8	0.62	0.98	2.74	1.76
*-īn > *-ī	1.85	0.53	0.97	2.66	1.69
dat., inst. > dat.	2.1	0.53	1.4	2.8	1.4
*-ī	1.78	0.56	0.8	2.49	1.69
*ijōz > *sijā	2.01	0.53	1.13	2.78	1.65
*unsiz > *uns, etc.	1.87	0.52	0.95	2.62	1.67
*-nVssī	1.72	0.53	0.92	2.56	1.64
1sg., 3sg. subj. > 3sg. subj.	1.97	0.61	0.87	2.72	1.85

Table A.25 Posterior estimates of feature occurrence times (cont.)

Feature	Mean	SD	Lower-89CI	Higher-89CI	HDI range
*-an	2.08	0.49	1.45	2.8	1.35
*-nd-ija- > *-nd-ijō-	1.8	0.58	0.8	2.57	1.77
inf. + *-ja-	1.91	0.62	0.99	2.8	1.81
*namô (neut.) > *namō (masc.)	1.92	0.62	0.86	2.59	1.73
2sg. *-s	1.88	0.58	0.94	2.67	1.73
2sg. past indic. > subj.	1.92	0.57	0.99	2.79	1.8
*-Ø > *-u/[+heavy] _	1.87	0.59	0.91	2.71	1.8
*i (cl. I) > *e (cl. IV/V)	1.87	0.66	0.95	2.78	1.83
*mati > *matja- : *sagjǫ-	2.06	0.56	1.02	2.8	1.78
*hehaww > *heuw	1.72	0.62	0.8	2.51	1.71
*hehēt > *heht	2.12	0.56	1.16	2.8	1.64
*-i- > Ø	1.98	0.54	1.24	2.79	1.55
*-dēs	1.72	0.47	0.92	2.36	1.44
*-st	1.95	0.52	1.34	2.8	1.46
*-ik	1.96	0.53	1.31	2.79	1.48
*-CijV- > *-CjV-	1.99	0.59	0.87	2.67	1.8
> [+voice]	1.87	0.62	0.8	2.67	1.87
*sī > *si(j)u	2.03	0.56	1.18	2.79	1.61
*ijē, *ijǭ	1.98	0.52	1.32	2.79	1.47
*wilī	1.65	0.44	0.8	2.09	1.29
*þits/*þitt(i)	1.89	0.44	1.24	2.65	1.41
*sa > *siz	1.87	0.52	1.25	2.8	1.55
*þrīz	1.81	0.62	0.95	2.72	1.77

Table A.26 Posterior estimates of feature occurrence times (cont.)

Feature	Mean	SD	Lower-89CI	Higher-89CI	HDI range
*twō + *n	1.72	0.62	0.8	2.57	1.77
*dēdē > *dādī	1.87	0.65	0.91	2.72	1.81
*þar > *þār; *hʷar > *hʷār	2.01	0.47	1.31	2.69	1.38
*þē	1.8	0.59	0.89	2.69	1.8
*baum	1.88	0.58	0.97	2.72	1.75
*obat	1.72	0.59	0.8	2.59	1.79
*rindā	1.75	0.58	0.89	2.63	1.74
*waskan	1.74	0.62	0.8	2.57	1.77
*wolkn	1.88	0.57	0.91	2.7	1.79
*gagang(?) > *gang	1.82	0.56	0.97	2.73	1.76
*waht	1.97	0.46	1.38	2.77	1.39
[+nasal] > Ø	1.49	0.56	0.8	2.33	1.53
*e > *i / _m	1.55	0.58	0.8	2.3	1.5
*a, *o > [+front]	1.69	0.61	0.8	2.59	1.79
*-lþ- > *-ld-	1.62	0.45	0.8	2.15	1.35
*sl > *ls	1.93	0.65	0.8	2.67	1.87
*ā, *ē > *ē	1.61	0.59	0.8	2.44	1.64
*h > Ø / _CC	1.34	0.54	0.8	2.23	1.43
*-z > Ø	1.96	0.51	1.3	2.79	1.49
*VfV, *VbV > *VbV	1.65	0.65	0.8	2.59	1.79
*-iw- > *-aw-	1.7	0.55	0.95	2.67	1.72
*-ō	1.43	0.54	0.8	2.14	1.34
*-i- ~ *-ija- > class II	1.54	0.58	0.8	2.46	1.66

Table A.27 Posterior estimates of feature occurrence times (cont.)

Feature	Mean	SD	Lower-89CI	Higher-89CI	HDI range
hund-	1.61	0.52	0.8	2.31	1.51
3pl.	1.71	0.54	0.91	2.67	1.76
*-ōs	1.62	0.58	0.8	2.4	1.6
*-ô > *-a	1.88	0.54	0.82	2.55	1.73
-ianne	1.55	0.55	0.8	2.31	1.51
*-nō- ~ *-na- > class III	1.7	0.59	0.8	2.39	1.59
*a, *o > [+nasal] / _ [+nasal]	1.59	0.48	0.8	2.21	1.41
*a > [+round]	1.59	0.45	0.82	2.09	1.27
*lagdun : *satte	1.89	0.52	1.28	2.8	1.52
*sindi	1.96	0.63	0.97	2.72	1.75
*sīn > Ø	1.67	0.58	0.87	2.62	1.75
*siz > Ø	1.99	0.52	1.17	2.72	1.55
*sek > Ø	1.52	0.51	0.8	2.19	1.39
*Þ- + *-s	1.76	0.65	0.9	2.75	1.85
*hi- ~ *he-	1.82	0.63	0.8	2.66	1.86
*stā-	1.64	0.54	0.8	2.39	1.59
*lais- ~ *laiz-	1.53	0.6	0.8	2.57	1.77
*i- ~ *e- > *hi- ~ *he-	1.5	0.55	0.8	2.39	1.59
*nigun	1.73	0.51	0.95	2.63	1.68
*hwat	1.85	0.54	0.98	2.58	1.6
*hwaþeraz	1.83	0.56	0.8	2.55	1.75
*a > [+front]	1.44	0.56	0.82	2.27	1.45
*ō > *ā / [-stress]	1.58	0.49	0.94	2.37	1.43

Table A.28 Posterior estimates of feature occurrence times (cont.)

Feature	Mean	SD	Lower-89CI	Higher-89CI	HDI range
*-w-	1.4	0.55	0.81	2.33	1.52
*-ē	1.32	0.42	0.8	1.77	0.97
*-s, -þ, -aþ	1.33	0.44	0.8	1.88	1.08
*þaizō, *þaimi	1.51	0.55	0.81	2.26	1.45
*hwa-	1.43	0.54	0.8	2.24	1.44
*hū	1.53	0.6	0.8	2.57	1.77
V > Ø / _(C)#	1.98	0.46	1.44	2.8	1.36
i-umlaut	1.84	0.55	0.95	2.67	1.72
V2	1.71	0.58	0.8	2.6	1.8
sé	1.45	0.61	0.8	2.47	1.67
*-hw-, *-h- > -h-	1.81	0.58	0.81	2.48	1.67
*-dē > *-dō	1.65	0.57	0.8	2.37	1.57
*au > ō	1.34	0.52	0.8	2.15	1.35
ao > ō	1.77	0.62	0.8	2.62	1.82
CR# > CVR#	1.32	0.49	0.8	2.04	1.24
*-anu	1.36	0.49	0.8	2.18	1.38
-īs	1.39	0.45	0.8	1.98	1.18
*-u > Ø / [+light] _	1.45	0.49	0.8	2.24	1.44
Ø > -u / [+heavy] _	1.35	0.47	0.8	2.01	1.21
1sg., 3sg. indic. > 3sg.	1.79	0.65	0.92	2.8	1.88
-ōno	1.17	0.36	0.8	1.71	0.91
*þi- ~ *þe-	1.39	0.44	0.8	1.9	1.1
*hwi- ~ *hwe-	1.6	0.52	0.8	2.34	1.54

Table A.29 Posterior estimates of feature occurrence times (cont.)

Feature	Mean	SD	Lower-89CI	Higher-89CI	HDI range
imu	1.53	0.53	0.8	2.34	1.54
-ta	1.46	0.48	0.8	2.05	1.25
*a > *æ	1.52	0.44	0.8	2.15	1.35
* $\hat{V}$ # > $\hat{V}$; * $\bar{V}$ # > V; *V# > $\emptyset$	1.34	0.49	0.8	2.09	1.29
*e, *i > i	1.44	0.5	0.82	2.34	1.52
* $\bar{e}_1$, * $\bar{e}_2$ > * $\bar{e}_1$	1.4	0.49	0.8	2.02	1.22
*i, *u > [ɛ, ɔ] / _ /r, h, h^w/	1.62	0.61	0.8	2.58	1.78
*h (/x/) > /h/	1.4	0.54	0.8	2.16	1.36
-ggw-, -ngw- > -/ngw/-	1.14	0.4	0.8	1.63	0.83
* $\bar{e}$ > a / [+stress] _	1.3	0.53	0.8	2.14	1.34
h > Cα / _ #Cα	1.49	0.52	0.82	2.26	1.44
*ai > /ɛ/	1.5	0.69	0.8	2.59	1.79
*au > /ɔ/	1.62	0.6	0.82	2.39	1.57
*z > s	1.35	0.51	0.8	2.03	1.23
*i > $\emptyset$ / _ *jV	1.4	0.53	0.8	2.25	1.45
*a > $\emptyset$ / _z#	1.56	0.58	0.8	2.39	1.59
*-(i)ji- > *-ī-	1.5	0.55	0.8	2.32	1.52
*-mz > -m	1.38	0.5	0.8	2.18	1.38
r/n > l	1.39	0.58	0.8	2.36	1.56
Thurneysen's Law	1.34	0.57	0.8	2.32	1.52
ē, ō > /ɛ, ɔ/ / / _ V	1.26	0.47	0.8	1.85	1.05
*-jj-, *-ww- > -ddj-/-ggj-, -ggw-	1.53	0.68	0.8	2.64	1.84
*-z > $\emptyset$ / V r/s _	1.43	0.54	0.8	2.33	1.53

Table A.30 Posterior estimates of feature occurrence times (cont.)

Feature	Mean	SD	Lower-89CI	Higher-89CI	HDI range
*fl- > þl-	1.27	0.58	0.8	2.44	1.64
*þ > t / _ s	1.22	0.49	0.8	2.02	1.22
-aiwa, -aima, -aina	1.5	0.6	0.8	2.4	1.6
Ø > j / _ i	1.5	0.57	0.8	2.27	1.47
*-n-	1.4	0.59	0.8	2.39	1.59
sijai-	1.26	0.48	0.8	1.94	1.14
siju-	1.23	0.5	0.8	2.03	1.23
-uh > -h	1.14	0.44	0.8	1.58	0.78
V > Ø / _-uh/-ei	1.61	0.59	0.8	2.6	1.8
*-aiz- > -ai	1.25	0.48	0.8	1.79	0.99
*-r-iz > -r-jus	1.31	0.55	0.8	2.18	1.38
-a, -o, -o	1.49	0.62	0.8	2.44	1.64
-o : -e	1.43	0.58	0.8	2.37	1.57
þata	1.38	0.51	0.8	2	1.2
*-īn- > Ø	1.19	0.44	0.8	1.87	1.07
*-at	1.64	0.49	0.8	2.28	1.48
*-assu-	1.16	0.38	0.8	1.63	0.83
*-ā-	1.33	0.52	0.8	2.04	1.24
*-es-	1.35	0.54	0.82	2.24	1.42
-and-s	1.67	0.59	0.8	2.54	1.74
1sg., 3sg. > 1sg.	1.13	0.36	0.8	1.82	1.02
hʷa	1.22	0.41	0.8	1.79	0.99
*hwō	1.37	0.51	0.8	2.11	1.31

Table A.31 Posterior estimates of feature occurrence times (cont.)

Feature	Mean	SD	Lower-89CI	Higher-89CI	HDI range
iusiza	1.2	0.48	0.8	1.91	1.11
godai	1.4	0.55	0.8	2.24	1.44
alþeis	1.3	0.51	0.8	2.08	1.28
*hir > her	1.36	0.54	0.8	2.17	1.37
sauil	1.42	0.64	0.8	2.56	1.76
*fōr ~ *fun- > fon ~ funin-	1.38	0.54	0.8	2.14	1.34
tunþus, fotus	1.43	0.67	0.8	2.44	1.64
sehʷun	1.43	0.63	0.8	2.5	1.7
wato, watins, etc.	1.2	0.41	0.8	1.72	0.92
iddj- ~ iddjed-	1.22	0.43	0.8	1.71	0.91
sitan, ligan	1.36	0.5	0.8	2.12	1.32
*anguz > aggwus	1.36	0.62	0.8	2.43	1.63
nahtam	1.33	0.47	0.8	2.25	1.45
*taujan	1.4	0.64	0.8	2.42	1.62
stōþ	1.37	0.54	0.8	2.27	1.47
wesun	1.38	0.59	0.8	2.28	1.48
ufar	1.47	0.62	0.8	2.51	1.71
hausjan	1.29	0.51	0.8	2.16	1.36
gadaúrsun	1.38	0.54	0.8	2.24	1.44
taihuntehund	1.44	0.61	0.8	2.36	1.56
*-ô, *-ō > -ō	1.41	0.53	0.8	2.16	1.36
*ār > er > ir / [-stress]	1.35	0.45	0.8	1.89	1.09
*eu, *iu > i > e	1.28	0.48	0.8	2.01	1.21

Table A.32 Posterior estimates of feature occurrence times (cont.)

Feature	Mean	SD	Lower-89CI	Higher-89CI	HDI range
*ai > ei	1.47	0.44	0.8	2.07	1.27
ǫ > u; a > e	1.54	0.58	0.8	2.52	1.72
*ai > á/ _ r/h	1.18	0.39	0.8	1.67	0.87
e > i	1.25	0.56	0.8	2.25	1.45
*eu, *iu > iu	1.14	0.42	0.8	1.64	0.84
V > Ø / _(C)#	1.33	0.46	0.8	2.24	1.44
Ṽ > V / [-stress]	1.14	0.39	0.8	1.67	0.87
R-umlaut	1.51	0.67	0.8	2.61	1.81
u-umlaut	1.17	0.44	0.8	1.64	0.84
*e > *ea > ja; *e > *eu > jo	1.21	0.41	0.8	1.86	1.06
*au > ó	1.17	0.44	0.8	1.9	1.1
iu > jú / f, g, k, p	1.23	0.49	0.8	2.06	1.26
V > Ṽ	1.26	0.43	0.8	1.88	1.08
V > Ṽ / _ CC	1.26	0.47	0.8	2.07	1.27
Ṽ > V / _CC	1.49	0.5	0.8	2.22	1.42
*ht > tt	1.44	0.5	0.8	2.12	1.32
*j > Ø / # _	1.18	0.4	0.8	1.67	0.87
w > Ø / # _	1.29	0.51	0.8	2.07	1.27
þ > Ø / _ l	1.23	0.37	0.8	1.69	0.89
*z, *r > *r	1.1	0.41	0.8	1.66	0.86
*kj, *gj > kkj, ggj	1.34	0.5	0.8	2.06	1.26
bera	1.28	0.51	0.8	2.03	1.23
*i > *e	1.48	0.57	0.8	2.24	1.44

Table A.33 Posterior estimates of feature occurrence times (cont.)

Feature	Mean	SD	Lower-89CI	Higher-89CI	HDI range
á, ǫ > ǫ	1.2	0.39	0.8	1.75	0.95
*d > ð / *r _	1.08	0.34	0.8	1.41	0.61
*zd, *zn > dd, nn	1.17	0.45	0.8	1.93	1.13
mn > fn	1.19	0.35	0.8	1.56	0.76
sá	1.12	0.43	0.8	1.6	0.8
-r > C / [+alveolar] _	1.41	0.59	0.8	2.31	1.51
*w > v	1.51	0.65	0.8	2.51	1.71
ðt > tt	1.52	0.62	0.8	2.58	1.78
Ø > t	1.33	0.6	0.8	2.55	1.75
berið	1.26	0.54	0.8	2.19	1.39
*ī	1.44	0.49	0.8	2.17	1.37
*hnut > hnot	1.48	0.72	0.8	2.62	1.82
*sezō, etc.	1.35	0.5	0.8	2.09	1.29
*-nnz > -ðr	1.24	0.52	0.8	2.18	1.38
3sg., 2sg. > 2sg.	1.45	0.58	0.8	2.41	1.61
-usi/-isi > -r	1.27	0.45	0.8	1.83	1.03
góðir	1.18	0.44	0.8	1.84	1.04
koma	1.33	0.55	0.8	2.27	1.47
cl. IV weak verbs > cl. II	1.29	0.47	0.8	1.93	1.13
-u(-)	1.26	0.57	0.8	2.5	1.7
-ar	1.3	0.59	0.8	2.37	1.57
-inn	1.28	0.48	0.8	1.97	1.17
-sk	1.35	0.63	0.8	2.59	1.79

Table A.34 Posterior estimates of feature occurrence times (cont.)

Feature	Mean	SD	Lower-89CI	Higher-89CI	HDI range
a-stems	1.18	0.43	0.8	1.77	0.97
i-stems	1.5	0.62	0.8	2.49	1.69
Cons. stems	1.34	0.46	0.8	1.93	1.13
an-stems	1.3	0.56	0.8	2.42	1.62
muga	1.2	0.43	0.8	1.55	0.75
nafn, vatn	1.21	0.45	0.8	1.98	1.18
lifa	1.39	0.52	0.8	2.19	1.39
þrettán	1.72	0.68	0.94	2.78	1.84
þér	1.41	0.55	0.8	2.35	1.55
vega	1.29	0.57	0.8	2.17	1.37
sé	1.82	0.58	0.8	2.6	1.8
hann	1.24	0.45	0.8	1.76	0.96
nǫkkurr	1.27	0.5	0.8	1.92	1.12
gøra	1.29	0.47	0.8	1.9	1.1
ugga	1.18	0.43	0.8	1.66	0.86
gamall	1.3	0.43	0.8	1.92	1.12
karl	1.51	0.61	0.8	2.39	1.59
eigi	1.43	0.49	0.8	2.23	1.43
kjǫt	1.4	0.57	0.8	2.42	1.62
eldr	1.46	0.59	0.8	2.4	1.6
margr	1.35	0.51	0.8	2.14	1.34
*p, *t, *k > pf, ʒ, hh	1.25	0.52	0.8	2.23	1.43
*w > Ø / _ r, l	1.53	0.55	0.8	2.31	1.51

Table A.35 Posterior estimates of feature occurrence times (cont.)

Feature	Mean	SD	Lower-89CI	Higher-89CI	HDI range
joh	1.22	0.41	0.8	1.77	0.97
*e > i / _ u	1.44	0.54	0.8	2.18	1.38
*CC > C	1.38	0.42	0.8	2.03	1.23
*h- > Ø / # _ C	1.13	0.34	0.8	1.57	0.77
*-hw-, *-h- > -h-	1.35	0.41	0.8	1.88	1.08
*-i- > Ø	1.33	0.49	0.8	2.07	1.27
Ø > -h-	1.17	0.45	0.8	1.84	1.04
i-umlaut	1.19	0.38	0.8	1.67	0.87
*ē > ie	1.13	0.4	0.8	1.74	0.94
-e > -ea, -ia > -a	1.14	0.41	0.8	1.61	0.81
*au > ou; *ai > ei; *eu > iu	1.2	0.4	0.8	1.8	1
*ō > uo	1.34	0.54	0.8	2.1	1.3
*au > ō	1.72	0.53	0.8	2.5	1.7
V > Ø / _(C)#	1.26	0.42	0.8	1.96	1.16
-w > -o	1.43	0.59	0.8	2.29	1.49
ao > ō	1.41	0.51	0.8	2.16	1.36
CR# > CVR#	1.29	0.5	0.8	2.12	1.32
Ø > V / l/r _ h/w	1.37	0.54	0.8	2.21	1.41
ga- > gi-	1.49	0.55	0.82	2.28	1.46
*i > *e / _ [+lab./+vel.] [+voc., -hi]	1.39	0.55	0.8	2.14	1.34
V1 > V2 / _ CV2(C)	1.38	0.48	0.8	2	1.2
*i > e / [-high] C0 _	1.41	0.56	0.8	2.31	1.51
*-ō > -u	1.4	0.57	0.8	2.32	1.52

Table A.36 Posterior estimates of feature occurrence times (cont.)

Feature	Mean	SD	Lower-89CI	Higher-89CI	HDI range
eo > io	1.43	0.48	0.82	2	1.18
-m > -n	1.28	0.46	0.8	1.92	1.12
iu > [yː]	1.13	0.41	0.8	1.74	0.94
sk	1.5	0.57	0.8	2.48	1.68
-V > -e	1.14	0.35	0.8	1.61	0.81
*Þ > [t]	1.4	0.55	0.8	2.28	1.48
*-dē > *-dō	1.43	0.49	0.8	2.24	1.44
*-dum > *-dōm, etc.	1.27	0.49	0.8	1.94	1.14
*-anu	1.73	0.61	0.87	2.57	1.7
-īs	1.4	0.5	0.8	2.25	1.45
1sg. -m	1.21	0.4	0.8	1.81	1.01
*-zz- > -zt-	1.45	0.61	0.8	2.32	1.52
-amu ~ -emu	1.32	0.54	0.8	2.07	1.27
*-u > Ø / [+light] _	1.47	0.55	0.8	2.46	1.66
Ø > -u / [+heavy] _	1.37	0.55	0.8	2.2	1.4
zi ērist	1.25	0.44	0.8	1.83	1.03
Abstracts in -ī	1.3	0.52	0.8	2.26	1.46
habēta	1.41	0.6	0.8	2.38	1.58
u-stem > i-stem	1.23	0.39	0.8	1.6	0.8
-ēs	1.11	0.37	0.8	1.69	0.89
*Þ rīz > drī	1.57	0.63	0.8	2.55	1.75
-ōnne, -ēnne	1.45	0.67	0.8	2.59	1.79
*-ai-	1.25	0.43	0.8	1.85	1.05

Table A.37 Posterior estimates of feature occurrence times (cont.)

Feature	Mean	SD	Lower-89CI	Higher-89CI	HDI range
nom. pl., acc. pl. > acc. pl.	1.33	0.56	0.8	2.26	1.46
-er-	1.22	0.48	0.8	2.05	1.25
-o	1.51	0.57	0.8	2.2	1.4
1sg., 3sg. indic. > 3sg.	1.5	0.58	0.8	2.34	1.54
2sg. -s > -st	1.47	0.57	0.8	2.17	1.37
-ōno	1.4	0.51	0.8	2.05	1.25
dual > Ø	1.19	0.43	0.8	1.78	0.98
-u > -o	1.26	0.53	0.8	2.01	1.21
-in > -en	1.33	0.46	0.8	1.77	0.97
fem. jō-stems ~ ī-stems	1.46	0.62	0.8	2.38	1.58
ō-stems	1.6	0.7	0.8	2.62	1.82
n-stems	1.2	0.44	0.8	1.79	0.99
*CReC- > class IV	1.42	0.57	0.8	2.33	1.53
-ta	1.42	0.52	0.8	2.13	1.33
*þi- ~ *þe-	1.31	0.47	0.8	2	1.2
*hwi- ~ *hwe-	1.49	0.54	0.8	2.39	1.59
sīn	1.24	0.5	0.8	1.99	1.19
wellen	1.27	0.51	0.8	2.17	1.37
imu	1.58	0.65	0.8	2.62	1.82
sāhun	1.22	0.47	0.8	1.8	1
fateres, fatere, etc.	1.3	0.54	0.8	1.91	1.11
*drī + o	1.29	0.44	0.8	1.83	1.03
zi	1.38	0.48	0.8	2.17	1.37

Table A.38 Posterior estimates of feature occurrence times (cont.)

Feature	Mean	SD	Lower-89CI	Higher-89CI	HDI range
ir(-)	1.42	0.58	0.8	2.34	1.54
doret	1.17	0.46	0.8	1.87	1.07
inan > in	1.43	0.6	0.8	2.55	1.75
drīzehan	1.32	0.55	0.8	2.09	1.29
(h)we-	1.2	0.38	0.8	1.67	0.87
sī	1.23	0.54	0.8	2.19	1.39
gitar	1.53	0.5	0.8	2.27	1.47
bim	1.38	0.56	0.8	2.32	1.52
habēt	1.69	0.67	0.8	2.45	1.65
gisehan	1.18	0.42	0.8	1.82	1.02
sluog	1.26	0.53	0.8	2.27	1.47
stuont, stuontun, gistantan	1.41	0.56	0.8	2.21	1.41
werdan, wesan	1.31	0.53	0.8	2.21	1.41
blint man	1.27	0.47	0.8	1.92	1.12
V2	1.66	0.64	0.8	2.61	1.81
*[awjwj] > *[auj]	1.43	0.62	0.8	2.4	1.6
*w > ∅ / _ i	1.24	0.41	0.8	1.78	0.98
*a > *æ	1.29	0.53	0.8	2.35	1.55
*ai > ā	1.14	0.36	0.8	1.57	0.77
ā > o / [-stress]	1.15	0.4	0.8	1.78	0.98
*au > ēa	1.31	0.5	0.8	2.01	1.21
[+front] > V1V2	1.47	0.63	0.8	2.55	1.75
*hs > x	1.41	0.54	0.8	2.35	1.55

Table A.39 Posterior estimates of feature occurrence times (cont.)

Feature	Mean	SD	Lower-89CI	Higher-89CI	HDI range
*k, *g > [+palatal]	1.17	0.36	0.8	1.71	0.91
*-kw- > -k-	1.34	0.44	0.8	2.1	1.3
i-umlaut	1.23	0.38	0.8	1.83	1.03
/f, þ, s/ > [v, ð, z] / [+stress]σ_	1.27	0.42	0.8	1.85	1.05
Ø / C_ C	1.41	0.42	0.8	1.97	1.17
*i, *u > Ø / _ #	1.26	0.46	0.8	2.03	1.23
*þs > *ss	1.32	0.53	0.8	2.19	1.39
*b > f / _ #	1.35	0.47	0.8	1.93	1.13
*h > Ø	1.32	0.44	0.8	2.02	1.22
*æ > a / _ C1 [+back]	1.19	0.48	0.8	1.83	1.03
i > io	1.33	0.49	0.8	2.07	1.27
CR# > CVR#	1.35	0.55	0.8	2.21	1.41
æ, i > e	1.3	0.43	0.8	1.77	0.97
*-azd- > *-ezd-	1.28	0.53	0.8	1.88	1.08
*C(l/r) > *CC(l/r)	1.39	0.54	0.8	2.26	1.46
*i > Ø / CV.C _ l	1.18	0.5	0.8	2.07	1.27
Ṽ > V / _ CC(C)	1.28	0.49	0.8	2.04	1.24
a ū	1.2	0.42	0.8	1.78	0.98
-sr- > -ss-	1.5	0.58	0.8	2.43	1.63
io, īo > eo, ēo	1.25	0.47	0.8	2.01	1.21
*-ēja- > *-ejV	1.11	0.39	0.8	1.6	0.8
*-iz	1.15	0.42	0.8	1.67	0.87
hettend	1.37	0.58	0.8	2.3	1.5

Table A.40 Posterior estimates of feature occurrence times (cont.)

Feature	Mean	SD	Lower-89CI	Higher-89CI	HDI range
wæter, wæteres	1.15	0.42	0.8	1.61	0.81
-CC-, -rġ-	1.15	0.31	0.8	1.5	0.7
*haubud, etc.	1.5	0.68	0.81	2.67	1.86
þā	1.46	0.63	0.8	2.52	1.72
Abstracts in *-u	1.51	0.65	0.8	2.61	1.81
-i	1.4	0.54	0.8	2.23	1.43
-æs, -æ, -um	1.28	0.54	0.8	2.25	1.45
*-æ-	1.44	0.64	0.8	2.59	1.79
heardra	1.02	0.3	0.8	1.3	0.5
*-z- ~ *-s-; *-d- ~ *-þ-	1.77	0.72	0.81	2.65	1.84
-e	1.56	0.55	0.8	2.22	1.42
1sg. subj.	1.31	0.46	0.8	1.85	1.05
acc. pl., nom. pl > nom. pl	1.19	0.44	0.8	1.78	0.98
-u	1.28	0.54	0.8	2.06	1.26
*-st	1.19	0.33	0.8	1.58	0.78
hæbbe wē	1.28	0.45	0.8	2.05	1.25
-tl > -ld	1.33	0.56	0.8	2.36	1.56
hrēaw(-), fēawe	1.34	0.58	0.8	2.34	1.54
dohtur	1.24	0.51	0.8	1.89	1.09
u-stems	1.27	0.39	0.8	1.72	0.92
gen. prons.	1.58	0.64	0.8	2.51	1.71
-tiġ	1.27	0.49	0.8	2.08	1.28
þȳ	1.55	0.66	0.8	2.57	1.77

Table A.41 Posterior estimates of feature occurrence times (cont.)

Feature	Mean	SD	Lower-89CI	Higher-89CI	HDI range
þrīora	1.37	0.59	0.8	2.35	1.55
*ni wi- > ny-	1.21	0.44	0.8	1.92	1.12
ēode	1.22	0.38	0.8	1.76	0.96
þreotīene	1.41	0.54	0.8	2.16	1.36
hwæs	1.3	0.5	0.8	1.96	1.16
wilt	1.24	0.46	0.8	1.95	1.15
*ar-	1.24	0.38	0.8	1.7	0.9
eam	1.48	0.51	0.8	2.28	1.48
guma	1.46	0.55	0.8	2.25	1.45
cwom > com	1.32	0.55	0.8	2.14	1.34
*hes > his	1.47	0.62	0.8	2.54	1.74
*her- > hir-	1.58	0.57	0.8	2.39	1.59
ēow	1.14	0.48	0.8	2.02	1.22
*gā-	1.22	0.55	0.8	2.08	1.28
ūre	1.25	0.43	0.82	1.76	0.94
miklǣ	1.18	0.53	0.8	2.33	1.53
sīe	1.32	0.54	0.8	2.2	1.4
dearr	1.39	0.57	0.8	2.32	1.52
hæbbe	1.4	0.61	0.8	2.54	1.74
tū	1.17	0.38	0.8	1.63	0.83
dæġ	1.37	0.55	0.8	2.31	1.51
dōm, dōð, etc.	1.15	0.41	0.8	1.67	0.87
dyde	1.18	0.46	0.8	2.09	1.29

Table A.42 Posterior estimates of feature occurrence times (cont.)

Feature	Mean	SD	Lower-89CI	Higher-89CI	HDI range
*ai,*au,*eu > ā, ē, iā	1.15	0.39	0.8	1.92	1.12
WGmc *a > PFris *æ	1.24	0.48	0.8	2.04	1.24
*g > j	1.38	0.51	0.8	2.16	1.36
k > kj > tj > ts	1.44	0.65	0.8	2.53	1.73
i-mutation	1.45	0.58	0.82	2.43	1.61
*i > iu	1.37	0.51	0.8	2.1	1.3
*e > *eu > iu	1.4	0.48	0.8	2.05	1.25
loss of u/w after iu	1.39	0.51	0.8	2.15	1.35
loss of intervoc. -h-, aha > a	1.19	0.35	0.8	1.62	0.82
loss of *ga-/*gi-	1.27	0.42	0.81	1.94	1.13
metathesis of r	1.26	0.45	0.8	1.81	1.01
loss of -n	1.45	0.56	0.8	2.29	1.49
-e- instead of -i-	1.19	0.42	0.8	1.73	0.93
1./2. ps. sg./pl. dat. = 1./2. ps. sg./pl. acc.	1.51	0.64	0.8	2.56	1.76
fem. -jon/-in-stems to str. fem. decl.	1.49	0.65	0.8	2.48	1.68
v drop after l/r	1.2	0.43	0.8	1.69	0.89
endings -ene/-ende	1.15	0.45	0.8	1.86	1.06
loss of distinct. feat. in u-/wo- adj.	1.26	0.53	0.8	2.01	1.21
stem vowel shortening	1.26	0.42	0.8	1.87	1.07
*ō > *ū/ [+stress]	1.31	0.51	0.8	2.33	1.53
-anh- > -ah-	2.25	0.42	1.81	2.8	0.99

References

Agee, Joshua (2018). "A glottometric subgrouping of the early Germanic languages". MA thesis. San Jose State University.

Aikhenvald, Alexandra Y. (2007). "Grammars in contact: A cross-linguistic perspective". In: *Grammars in contact: A cross-linguistic typology* Ed. by Alexandra Y. Aikhenvald and Robert M. W. Dixon. Oxford: Oxford University Press, 1–54.

Alkire, Ti and Carol Rosen (2010). *Romance languages: A historical introduction.* Cambridge: Cambridge University Press.

Andersen, Henning (2006). "Synchrony, diachrony, and evolution". In: *Competing models of linguistic change: Evolution and beyond* Ed. by Ole Nedergaard Thomsen. Vol. 279. Amsterdam: John Benjamins Publishing, 59–90.

Antonsen, Elmer H. (1965). "On Defining Stages in Prehistoric Germanic". In: *Language* 41.1, 19–36.

Anttila, Raimo (1989). *Historical and comparative linguistics* Amsterdam/Philadelphia: John Benjamins.

Atkinson, Quentin D. and Russell D. Gray (2005). "Curious parallels and curious connections—phylogenetic thinking in biology and historical linguistics". In: *Systematic biology* 54.4, 513–526.

Barido-Sottani, Joëlle et al. (2020). "Estimating a time-calibrated phylogeny of fossil and extant taxa using RevBayes". In: *Phylogenetics in the genomic era* Ed. by Céline Scornavacca, Frédéric Delsuc, and Nicolas Galtier. Authors open access book, 5.2:1–5.2:23.

Barrack, Charles M. (1987). "The fate of Protogermanic ∗x". In: *Zeitschrift für Dialektologie und Linguistik* 54.3, 340–344.

Bergsland, Knut and Hans Vogt (1962). "On the validity of glottochronology". In: *Current anthropology* 3.2, 115–153.

Bergstra, James, Daniel Yamins, and David Cox (2013). "Making a science of model search: Hyperparameter optimization in hundreds of dimensions for vision architectures". In: *Proceedings of the 30th international conference on machine learning* Vol. 28.1, 115–123.

Bhavnani, Ravi et al. (2014). "Group segregation and urban violence". In: *American journal of political science* 58.1, 226–245.

Bishop, Christopher M. (2006). *Pattern recognition and machine learning* New York: Springer.

Bleiker, Jürg (1963). "Das Burgunderproblem in germanistischer Sicht". In: *Vox Romanica* 22, 13–58.

Bouckaert, Remco et al. (2012). "Mapping the origins and expansion of the Indo-European language family". In: *Science* 337.6097, 957–960.

Bowern, Claire (2006). "Punctuated equilibrium and language change". In: *Encyclopedia of language and linguistics* 286–289.

Bowern, Claire (2012). "The riddle of Tasmanian languages". In: *Proceedings of the Royal Society B: Biological sciences* 279.1747, 4590–4595.

Bowern, Claire (2013). "Relatedness as a Factor in Language Contact". In: *Journal of language contact* 6.2, 411–432.

Bowern, Claire (2018). "Computational phylogenetics". In: *Annual review of linguistics* 4, 281–296.

Bowern, Claire and Quentin D. Atkinson (2012). "Computational phylogenetics and the internal structure of Pama-Nyungan". In: *Language* 817–845.

Boyd, Robert and Peter J. Richerson (2005). *The origin and evolution of cultures*. Oxford: Oxford University Press.

Brandt, Jochen (2014). "Soziologische Aspekte des Jastorf-Konzepts". In: *Das Jastorf-Konzept und die vorrömische Eisenzeit im nördlichen Mitteleuropa* Ed. by Jochen Brandt and Björn Rauchfuß. Hamburg: Archäologisches Museum Hamburg, 69–80.

Braune, Wilhelm and Hans Eggers (1987). *Althochdeutsche Grammatik* Tübingen: de Gruyter.

Braune, Wilhelm and Frank Heidermanns (2004). *Gotische Grammatik: Mit Lesestücken und Wörterverzeichnis* 20. Aufl. Vol. 1. Sammlung kurzer Grammatiken germanischer Dialekte A, Hauptreihe. Tübingen: Niemeyer.

Braune, Wilhelm and Ingo Reiffenstein (2004). *Althochdeutsche Grammatik* 15th ed. Tübingen: Niemeyer.

Bremmer, Rolf H. (2009). *An introduction to Old Frisian: History, grammar, reader, glossary* Amsterdam: John Benjamins Publishing.

Brumlich, Markolf (2020). "The Teltow—an early iron smelting district of the Jastorf Culture". In: *The coming of iron. The beginnings of iron smelting in central Europe* Ed. by Markolf Brumlich, Enrico Lehnhardt, and Michael Meyer. Rahden: Marie Leidorf, 127–154.

Bryant, David and Vincent Moulton (2002). "NeighborNet: An agglomerative method for the construction of planar phylogenetic networks". In: *2nd international workshop on algorithms in bioinformatics*, 375–391.

Bürkner, Paul-Christian (2017). "brms: An R Package for Bayesian Multilevel Models Using Stan". In: *Journal of statistical software* 80.1, 1–28.

Bussmann, Kathrin S. (2004). *Diphthongs in Frisian: A comparative analysis of phonemic inventories past and present*. Heidelberg: Winter.

Campbell, Lyle (2013). *Historical linguistics: An introduction* 3. ed. Edinburgh: Edinburgh University Press.

Chang, Will et al. (2015). "Ancestry-constrained phylogenetic analysis supports the Indo-European steppe hypothesis". In: *Language* 91.1, 194–244.

Clackson, James (2007). *Indo-European linguistics: An introduction* Cambridge textbooks in linguistics. Cambridge: Cambridge University Press.

Colleran, Rebecca Anne Bills (2017). "Keeping it in the family: Disentangling contact and inheritance in closely related languages". PhD Thesis. The University of Edinburgh.

Condamine, Fabien L., Jonathan Rolland, and Helene Morlon (2013). "Macroevolutionary perspectives to environmental change". In: *Ecology letters* 16, 72–85.

Croft, William (2000). *Explaining language change: An evolutionary approach* Harlow: Pearson Education.

Crowley, Terry and Claire Bowern (2010). *An introduction to historical linguistics* Oxford: Oxford University Press.

Daniels, Don, Danielle Barth, and Wolfgang Barth (2019). "Subgrouping the Sogeram languages: A critical appraisal of historical glottometry". In: *Journal of historical linguistics* 9.1, 92–127.

Dixon, Robert M.W. (1997). *The rise and fall of languages* Cambridge: Cambridge University Press.

Drinka, Bridget (2013). "Phylogenetic and areal models of Indo-European relatedness: The role of contact in reconstruction". In: *Journal of language contact* 6.2, 379–410.

Dunn, Michael et al. (2008). "Structural phylogeny in historical linguistics: Methodological explorations applied in Island Melanesia". In: *Language* 84.4, 710–759.

Euler, Wolfram (2009). *Sprache und Herkunft der Germanen* Hamburg, London: Inspiration Un Limited.

Fortson, Benjamin W. IV. (2010). *Indo-European language and culture: An introduction* Chichester: Wiley-Blackwell.

Fox, Anthony (1995). *Linguistic reconstruction: An introduction to theory and method* Oxford: Oxford University Press.

François, Alexandre (2015). "Trees, waves and linkages: Models of language diversification". In: *The Routledge handbook of historical linguistics* Ed. by Claire Bowern and Bethwyn Evans. New York: Routledge, 161–189.

Francovich Onesti, Nicoletta (2002). *I Vandali: Lingua e storia* Vol. 14. Lingue e letterature Carocci. Roma: Carocci.

Francovich Onesti, Nicoletta (2008). "Ostrogothic and Burgundian personal names in comparison: A contrastive study". In: *Studien zu Literatur, Sprache und Geschichte in Europa: Wolfgang Haubrichs zum 65. Geburtstag gewidmet* Ed. by Albrecht Greule et al. St. Ingbert: Röhrig Universitätsverlag, 267–280.

Frey, Benjamin and Joseph Salmons (2012). "Dialect and language contact in emerging Germanic". In: *Archaeology and language: Indo-European studies presented to James P. Mallory* Ed. by Martin E. Huld, Karlene Jones-Bley, and Dean Miller. Washington, D.C.: Institute for the Study of Man, 95–120.

Fulk, Robert Dennis (2018). *A comparative grammar of the early Germanic languages* Vol. 3. Amsterdam/Philadelphia: John Benjamins Publishing Company.

Garamszegi, László Zsolt (2014). *Modern phylogenetic comparative methods and their application in evolutionary biology: Concepts and practice* Berlin: Springer.

Gelman, Andrew et al. (2013). *Bayesian data analysis* New York: CRC press.

Giles, Howard, Nikolas Coupland, and Justine Coupland (1991). *Contexts of accommodation: Developments in applied sociolinguistics* Studies in Emotion and Social Interaction. Cambridge: Cambridge University Press.

Gong, Tao, James W. Minett, and W.S.-Y. Wang (2006). "Language origin and the effects of individuals' popularity". In: *2006 IEEE international conference on evolutionary computation* IEEE, 999–1006.

Grant, Anthony P. (2020). "Contact and convergence". In: *The handbook of language contact* Ed. by Raymond Hickey. Hoboken: John Wiley & Sons, 113–128.

Gray, Russell D. and Quentin D. Atkinson (2003). "Language-tree divergence times support the Anatolian theory of Indo-European origin". In: *Nature* 426.6965, 435–439.

Gray, Russell D., David Bryant, and Simon J. Greenhill (2010). "On the shape and fabric of human history". In: *Philosophical transactions of the Royal Society B: Biological sciences* 365.1559, 3923–3933.

Gray, Russell D., Simon J. Greenhill, Quentin D. Atkinson, et al. (2013). "Phylogenetic models of language change: Three new questions". In: *Cultural evolution: Society, technology, language, and religion* Ed. by Peter J. Richerson and Morten H. Christiansen. Cambridge: MIT Press, 285–300.

Gray, Russell D., Simon J. Greenhill, and Robert M. Ross (2007). "The pleasures and perils of Darwinizing culture (with phylogenies)". In: *Biological theory* 2.4, 360–375.

Greenhill, Simon J., Alexei J. Drummond, and Russell D. Gray (2010). "How accurate and robust are the phylogenetic estimates of Austronesian language relationships?" In: *PloS one* 5.3.

Greenhill, Simon J. and Russell D. Gray (2012). "Basic vocabulary and Bayesian phylolinguistics: Issues of understanding and representation". In: *Diachronica* 29.4, 523–537.

Greenhill, Simon J., Russell D. Gray, et al. (2009). "Austronesian language phylogenies: myths and misconceptions about Bayesian computational methods". In: *Austronesian historical linguistics and culture history: A festschrift for Robert Blust* Ed. by Alexander Adelaar, Andrew Pawley, et al. Canberra: Pacific Linguistics, 375–397.

Grønvik, Ottar (1983). *Die dialektgeographische Stellung des Krimgotischen und die krimgotische cantilena* Oslo/Bergen/Stavanger/Tromsø: Univ.-Forl.

Grønvik, Ottar (1998). *Untersuchungen zur älteren nordischen und germanischen Sprachgeschichte.* Vol. 18. Frankfurt am Main: Peter Lang.

Hachmann, Rolf (1970). *Die Goten und Skandinavien* Berlin: de Gruyter.

Harbert, Wayne (2007). *The Germanic languages* Cambridge language surveys. Cambridge: Cambridge University Press.

Hartmann, Frederik (2020). *The Vandalic language—Origins and relationships* Heidelberg: Winter.

Hartmann, Frederik (2021). Old Frisian Breaking and Labial Mutation Revisited, Amsterdamer Beiträge zur älteren Germanistik, 80(4), 462–475.

Hartmann, Frederik and Chiara Riegger (2022). "The Burgundian language and its phylogeny. A cladistical investigation". In: *North-Western European language evolution (NOWELE)* 75.1, 42–80.

Hasegawa, Masami, Hirohisa Kishino, and Taka-aki Yano (1985). "Dating of the human-ape splitting by a molecular clock of mitochondrial DNA". In: *Journal of molecular evolution* 22.2, 160–174.

Haubrichs, Wolfgang (2014). "Personennamen sprachlich ostgermanischer Provenienz". In: *Studia anthroponymica scandinavica* 32, 5–35.

Haubrichs, Wolfgang and Max Pfister (2008). "Burgundisch (Burgundian)". In: *Wieser Enzyklopädie. Sprachen des europäischen Westens* Ed. by Ulrich Ammon and Harald Haarmann. Klagenfurt: Wieser Verlag, 73–80.

Haugen, Einar (1982). *Scandinavian language structures: A comparative historical survey* Tübingen: Niemeyer.

Haugen, Einar (1984). *Die Skandinavischen Sprachen* Hamburg: Helmut Buske Verlag.

Heath, Tracy A., John P. Huelsenbeck, and Tanja Stadler (2014). "The fossilized birth–death process for coherent calibration of divergence-time estimates". In: *Proceedings of the National Academy of Sciences* 111.29, 2957–2966.

Heather, Peter (1996). *The Goths* Oxford: Blackwell.

Heather, Peter (2009). *Empires and barbarians: The fall of Rome and the birth of Europe* Oxford: Oxford University Press.

Heggarty, Paul (2021). "Cognacy databases and phylogenetic research on Indo-European". In: *Annual review of linguistics* 7, 371–394.

Heggarty, Paul, Warren Maguire, and April McMahon (2010). "Splits or waves? Trees or webs? How divergence measures and network analysis can unravel language histories". In: *Philosophical transactions of the Royal Society B: Biological sciences* 365.1559, 3829–3843.

Heine, Bernd and Tania Kuteva (2020). "Contact and grammaticalization". In: *The handbook of language contact* Ed. by Raymond Hickey. Hoboken: John Wiley & Sons, 93–112.

Heled, Joseph and Alexei J. Drummond (2012). "Calibrated tree priors for relaxed phylogenetics and divergence time estimation". In: *Systematic biology* 61.1, 138–149.

Hickey, Raymond (2020). "Contact and language shift". In: *The handbook of language contact* Ed. by Raymond Hickey. Hoboken: John Wiley & Sons, 149–168.

Ho, Simon Y. W. and Matthew J. Phillips (2009). "Accounting for calibration uncertainty in phylogenetic estimation of evolutionary divergence times". In: *Systematic biology* 58.3, 367–380.

Hock, Hans Henrich (1991). *Principles of historical linguistics* Berlin: Walter de Gruyter.

Höhna, Sebastian (2014). "Likelihood inference of non-constant diversification rates with incomplete taxon sampling". In: *PLoS one* 9.1.

Höhna, Sebastian (2015). "The time-dependent reconstructed evolutionary process with a key-role for mass-extinction events". In: *Journal of theoretical biology* 380, 321–331.

Höhna, Sebastian and Will A. Freyman (2016). *RevGadgets: Process output generated by RevBayes* R package version 1.0.0.

Höhna, Sebastian, Michael J. Landis, et al. (2017). *Statistical phylogenetic inference using RevBayes* Accessed: 18.5.2021.

Holm, Hans J. (2000). "Genealogy of the main Indo-European branches applying the separation base method". In: *Journal of quantitative linguistics* 7.2, 73–95.

Huson, Daniel H. and David Bryant (2006). "Application of phylogenetic networks in evolutionary studies". In: *Molecular biology and evolution* 23.2, 254–267.

Hutterer, Claus Jurgen (1975). *Die germanischen Sprachen* Budapest: Akadémiai Kiadó.

Iverson, Gregory K., Garry W. Davis, and Joseph C. Salmons (1994). "Blocking environments in Old High German umlaut". In: *Folia linguistica historica* 15, 131–148.

Jacques, Guillaume and Johann-Mattis List (2019). "Save the trees: Why we need tree models in linguistic reconstruction (and when we should apply them)". In: *Journal of historical linguistics* 9.1, 128–167.

Jukes, Thomas H., Charles R. Cantor, et al. (1969). "Evolution of protein molecules". In: *Mammalian protein metabolism* Ed. by H. N. Munro. New York: Academic Press, 21–132.

Karstien, Carl (1939). *Historische deutsche Grammatik* Vol. 20. Heidelberg: Winter.

Kassambara, Alboukadel and Fabian Mundt (2020). *factoextra: Extract and visualize the results of multivariate data analyses* R package version 1.0.7. URL: https://CRAN.R-project.org/package=factoextra.

Koch, John (2020). *Celto-Germanic. Later prehistory and post-Proto-Indo-European vocabulary in the north and west* Aberystwyth: University of Wales Centre for Advanced Welsh and Celtic Studies.

König, Ekkehard and Johan van der Auwera (1994). *The Germanic languages* London: Routledge.

König, Werner (2007). *dtv-Atlas deutsche Sprache* 16th ed. München: Deutscher Taschenbuch Verlag.

Kortlandt, Frederik (2001). "The origin of the Goths". In: *Amsterdamer Beiträge zur älteren Germanistik* 55.1, 21–25.

Kortlandt, Frederik (2017). "Old English and Old Frisian". In: *Us Wurk* 66.3–4, 122–127.

Krahe, Hans (1948). *Historische Laut-und Formenlehre des Gotischen* Heidelberg: Winter.

Krahe, Hans and Wolfgang Meid (1969). *Germanische Sprachwissenschaft* Berlin: De Gruyter.

Krause, Wolfgang (1953). *Handbuch des Gotischen: Handbücher für das germanistische Studium* München: Beck.

Krogh, Steffen (1996). *Die Stellung des Altsächsischen im Rahmen der germanischen Sprachen* Vol. 29. Göttingen: Vandenhoeck & Ruprecht.

Krogh, Steffen (2013). "Die Anfänge des Altsächsischen". In: *NOWELE* 66.2, 141–168.

Kufner, Herbert L. (1972). "The grouping and separation of the Germanic languages". In: *Toward a grammar of Proto-Germanic* Ed. by Frans van Coetsem and Herbert L. Kufner. Tübingen: Niemeyer, 71–98.

Kuhn, Hans (1955). "Zur Gliederung der germanischen Sprachen". In: *Zeitschrift für deutsches Altertum und deutsche Literatur* 86.1, 1–47.

Labov, William (2001). *Principles of linguistic change Volume 2: Social factors.* Malden: Blackwell.

Landis, Michael J. et al. (2013). "Bayesian analysis of biogeography when the number of areas is large". In: *Systematic biology* 62.6, 789–804.

Lass, Roger (1994). *Old English: A historical linguistic companion* Cambridge: Cambridge University Press.

Lê, Sébastien, Julie Josse, and François Husson (2008). "FactoMineR: A package for multivariate analysis". In: *Journal of statistical software* 25.1, 1–18.

Lehmann, Winfred P. (1961). "A definition of Proto-Germanic: A study in the chronological delimitation of languages". In: *Language* 37.1, 67–74.

Lehmann, Winfred P. (1966). "The grouping of the Germanic languages". In: *Ancient Indo-European dialects: Proceedings of the conference on Indo-European linguistics held at the University of California, Los Angeles, April 25–27, 1963* Ed. by Henrik Birnbaum and Jaan Puhvel. Berkeley: University of California Press, 13–28.

Lekvam, Torvald, Björn Gambäck, and Lars Bungum (2014). "Agent-based modeling of language evolution". In: *Proceedings of the 5th workshop on cognitive aspects of computational language learning (CogACLL)* 49–54.

Levy, Dan and Lior Pachter (2011). "The neighbor-net algorithm". In: *Advances in applied mathematics* 47.2, 240–258.

Longobardi, Giuseppe and Cristina Guardiano (2009). "Evidence for syntax as a signal of historical relatedness". In: *Lingua* 119.11, 1679–1706.

Longobardi, Giuseppe, Cristina Guardiano, et al. (2013). "Toward a syntactic phylogeny of modern Indo-European languages". In: *Journal of historical linguistics* 3.1, 122–152.

Mallory, James P. (1989). *In search of the Indo-Europeans: Language, archaeology and myth* Vol. 186. London: Thames and Hudson.

Manczak, Witold (1982). "Kamen die Goten aus Skandinavien?" In: *Indogermanische Forschungen* 87, 127.

Manczak, Witold (1987). "On the Ausgliederung of Germanic languages". In: *Journal of Indo-European studies* 15.1–2, 1–17.

Markey, Thomas (1976). *Germanic dialect grouping and the position of Ingvæonic.* Vol. 15. Institut für Sprachwissenschaft der Universität Innsbruck.

Martens, Jes (2014). "Jastorf and Jutland". In: *Das Jastorf-Konzept und die vor-römische Eisenzeit im nördlichen Mitteleuropa* Ed. by Jochen Brandt and Björn Rauchfuß. Hamburg: Archäologisches Museum Hamburg, 245–266.

Martens, Jes (2017). "Continuity or rupture? Some remarks on the transition from the Early to the Late Pre-Roman Iron Age in Northern Central Europe". In: *Settlements pottery of the pre-Roman Iron Age in central European Barbaricum—new research perspectives* Ed. by Andrzej Michalowski et al. Poznań: Biblioteka Telgte Wydawnictwo, 31–39.

Maurer, Friedrich (1952). *Nordgermanen und Alemannen, Studien zur germanischen und frühdeutschen Sprachgeschichte, Stammes-und Volkskunde* 3rd ed. Bern/München: Francke/Lehnen.

McElreath, Richard (2020). *Statistical rethinking: A Bayesian course with examples in R and Stan* Boca Raton: CRC press.

McMahon, April and Robert McMahon (2008). "Genetics, historical linguistics and language variation". In: *Language and linguistics compass* 2.2, 264–288.

Mesoudi, Alex, Andrew Whiten, and Kevin N. Laland (2004). "Perspective: Is human cultural evolution Darwinian? Evidence reviewed from the perspective of *The Origin of Species*". In: *Evolution* 58.1, 1–11.

Mesoudi, Alex, Andrew Whiten, and Kevin N. Laland (2006). "Towards a unified science of cultural evolution". In: *Behavioral and brain sciences* 29.4, 329.

Miller, D. Gary (2019). *The Oxford Gothic grammar* Oxford: Oxford University Press.

Nedoma, Robert (2017). "The documentation of Germanic". In: *Handbook of comparative and historical Indo-European linguistics* Ed. by Jared Klein, Brian Joseph, and Matthias Fritz. Vol. 2. Berlin: De Gruyter Mouton, 875–888.

Nee, Sean, Robert Mccredie May, and Paul H. Harvey (1994). "The reconstructed evolutionary process". In: *Philosophical transactions of the Royal Society of London. Series B: Biological sciences* 344.1309, 305–311.

Nichols, Johanna and Tandy Warnow (2008). "Tutorial on computational linguistic phylogeny". In: *Language and linguistics compass* 2.5, 760–820.

Nielsen, Hans Frede (1981). *Old English and the continental Germanic languages: a survey of morphological and phonological interrelations* Vol. 33. Innsbruck: Institut für Sprachwissenschaft der Universität Innsbruck.

Nielsen, Hans Frede (1989). *The Germanic languages: Origins and early dialectal interrelations* Tuscaloosa: University of Alabama Press.

Nielsen, Hans Frede (1995). "Methodological problems in Germanic dialect grouping". In: *Nord-westgermanisch* Ed. by Edith Marold and Christiane Zimmermann. Berlin: de Gruyter, 115–124.

Nielsen, Hans Frede (2000). *The early runic language of Scandinavia* Heidelberg: Winter.

Nielsen, Hans Frede (2017). "The phonological systems of Biblical Gothic and Crimean Gothic compared". In: *Die Faszination des Verborgenen und seine Entschlusselung-Rāð i sāR kunni: Beiträge zur Runologie, skandinavistischen Mediävistik und germanischen Sprachwissenschaft* Ed. by Jana Krüger et al. Berlin/Boston: De Gruyter, 277–290.

Noreen, Adolf (1923). *Altisländische und altnorwegische Grammatik (Laut- und Flexionslehre): Unter Berücksichtigung des Urnordischen* 4th ed. Vol. I. Halle (Saale): Niemeyer.

Penzl, Herbert (1985). "Zur gotischen Urheimat und Ausgliederung der germanischen Dialekte". In: *Indogermanische Forschungen* 90.1985, 147–167.

Penzl, Herbert (1989). "Die Gallehusinschrift: Trummer der nordisch-westgermanischen Ursprache". In: *Germanische Rest- und Trümmersprachen* Ed. by Heinrich Beck. Berlin/Boston: De Gruyter, 87–96.

Pereltsvaig, Asya and Martin W. Lewis (2015). *The Indo-European controversy* Cambridge: Cambridge University Press.

Pickering, Martin J. and Simon Garrod (2004). "The interactive-alignment model: Developments and refinements". In: *Behavioral and brain sciences* 27.2, 212225.

Plassmann, Alheydis (2009). *Origo gentis* Berlin: Akademie Verlag.

Plummer, Martyn et al. (2006). "CODA: Convergence diagnosis and output analysis for MCMC". In: *R News* 6.1, 7–11.

Polomé, Edgar C. (1992). "Zur Chronologie des Germanischen". In: *Rekonstruktion und relative Chronologie: Akten der VIII. Fachtagung der Indogermanischen Gesellschaft, Leiden, 31. August–4. September 1987* Ed. by Robert Stephen Paul Beekes, Alexander Lubotsky, and Joseph Johannes Sicco Weitenberg. Vol. 65. Innsbruck: Institut für Sprachwissenschaft der Universität Innsbruck, 55–73.

Prokosch, Eduard (1939). *A comparative Germanic grammar* Vol. 4. Philadelphia: Linguistic Society of America.

Pyron, R. Alexander (2011). "Divergence time estimation using fossils as terminal taxa and the origins of Lissamphibia". In: *Systematic biology* 60.4, 466–481.

Railsback, Steven F. and Volker Grimm (2019). *Agent-based and individual-based modeling: A practical introduction* Princeton: Princeton University Press.

Rauch, Irmengard (1992). *The Old Saxon language: Grammar, epic narrative, linguistic interference* Vol. 1. New York: Peter Lang.

Ree, Richard H. et al. (2005). "A likelihood framework for inferring the evolution of geographic range on phylogenetic trees". In: *Evolution* 59.11, 2299–2311.

Reichert, Hermann (2009). "Sprache und Namen der Wandalen in Afrika". In: *Namen des Frühmittelalters als sprachliche Zeugnisse und als Geschichtsquellen*. Ed. by Albrecht Greule and Matthias Springer. Reallexikon der Germanischen Altertumskunde—Ergänzungsbände. Berlin/Boston: De Gruyter, 43–120.

Ren, Chuanjun, Chenghui Yang, and Shiyao Jin (2009). "Agent-based modeling and simulation on emergency evacuation". In: *International conference on complex sciences* 1451–1461.

Ringe, Donald A. (2017). *From Proto-Indo-European to Proto-Germanic* Second edition. Vol. 1. A linguistic history of English. Oxford: Oxford University Press.

Ringe, Donald A. and Ann Taylor (2014). *The development of Old English* 1st ed. Vol. 2. *A linguistic history of English* Oxford: Oxford University Press.

Ringe, Donald A., Tandy Warnow, and Ann Taylor (2002). "Indo-European and Computational Cladistics". In: *Transactions of the Philological Society* 100.1, 59–129.

Roberge, Paul (2020). "Contact and the history of Germanic languages". In: *The handbook of language contact* Ed. by Raymond Hickey. Hoboken: John Wiley & Sons, 406–431.

Robinson, Orrin W. (1993). *Old English and its closest relatives: a survey of the earliest Germanic languages* Stanford: Stanford University Press.

Ronquist, Fredrik, Seraina Klopfstein, et al. (2012). "A total-evidence approach to dating with fossils, applied to the early radiation of the Hymenoptera". In: *Systematic biology* 61.6, 973–999.

Ronquist, Fredrik, Paul van der Mark, and John P. Huelsenbeck (2009). "Bayesian phylogenetic analysis using MrBayes". In: Cambridge: Cambridge University Press, 210–266.

Rübekeil, Ludwig et al. (2017). "The dialectology of Germanic". In: *Handbücher zur Sprach- und Kommunikationswissenschaft/Handbooks of linguistics and communication science* 41.2, 986–1002.

Saitou, Naruya and Masatoshi Nei (1987). "The neighbor-joining method: a new method for reconstructing phylogenetic trees." In: *Molecular biology and evolution* 4.4, 406–425.

Salmons, Joseph (2018). *A history of German: What the past reveals about today's language* 2nd ed. Oxford: Oxford University Press.

Schleicher, August (1860). *Die deutsche Sprache* Stuttgart: Cotta.

Schliep, Klaus P. (2011). "phangorn: phylogenetic analysis in R". In: *Bioinformatics* 27.4, 592–593.

Schmidt, Johannes (1872). *Die Verwandtschaftsverhältnisse der indogermanischen Sprachen* Weimar: Bohlau.

Schulte, Kim (2011). "Romanian studies: Language and linguistics". In: *The year's work in modern language studies* 73.1, 266–283.

Schulze, Christian, Dietrich Stauffer, and Søren Wichmann (2007). "Birth, survival and death of languages by Monte Carlo simulation". In: *arXiv preprint arXiv:0704.0691*.

Schwartz, Stephen P. (1968). "The use of onomastics in Germanic linguistics: The first steps". In: *Names* 16.2, 119–126.

Schwarz, Ernst (1951). *Goten, Nordgermanen, Angelsachsen: Studien zur Ausgliederung der germanischen Sprachen* Vol. 2. Bibliotheca Germanica. Bern: Francke.

Seebold, Elmar (2013). "Die Aufgliederung der germanischen Sprachen". In: *NOW-ELE* 66.1, 55–77.

Shahriari, Bobak et al. (2016). "Taking the human out of the loop: A review of Bayesian optimization". In: *Proceedings of the IEEE* 104.1, 148–175.

Smith, Jeremy J. (2009). *Old English: A linguistic introduction* Cambridge: Cambridge University Press.

Sokal, Robert R. and Charles D. Michener (1958). *A statistical method for evaluating systematic relationships.* Lawrence: University of Kansas.

Sonderegger, Stefan (2012). *Althochdeutsche Sprache und Literatur: Eine Einführung in das älteste Deutsch. Darstellung und Grammatik* Berlin: Walter de Gruyter.

Sóskuthy, Márton (2015). "Understanding change through stability: A computational study of sound change actuation". In: *Lingua* 163, 40–60.

Stearns, MacDonald (1989). "Das Krimgotische". In: *Germanische Rest- und Trümmersprachen* Ed. by Heinrich Beck. Berlin: de Gruyter, 175–194.

Steels, Luc (2011). "Modeling the cultural evolution of language". In: *Physics of life reviews* 8.4, 339–356.

Steinacher, Roland (2020). "Rome and its created northerners". In: *Interrogating the 'Germanic'* Ed. by Matthias Friedrich and James M. Harland. Berlin/Boston: De Gruyter, 31–66.

Stiles, Patrick V. (1995). "Remarks on the "Anglo-Frisian" thesis". In: *Friesische Studien II.* Ed. by Volkert F. Faltings, Alastair G. H. Walker, and Ommo Wilts. Odense: Odense University Press, 177–220.

Stiles, Patrick V. (2013). "The Pan-West Germanic isoglosses and the sub-relationships of West Germanic to other branches". In: *North-Western European language evolution (NOWELE)* 66.1, 5–38.

Streitberg, Wilhelm (1896). *Urgermanische Grammatik: Einführung in das vergleichende Studium der altgermanischen Dialekte* Vol. 1. Heidelberg: Winter.

Tavaré, Simon et al. (1986). "Some probabilistic and statistical problems in the analysis of DNA sequences". In: *Lectures on mathematics in the life sciences* 17.2, 57–86.

Tischler, Daniel and Rudolf Moosbrugger-Leu (1982). "Die Aufschriften auf burgundischen Danielschnallen: Mit Zeichnungen von R. Moosbrugger-Leu". In: *Beiträge zur Namenforschung* 17.2, 113–160.

Todd, Malcolm (2009). *The early Germans* New York: John Wiley & Sons.

Turchin, Peter et al. (2013). "War, space, and the evolution of Old World complex societies". In: *Proceedings of the National Academy of Sciences* 110.41, 16384–16389.

Van Coetsem, Frans and Alfred Bammesberger (1994). *The vocalism of the Germanic parent language: Systemic evolution and sociohistorical context* Vol. 4. Heidelberg: Winter.

Van Gelderen, Elly (2014). *A history of the English language* 2nd ed. Amsterdam/Philadelphia: John Benjamins.

Verkerk, Annemarie (2019). "Detecting non-tree-like signal using multiple tree topologies". In: *Journal of historical linguistics* 9.1, 9–69.

Versloot, Arjen P. (2004). "Why Old Frisian is still quite old". In: *Folia linguistica historica* 25.1–2, 253–304.

Von Der Leyen, Friedrich (1908). *Einführung in das gotische: Althochdeutsche und mittelhochdeutsche* Munchen: C.H. Beck'sche Verlagsbuchhandlung.

Voyles, Joseph B. (1968). "Gothic and Germanic". In: *Language* 44.4, 720–746.

Voyles, Joseph B. (1971). "The Problem of West Germanic". In: *Folia Linguistica* 5.1–2, 117–150.

Voyles, Joseph B. (1992). *Early Germanic grammar: Pre-, proto-, and post-Germanic languages*. San Diego: Acaddemic press Press.

Walkden, George (2012). "Against inertia". In: *Lingua* 122.8, 891–901.

Walkden, George (2019). "The many faces of uniformitarianism in linguistics". In: *Glossa: A journal of general linguistics* 4.1, 1–17.

Warnock, Rachel C. M. et al. (2015). "Calibration uncertainty in molecular dating analyses: there is no substitute for the prior evaluation of time priors". In: *Proceedings of the Royal Society B: Biological sciences* 282.1798, 20141013.

Wei, Taiyun and Viliam Simko (2017). *R package "corrplot": Visualization of a correlation matrix* (Version 0.84). URL: https://github.com/taiyun/corrplot.

Weidmann, Nils B. and Idean Salehyan (2013). "Violence and ethnic segregation: A computational model applied to Baghdad". In: *International studies quarterly* 57.1, 52–64.

Wichmann, Søren (2008). "The emerging field of language dynamics". In: *Language and linguistics compass* 2.3, 442–455.

Wickham, Hadley (2016). *ggplot2: Elegant graphics for data analysis* Springer-Verlag New York. ISBN: 978-3-319-24277-4. URL: https://ggplot2.tidyverse.org.

Winter, Bodo and Andrew Wedel (2016). "The co-evolution of speech and the lexicon: The interaction of functional pressures, redundancy, and category variation". In: *Topics in cognitive science* 8.2, 503–513.

Wolfram, Herwig (1990). "Einleitung oder Überlegungen zur origo gentis". In: *Typen der Ethnogenese unter besonderer Berücksichtigung der Bayern* Ed. by Herwig Wolfram and Walter Pohl. Wien: Verlag d. Österreichischen Akad. d. Wiss., 19–34.

Wolfram, Herwig (1997). *The Roman empire and its Germanic peoples* Berkeley: University of California Press.

Wrede, Ferdinand (1886). *Über die Sprache der Wandalen. I. Teil* Strassburg: K. J. Trübner.

Wrede, Ferdinand (1924). "Ingwäonisch und Westgermanisch". In: *Zeitschrift für deutsche Mundarten* 19.3/4, 270–284.

Xie, Wangang et al. (2011). "Improving marginal likelihood estimation for Bayesian phylogenetic model selection". In: *Systematic biology* 60.2, 150–160.

Yang, Ziheng (1994). "Maximum likelihood phylogenetic estimation from DNA sequences with variable rates over sites: Approximate methods". In: *Journal of molecular evolution* 39.3, 306–314.

Yanovich, Igor (2020). "Phylogenetic linguistic evidence and the Dene-Yeniseian homeland". In: *Diachronica* 37.3, 410–446.

Index of languages and clades

Index of subjects

OXFORD STUDIES IN DIACHRONIC AND HISTORICAL LINGUISTICS

General editors
Adam Ledgeway and Ian Roberts, University of Cambridge

Advisory editors
Cynthia L. Allen, *Australian National University*; Ricardo Bermúdez-Otero,
University of Manchester; Theresa Biberauer, *University of Cambridge*;
Charlotte Galves, *University of Campinas*; Geoff Horrocks, *University of Cambridge*;
Paul Kiparsky, *Stanford University*; David Lightfoot, *Georgetown University*;
Giuseppe Longobardi, *University of York*; George Walkden, *University of Konstanz*;
David Willis, *University of Oxford*